MAN KIND?

Our Incredible War on Wildlife

A Curtis Brown BOOK

BOOKS BY
CLEVELAND AMORY

NONFICTION

The Proper Bostonians

The Last Resorts

Who Killed Society?

Man Kind? Our Incredible
    War on Wildlife

FICTION

Home Town

MAN KIND?

Our Incredible War on Wildlife

**CLEVELAND
AMORY**

HARPER & ROW, PUBLISHERS

NEW YORK, EVANSTON
SAN FRANCISCO, LONDON

Designed by Janice Willcocks Stern

LIBRARY OF CONGRESS CATALOGING IN PUBLICATION DATA
Amory, Cleveland.
    Man kind? Our incredible war on wildlife.
    1. Wildlife conservation. 2. Hunting—Moral and religious aspects. I. Title.
QL82.A45   179′.3   76-181605
ISBN 0-06-010092-3

To Marian
Assistant-in-Chief
For Judgment under Pressure

The author also wishes to express thanks to Regina Bauer Frankenberg, without whom the book would not have been possible, to Lewis Regenstein, the bright star on the animal horizon, and to Ed Walsh, councilor as well as counselor. There are many others—among them Marion Schaefer, Patt Mitchell, Patti Forkan, Doris Dixon, Virginia Handley, Carol Koury, Sandy Rowland, Norma Hansen, Sid and Carolyn Rosenthal, Allen and Diana Manning, Frances Scaife, Jane Volk, Maria Lloyd, Eleanor Moore, Margaret Scott, Sharon Gaiser, Caskie Stinnett, George Campbell, Sharon Acker, Gretchen Wyler, Jack Silverman, Philo Higley, Winthrop Wadleigh, Kitty Hunt, Ted Steele, Ed Ney, Edward Block, Jeanne Adlon, Alice Brown and Phyllis Silverberg. Then, too, the author wishes to acknowledge, at Harper & Row, the indefatigable assistance of Beulah Hagen, Maria Guarnaschelli, and James Fox. And finally the author wishes to state that it is a source of deep pride to him that this book bears the incomparable imprimatur of that grand gentleman of publishing, Mr. Cass Canfield.

Contents

Introduction   ix

I

FOR FUN

Support Your Right to Arm Bears   7

II

FOR MONEY

Real People Wear Fake Furs   193

III

FOR REVENGE

The Most-Persecuted List   321

Index   359

A section of photographs
will be found following p. 180

Introduction

There is no better place to begin an examination of our treatment of our fellow creatures than with our language.

Take the word "animal." One of the dictionary definitions for "animal" is "a bestial person; a brute." On the other hand, one of the dictionary definitions of "beast" is "a brutal *person*" —italics ours.

Television is a particular offender. "He's an animal," says a character on one program. "He deserves to be killed." Meanwhile, on another program, a woman shouts to another, in utter contempt, "You're an animal!" Later in the same episode, when she learns she has misjudged that particular person, she apologizes, then points to someone else. "*He's* an animal," she says. And, as if this weren't enough, another program—an interview show—is promoted as follows: "A Tough Judge Says 'Don't Coddle Criminals. They're Punks, Vermin and Animals.' "

In real life the situation is, if anything, worse. One Illinois woman, Mrs. Florence Linzmeier, has made a habit of noting all unfavorable public uses of the word "animal." She observed that when a new U.S. attorney vowed war on Chicago's crime syndicate, he literally spat out, on TV news, the words "They're animals!" Mrs. Linzmeier wrote in protesting. "A few weeks later," she wrote me, "I was gratified to hear the district attorney refer to the hoodlum element as 'the scum of society.' "

But the mindless maligning goes on. In the Detroit riots of a few years ago, according to a news report, a National Guardsman steadied his carbine on the trunk of a new car and squeezed the trigger. "They're not Negroes," he said. "They're animals." And, of course, the situation was as easily reversed when LeRoi Jones, commenting on the Newark police, managed to use two anti-animal expressions at once. "These pigs," he was quoted as saying, "treat us like animals."

In sports, the Boston Bruin hockey team, playing roughly, are known around the league as "The Animals." But so are tough teenagers, particularly motorcycle gangs. And even younger children get it. In fact, if your own act up at a party, what do you say to them? "Why," you say, "you behaved like wild animals." Wild, of course, not in the sense of living in the wild but just *acting* wild.

On an individual basis, the situation is just as bad. We call each other names by animals—"You pig," "you swine," "you weasel," "you rat," "you skunk," "you baboon" or "you jackal." And we do it in the hope, of course, that as we do it we don't make too much of "a jackass," or perhaps just "an ass," out of ourselves. The second dictionary definition of "coyote" is "a contemptible sneak," of "bear," "a clumsy, ill-mannered *person*"—again, italics ours.

And how many of our similes are unfavorably animal-oriented? For every "brave as a lion," "busy as a beaver" or even "wise as an owl" or "cute as a bug," there are literally dozens of "cross as a bear," "mean as a snake," "sly as a fox," "dumb as an ox," "slippery as an eel," "stubborn as a mule," "silly as a goose," "crazy as a loon," "greedy as a pig" and so on. You may cry "crocodile tears," but if you're hurt, you'll squeal "like a stuck pig." You may be "hog tied," but it depends on "whose ox is being gored."

You "badger" someone; someone in turn "buffaloes" you. You're either "chicken" or "sheepish" or you "toady" to someone, or you "go ape." You're "bull-headed" or a "dumb bunny" or "mousy." You have "bats in your belfry" or you're "batty" or you're up to "monkey business." If something is wrong, there's something "fishy." One animal, the lovable sloth, we have even named after one of the seven deadly sins.

A man is either a "wolf"—who will, of course, "turn"—or else he's an "old goat"; a woman can "look like a horse," or be "horse-faced," or, worse still, "a cow." She can also be a "shrew" or a "vixen." And, last but not least, we come to the animals closest to us of all—the cat and the dog. And we have words for them galore, all the way from our worst stocks— even stock-market officials refer to them as "cats and dogs"— to our lowest form of living—which would either be "in the doghouse" or, horror of horrors, the "cathouse."

And what are we when we are "catty"? Why, obviously, being mean. And if a woman is unattractive, what is she? Why, a "dog." Someone is "nervous as a cat" or "fraidy cat." Someone else "lets the cat out of the bag." Still a third person declares, "There are more ways than one to skin a cat."

We may "put on the dog," but more likely someone treats you "like a dog." You may "go to the dogs," or something may happen to you that "shouldn't happen to a dog." Our least important public office is all too clear in the expression "He couldn't get elected dog catcher." And, finally, if a woman can be a "bitch," surely our No. 1 epithet is someone who is the son of same.

As for man, of course, he doesn't even consider himself an animal—which, considering the way he considers them, is probably, all things considered, the only considerate thing about him.

I: For Fun

Some years ago, on the NBC *Today* show, I did my first essay on the virtues of hunting. The script follows:

INTRO (FRANK BLAIR): Our guest has been out hunting society in various places for you, but today he's decided to take the bull by the horns, so to speak, and bring you the story of hunting society itself.

AMORY: Some of you may have seen the stories of the "sticks and stones" rabbit hunts which have been put on by the local American Legion post in the curiously named town of Harmony, North Carolina.

The reason for these hunts was that the Legion felt that since the number of hunters nowadays had swelled to such proportions, it was dangerous for the hunters to use firearms—and therefore safer to kill the rabbits with sticks and stones and clubs.

Of course, there has been some criticism of the cruelty of these hunts—which the Legion has answered with the usual pro-hunting arguments—i.e. (1) that such complaints *always* come from all the "bleeding hearts" and "animal lovers" anyway, and (2) that hunting is *absolutely necessary* to keep down the overpopulation of animals. It is all, in other words, a matter of conservation. Conservation, as the hunters use the word, means killing the animals for their own good, but some of the animals apparently are so selfish they refuse to take the long-term view of it.

On the other hand, what the *hunters* don't seem to understand is that the chief problem isn't the overpopulation of *animals*—it's the overpopulation of *hunters*. There are now 15,000,000 hunters in this country. They're breeding like flies and they're overcrowding our farms and our woods and even our highways. And what is needed, of course, is an intelligent, long-term program for the conservation of *them*.

Halfway measures are simply not enough. All of us, of course, applaud hunting accidents. There has been a nice, healthy increase here. Our own favorite statistic is that an average of five hunters a year are killed by rabbits—in other words, while the hunter was clubbing the rabbit to death with his gun butt, the little rascal moved or something and the trigger accidentally went off and the hunter was killed.

This is good news, of course, but this morning I have some really exciting news for you. It's the story of the formation of a new club—hunters *do* love clubs—the Hunt-the-Hunters Hunt Club. It's a world wild organization—and it even has its own motto—"If you can't play a sport, shoot one." It has, of course, been criticized by the "bleeding hearts" and "people lovers," but it has *never* proposed, as has been said, the extermination of all hunters. All it proposes, in the hunters' own words, is "trimming the herd." It proposes a carefully regulated regular open season on hunters where you and your club-mates, in a carefully regulated, gentlemanly club atmosphere, can have a really first-rate weekend shoot.

Above all, it's an absolutely fair club. Hunters who shoot with a bow and arrow, for example, will themselves be shot with a bow and arrow—and we'll be able to see how truly sporting this form of shooting really is. Trappers will be trapped—humanely, of course—and if they're too small, they'll be thrown back to live to play again another day. Fox-hunters in particular will be glad to know they'll be ridden down by nothing but thorough-bred horses and pure-bred dogs, and members of that branch of the club, hunting fox-hunters, will dress correctly in clean pink coats. There'll be no letting down the bars. However you prefer to hunt, the club asks only that you use your discretion. Please do not, for example, simply go out and take pot shots at hunters—within city limits, say, or in parked cars, or in their dating season.

Now some members of the Hunt-the-Hunters Hunt Club have already complained that hunters do not make good sporty game—that they are inclined to be stealthy and hide behind trees, and don't leap about and jump properly, and are difficult to flush. Also, that they have a tendency to get cross when they are shot at.

Those hunters don't seem to understand that it's all being done for their own conservation—and the club has a special program for them. "Improving the breed," it's called. This is specially good for hunters who like to hunt animals specially raised for hunting. They themselves will be specially raised—in regular club preserves where they will be hunted only with the kind of people they would like to be hunted with. Again, only a nice gentlemanly club atmosphere.

The important thing here, of course, is to get good specimens to begin with—sound of wind and limb and with a good head of hair and a good scent. To get these specimens, of course, you need the proper calls. I have here a variety of calls that hunters regularly use. This one is for ducks (demonstrates), this one is for deer (demo), this for quail (demo), and these for two different kinds of varmints (two demos). The Hunt-the-Hunters Hunt Club will also, of course, have calls. The simplest of these—and extraordinarily effective around 6 o'clock in the evening—is (demonstrates cocktail shakers).

Last but not least, the Hunt-the-Hunters Hunt Club wishes to make clear that it never countenances going to excess in any way. For example, after your "bag" or your "take," or your kill, *don't* drape your hunter on your automobile. And when you get home, don't mount your head. Mounting heads is considered, by the club, in very bad taste. They recommend, instead, merely mounting the cap, or the jacket, or perhaps the gun itself. Just use your judgment, and the inherent good taste of all sportsmen.

Finally, there have already been some complaints by members of the club that hunters are tough. This, we can state unequivocally, is simply not true. If you shoot them in season, and season them properly, they can be quite tasty.

Support Your Right to Arm Bears

What occasioned this broadcast, as stated in the beginning of the script, was the so-called "Bunny Bop" in Harmony, North Carolina. The town of Harmony, population three hundred, lies in the foothills of the Blue Ridge. Harmony won its quaint name, I was informed by Homer Keever, Director of History for the Western North Carolina United Methodist Church Conference, because it was once upon a time a camping ground—and, in those days at least, the atmosphere was relatively harmonious.

It has been less so since. In fact, for years it was the scene of an infamous annual "sticks and stones hunt"—one which was held each December, ironically just before Christmas. This hunt was sponsored by Harmony Post 113 of the American Legion, which afterward held a barbecue (rabbit, of course) for the benefit of various good causes. These ranged from feeding the hungry to raising money for the battleship *North Carolina*.

During this event, Harmonians gathered together with their dogs, in many cases with children and in some cases with wives; everybody then surrounded a field and drove the rabbits toward a central area. When the rabbits attempted to turn back to the places from which they had been driven—bushes, holes and so forth—they were beaten to death and the scene turned into a wild, yelling, bloody melee. There was no set plan, no orderly procedure, not even any noticeable effort to get the job over with as quickly as possible. Some people used sticks, some clubs, some stones, some their feet and some even their hands. In certain cases, the dogs chewed up the rabbits by themselves; in other cases, the people stunned the rabbits and then threw them to the dogs. Sometimes more than one person clubbed a single rabbit. At another time one lone person would club half a dozen rabbits half to death, and then leave them to hobble off on broken legs or simply to lie on the ground, unable to move, with blinded eyes, fractured skulls, and broken backs —their only hope that in the confusion somebody else would see they were not quite dead and finish them off by more smashing, pounding or stomping.

The history of the hunt is not easy to come by—at least in Harmony proper. Entering Harmony and leaving it amount to almost the same thing, unless you happen to stop in a small café located at Harmony's main crossroads. What, I asked a pretty girl in back of a counter, is Harmony famous for? "Pretty girls," she answered, smiling. A customer wondered if I knew what time it was when there were twenty-six dogs in the backyard. I shook my head. "Twenty-five after one," he said, laughing.

I asked if they thought the Bunny Bop was cruel. Both of them did. Meanwhile, a man sitting at a table said he didn't think I understood why the hunt had to be held that way. "Once they used guns," he explained, "but the hunt got so popular that one day someone was shot, so they decided to do it this way." Didn't he think it was cruel? "I don't know," he said. "I never took part in it. But there was all these humane people from all over who got ahold of it—and they said it was."

At the café I was directed for further information about the hunt to "Reavis' place," run by a man named Reavis who was sergeant-at-arms of the American Legion. I found him down the road at a combination beer parlor, pool hall, and general store. He was sitting on the counter. I felt I was in the middle of *In the Heat of the Night*. Did he know anything about the Bunny Bop? "No," he said, "I don't." Did he know anyone who did? "Not that I know of." Was he connected, I persisted, with the American Legion? "Sometimes I is, sometimes I isn't." How, I asked finally, could he tell which was which? "Mostly," he said, "by tending to my own business, and wishing other people would tend to theirs." As I went out the door, I heard him say, "That's the same s.o.b. came down here before about those damn rabbits."

Mr. Reavis was correct. It was not my first trip to Harmony. Two years before, the Legion had invited me to debate two Legion lawyers on the merits of the hunt—the debate to be held before a large local audience. As I entered the hall, the Legion commander, Pierce Van Hoy, was talking. "This here hunt," he was saying, "has been distorted by the press. You will find on the scrolls of the American Legion Post 113 some of the most bravest soldiers who have fought in the Confederate Army, in World War I, in World War II, in Korea and in Vietnam. As a matter of fact, the timekeeper for this debate has to return to Vietnam tomorrow."

"This here hunt," Commander Van Hoy went on, "has helped Post 113. But there are other methods, other means, of us associating together and having fun. And if there is anything wrong about what we are doing, we want to know about it."

Commander Van Hoy next introduced our moderator, Mr. Hugh G. Mitchell, from nearby Statesville. Mr. Mitchell was, he said, the national president of the American Coalition of Patriotic Societies, and had, Commander Van Hoy noted, "done more than any other man for the cultural development of Statesville." He had also, he said, "represented us at the United Nations."

Next Mr. Mitchell introduced the judges—the mayor, a leather tycoon; the sales representative of a chemical company; and "two college students." To prove, of course, that Harmony wasn't anti-intellectual. When Mr. Mitchell introduced me, he said, "Mr. Amory is a graduate of Harvard and many other universities."

One of my opponents, lawyer Arthur Beckham, referred to me as a "bleeding heart," and declared that rabbits were good for only three things—for food, for destroying crops and for producing more rabbits. Mr. Beckham also declared North Carolina was not a "brutal state." "We suffered," he offered in evidence of this, "the highest proportionate losses of any State in the Confederacy. And," he added, "a North Carolina flag went farther than any other at Gettysburg, and a North Carolina flag was on the first tank into Tokyo."

On, I presumed, our side.

My next opponent, lawyer Douglas Eisele, was firm. "Brutality," he said, "like beauty, is in the eyes of the beholder. A dumb animal, who has no emotion and very little sense of pain, cannot experience brutality. The proper hunting of animals, like it's done here, *helps* animals."

When it came to my turn I expressed the wish that the debate could be decided by the vote of the rabbits. I told them that I had seen all sorts of animals in laboratories but to me the most pathetic—because they were the most frightened—were the rabbits. I said that I had seen in one laboratory rows upon rows of rabbits, in stocks as it were, awaiting the testing on their naked eyes, without anesthesia, of hair dyes and cosmetics, even those rabbits, I concluded, seemed to be fortunate compared to Harmony's rabbits.

Nevertheless the vote was unanimous—for the hunt. The Legion, however, voted for the first time in the history of the hunt to ban stones, to use nets, to hold rabbits "in the proper position for clubbing" and, finally, to kill them "in the most humane manner possible." And this too represented a small victory—it was the first time anyone on their side had used, any way but sarcastically, the word "humane."

The next day the hunt was held, but there were so many representatives from newspapers, magazines, television and radio, as well as curiosity seekers, that they not only outnumbered the hunters (twenty) but also the rabbits (nine). Some of the hunters blamed "outside meddlin'," some blamed humane societies in general, some blamed me in particular. "We're members of the *human* society, not the humane society," one hunter told me. "We wouldn't be here today if somebody back then didn't go hunting."

There has never been a humane society in Iredell County, where the hunt takes place. In neighboring Mecklenburg County, however, there is a humane society. Its officers, Mrs. George Rawlins and Mrs. Martha Boyce, deserve prime credit for attempting to stop the Bunny Bop. So does Mr. James Yandell, who is a nonpaid agent for all humane societies.

"I had calls from all over about that hunt," he told me. "Is there a Chicago *Tribune?* Well, anyway, I had calls from that too. And even Australia. The American Humane Association called me and said if there was anything cruel going on up there to go on up and arrest somebody. But, shucks, I told

them, you couldn't even *get* anybody to arrest anybody. I remember one man I called up there—believe me he was eighty-
two. He told me they weren't doing what I thought they were
doing. Well, I told him, you're killing rabbits with sticks and
stones. That's what I think you're doing. 'What's the difference,
Jim,' he asked me, 'between sticks and stones and a gun? The
rabbit's daid anyway, isn't he?' Well, I told him, you have high
glee doing it, and I contend that isn't right. And then he told
me, 'Listen, Jim, why do you take on so much about this? I've
lived a good deal longer than you have and if you don't do
anything worse than kill a rabbit with a stick, you'll make it
in all right.'

"The funny thing is," Mr. Yandell continued, "if a North
Carolina mother sees a little kid beating a rabbit, she'll about
drop her dishes to tell that kid to quit. But then you have these
kids and they go out with their daddy—and then the Legion
uses it as a drawing card for members. One man got himself
so worked up about it he said the hunt would go on even if he
had to do it alone."

Mr. Yandell, however, is not only a remarkable man, but a
brave one too. And it was he who saw eventually that the
bunny boppers were brought to court. He admitted, though,
that it wasn't easy. "I worked a day and a half every day to get
any kind of law firm to represent us up there," he told me.
"They all told me to a man that those people were their friends
and their clients. 'We live with them, Jim,' they said. 'You're a
foreigner and anyway this is a one-shot deal.' I even called
several lawyers in Charlotte, but they didn't want it either.
Some weren't in sympathy and some just didn't think they
should fool with it."

Finally, a law firm was procured but, despite the fact that
the North Carolina law on cruelty to animals uses such words

as "overdrive," "overload," "wound," "injure," "torture," "torment," "deprive of necessary sustenance," "cruelly beat," "needlessly mutilate or kill," the case was lost. Furthermore, it was lost not only once but again after an appeal and after that still a third time in the North Carolina Supreme Court. One reason for this is that our animal laws, as far as hunting is concerned, are meaningless. Another factor is that fish and game departments are run not for any benefit to animals but entirely for hunters. Still a third factor is that North Carolina officials, from then Governor Terry Sanford on down, showed an extraordinary disinclination to get involved. A fourth reason was that the letter sent by William W. Burton, National Commander of the American Legion, was not allowed to be introduced as evidence because it was a copy and not signed. This letter, remarkably enough, specifically instructed Harmony Post 113 not to sponsor the Bunny Bop and declared that, if they continued to sponsor it, they would have to surrender their charter.

Before leaving Harmony I paid a final call on Commander Pierce Van Hoy. He showed me a picture the Pontiac Motor Division of General Motors had given him. It depicted Hopi Indians using nets and curved boomerang-like sticks to kill rabbits. "Sticks-and-stones hunts," he told me, "were prevalent in this country long before Columbus. The rabbit can take care of himself. He's endowed by nature to get away. Do you know how many rabbits you'd have if you started with a pair and left them alone for two years? Do you know how many you'd end up with? You'd have," he said triumphantly, "thirteen million rabbits."

"And if you want the source for that," he said proudly, "it's right in your V.F.W. magazine."

I asked Mr. Van Hoy if the hunt had been held last year—

the year after our debate. "I really don't know," he said. "I'm a pretty busy man. But I'll tell you one thing—every prominent Legionnaire in North Carolina was excited about it one way or the other. They all knew it was a publicity stunt and they looked on it neither with favor nor disfavor. If it was held last year, it wasn't part of Legion business."

I asked him if he was planning to hold the hunt this year. "I wouldn't make any predictions," he said. "It is not the mark of a man to mistreat an animal, but when it comes to hunting, that's something else again. It's just not right to blow this thing up as cruel. Basically all we do is go out and observe nature and tell tales to each other and listen to the music of the hounds baying.

"Yessir," he repeated, "the music of the hounds baying. And now I want to ask you something. What would all these rabbit hunters be doing if they weren't letting off all this steam? I'll tell you what they'd be doing. They'd be drinking and carousing and beating their wives."

At this juncture, Mrs. Van Hoy appeared on the scene. "The thing about a rabbit, you know," she said, "is that you either hit it or miss it."

I am still working on that one.

*

Why do people hold such events as the "Bunny Bop"? Obviously, because they like to. They like to "hunt"—i.e., kill. Other reasons, such as that they have to kill rabbits because there are too many of them, are suspect. Man has an infinite capacity to rationalize his own cruelty. The reason there are too many rabbits is that the hunters, however much they love potting at rabbits and squirrels and woodchucks and chipmunks and virtually anything that moves, like even better potting bigger and better things—such as all the animals of which the rabbits are the natural prey, and which hunters have shot off to virtual extinction.

Hunters are fond of protesting that they have never been responsible for the endangerment of any species. It is a difficult argument to maintain. In the first place, it seems a reasonable assumption that the animals did not shoot each other. In the second place, although loss of habitat and changing environmental pressures were obviously responsible for much endangerment, the fact remains that the Endangered Species Act of 1973 begins, and I quote, "The two major causes of extinction are hunting and destruction of natural habitat." And in the Endangered List itself—all the way from the Aleutian Canada goose to the Mexican duck—one of the chief problems remaining is that hunting is still allowed by the Bureau of Sport Fisheries and Wildlife.

In the third and final place, take the tables extracted from the Red Data Book of the International Union for the Conservation of Nature. These, as Roger Caras has pointed out, clearly demonstrate that, in the case of literally dozens and dozens of animal species, hunting has been not just "a major factor" in the endangerment, but the *only* major factor—and it has been listed as such. These species include such strange "game" as the giant armadillo, the Indochinese lar gibbon and the glacier bear—the latter's "reasons for decline" being listed in the U.S. Endangered Species Act as "over-hunting as a curio." Other equally curious game animals for which hunting is listed as the only major factor are the Amazonian manatee and the Syrian and Somali wild asses. The list also includes such prize "trophies" as the grizzly bear, the Bali tiger, the rhino, the snow leopard and the giant otter. Hunting as the only major factor is also credited with the endangerment of a wide variety of stag, deer, sikas, yaks, gazelles, antelopes, oryxes, ibexes, etc. As for animals for which hunting is listed as not "the *only* major factor," but *a* major factor, virtually all the Endangered Species are so included.

Hunters reply that much of this endangerment is due not to sport hunting but to "market" hunting, that it was not the sport hunter who was responsible for the extinction of the buffalo, the passenger pigeon, the great auk, etc. But take, for example, the buffalo. Market hunted, yes, but how many hunters who decry what the market hunter did to the buffalo themselves line up to pay $45 or more for permits for the annual buffalo hunt put on each year at House Rock Valley, Arizona. Here, "surplus" buffalo, brought back from extinction, are penned in and driven toward the hunters' guns—memorably depicted in Glendon Swarthout's book and in Stanley Kramer's movie *Bless the Beasts and Children.* A hunt? It is not, of course. It is an execution—one which any up-to-date slaughter plant would deplore. The buffaloes are driven down to the hunters who, three by three, are checked into the ring to hunt—i.e., take two shots at—the docile, bewildered animals, old ones, cows and young, a few feet from them. Two shots only. Then, if the job is botched—which, buffalo being difficult animals to kill, it usually is—it is then up to a man from the Arizona Game and Fish Department to finish off the animals.

The cruelty of this hunt, with the animals old and young killed beside each other, or wounded and writhing on the ground, has occasioned world-wide protest. But Arizona's Attorney General Garry Nelson has declared that he saw nothing inhumane about it, adding that it had, as he put it, "been done for years as a game management method." Robert L. Thomas, in the *Arizona Republic,* wrote, "I lose patience with bleeding hearts, because I suspect they are hypocrites who are not really concerned with the life or death of an animal, but wish only to end the enjoyment of others who hunt for pleasure and meat." And when a local humanitarian, Patrick Shields, suggested at least two viable alternatives—the gelding of young male buffaloes and the establishment of a sperm bank and the opening of the range to tourists who would, in turn, pay for the herd, he was immediately taken to task by the *Arizona Republic*'s outdoor writer Ben Avery:

> I don't know, but if I were a buffalo, I would tell Mr. Shields to take his proposal back to New York City or wherever such things are hatched. . . . As for the Kramer movie, my wife and I have not attended a motion picture since they started using foul language and showing immoral scenes. I received a free pass to see this one, but I have better things to do. However, reports I received from those who did go are that it was full of foul language and at least one suggestive, filthy scene.

It sure was—the buffalo hunt itself.

✳

Looking through the literature of the hunt is an exercise in frustration for animal people. It is also an education in either mindless savagery or heartless indifference, it is hard to know which. In any case, there is no better place to start than right with the buffalo hunt—and with Buffalo Bill himself. Take "Quick Trigger," from the *Field & Stream Treasury*:

> One of the most spectacular of Buffalo Bill's hunting stunts was when he challenged his bitter rival, Bill Comstock, to a competition for the championship of the world in buffalo hunting. There was also a side bet of $500 between rival contestants. This was the first "world's

championship" contest staged in America—the forerunner of ballyhooed boxing, baseball, and other promoted events. It was widely publicized and even a special train from St. Louis carried approximately one hundred persons who made the trip especially to witness the contest. There was also much betting throughout that part of the West on the outcome.

Comstock was also a noted hunter and chief of the scouts at Fort Wallace. He was backed by most of the Army men, while the railroad men favored Cody.

The rules of the march were few and simple. The hunt was to begin at eight o'clock in the morning and last eight hours. Each hunter had a referee who was to follow his man to keep count of the number of buffaloes he killed. The one with the largest score was to be the winner.

The gallery rode out to the hunting grounds in wagons and on horseback and were to be kept a sufficient distance away so that they would not interfere with the contest. An elaborate lunch was to be served on the location, and even champagne was included in the liquid refreshments taken along.

At precisely 8 A.M. the two hunters and their referees galloped away from the gallery of observers. There were plenty of buffaloes in the distance and they quickly sighted a herd. It split into two sections. Cody went after one and Comstock gave chase to the other, each stripped for action and riding at the utmost, for a title was at stake.

At the end of their first "run," Comstock had felled 23 buffaloes and Cody had accounted for 38. Soon thereafter they sighted another herd, and the second run was launched. By the end of this sortie it was high noon, and they decided to return to the wagons for lunch with the audience. At this stage of the contest, Comstock had a score of 37 and Cody had 56.

During the lunch, drinks were generously served; and when it came time for the two contestants to resume the

contest, Cody announced in loud tones that in view of
the fact that he was well in the lead he would give his
adversary an added advantage—he would complete the
contest riding his horse without saddle, reins or bridle.
As Comstock did not protest, Buffalo Bill leaped on the
bare back of Brigham and, with a war whoop and waving
Lucretia high over his head, away he went.

At the end of the first afternoon's run Bill Comstock
voluntarily conceded Cody the victory and they returned
to where the audience still waited to cheer the winner.
The final score was: Buffalo Bill, 69 buffaloes, Bill Comstock, 46. Thus was won the "buffalo hunting championship of the world."

Move on to elephants, and the feats of the greatest killer
of them all—an Englishman named W. D. M. Bell. He personally killed a total of 1,011 elephants, of which 983 were bulls.
One day he shot 19. But all days were not so good. Continue
with the *Field & Stream Treasury:*

His book, *The Wanderings of an Elephant Hunter,*
is one of the most fascinating ever published about
Africa. It is written with a modesty that is refreshing.
One incident which he relates as "his most disappointing
day" describes his locating a herd of 54 bull elephants
(mostly huge ones) that were steadily on the march
through the jungle. With great exertion and difficulty he
managed to locate himself alone right in the path of their
course. As he waited for them to come upon him, his
impulse was to hurry back to camp as soon as it was
over to paint a picture of the scene. Silently he waited,
until the herd had pushed their great hulks only a few
paces right in front and to either side of him. Then he
opened fire. But, to his dismay, he succeeded in dropping
"only five out of that magnificent millionaire herd. They
split up in all directions and at hell's own gait. Alas! what
should I have done?"

We have some suggestions. In any case, Mr. Bell was rarely at a loss. What he calls his "most unpleasant experience" he describes very briefly:

> Traveling hot-foot 8½ hours at 6 miles per hour on an enormous track in wet season to find a tuskless bull! Killed to prevent a recurrence!

So that another hunter, of course, would not have to waste his valuable time. Like, say, Gordon Cumming, who makes certain, in his book, *Five Years of a Hunter's Life in South Africa,* that each of his encounters with elephants gets the full, gladiatorial treatment:

> I fought one of the former [an elephant] in dense wait-a-bit jungle from half-past eleven till the sun was under, when his troubled spirit fled, and he fell, pierced with 57 balls.

Again:

> I was therefore obliged to hunt him on foot, and slew him with 30 bullets, after an extremely severe and dangerous combat of about four hours.

And still again:

> In the afternoon, I was engaged for three to four hours combatting with a vicious elephant which I finished with 35 bullets in the shoulder, in an impracticable jungle of wait-a-bit thorns.

J. A. Hunter, in his briefly entitled book, *Hunter,* did not favor the shoulder shot:

> The frontal skull is my favorite target. An elephant hit there crashes to earth on his knees. This is my favorite shot, possibly because I have used it so much, and with telling results. When the elephant is ten yards or so away it is very effective. The bullet crashes through the skull

and enters the brain, bringing instant death. But at less than ten yards, the great difference in height between a man and an elephant makes this shot difficult and frequently impossible. The hunter is forced to shoot upward and the bullet enters the elephant's head at an angle, missing the brain. When this happens the hunter rarely has time to fire again, for the elephant can whirl around in a flash and be off—or the reverse, as the mood takes him.

Lions, of course, are, in these books, great "game." "There are few sights in nature," writes J. A. Hunter, "more terrible than that of a charging lion." Then, in the next breath, he writes of "dumb killing"—which he explains as follows:

> A dumb killer is a rifle lashed into position against a tree with a string leading from the trigger to a bit of bait. When a lion comes to eat the bait, he pulls the string and shoots himself.

The Maharajah of Datia in Laikitia in 1921 killed eighteen lions in one night, shooting from a *boma* of thorn over a zebra carcass. Elephant hunter Bell, however, scorned this. "With regard to lions," he wrote modestly, "I merely killed any that caused annoyances, such as roaring around camp, stampeding porters, and so forth."

To teach them, obviously, a good lesson. Tigers are, on the other hand, praised as "game" by virtually all hunters—in fact, the secrets of tiger hunting are told in book after book. These involve three basic methods. In the first, you sit up in a *machan* (treehouse) over a *boda* (a tied live buffalo or goat or whatever) until the tiger appears. In the second, you sit up in a *machan* while beaters drive the tiger by and/or under you. In the third, you sit up on your elephant and shoot from either a howdah or a mattress. Some hunters, of course, asked even more. The Nawab Vizier of Oudh used to go tiger hunting with ten thousand cavalry, ten thousand foot soldiers, eight hundred elephants and "a host of retainers." Accountants, presumably. Lieutenant Colonel John Champion Faunthorpe was evidently terrific. States *Big Game Shooting Records,* "The exact number of tigers that Faunthorpe killed does not appear to be definitely known, but it is stated in that excellent biographical sketch which appeared in *The Hoghunters' Annual* that the number that he shot must be over 300."

Who could dispute the *Hoghunters' Annual?* And, while we're at it, let's take a look at hog hunting. Or, more properly, pig sticking—from an account in *The Field* of two days in Moescoondie in 1906 when 17 "spears" accounted for 149 boars:

> The plan of action was simple. The spears were divided into parties of three. The patches of jungle were enormous and the line was made up of 200 men with Crawford himself in charge, ably backed by Billy Barker and assistants from the outlying factories. Most of the parties rode with the line, but some of them were posted outside the jungle. The line was most skilfully worked and there were no gaps in it, but for some time nothing showed. Then a few smallish pig began to break across the plain toward the next cover, and suddenly the plain was black with hundreds of pig of every size making their way across the open. Never have I seen such a sight. Portly matrons, followed by strings of striped piglings no bigger than rabbits; young boars still showing the brown coat of the yearling, 26 in. pig, black as night, quick on their feet, more ready to run than fight; and then the lords of the harem, ploughing their way through the press like great galleons, shouldering the smaller fry to right and left. Truly a sight to dream of, but only to be seen once in a lifetime!

All idea of parties was forgotten. Each man picked his board, let in the spurs and rode him, the trouble being to avoid the smaller pig, which were continually getting in the way.

George Paris was brought down like this by a crossing pig early in the day, and retired with concussion and a cheek split from chin to ear, so that the subsequent proceedings interested him no more.

It was no place for children. In the open the odds were in favour of horse and man, but in cover it was different. The grass and jhow was almost up to the waist of a mounted man, and a hunted boar had a habit of squatting so that the rider overshot the mark, and the boar charged in behind. The going was quite blind and full of holes, and the only thing to do was to leave the horse's head alone, harden one's heart and drive him through it. The man who pulled rein and rode with caution always met with disaster.

Most of the men and horses knew the game and could be backed to ride and kill their quarry single-handed, but that was not the only reason for the tremendous bag of 149 boar killed in the two days. The main reason was that these magnificent hog seemed to prefer to fight than to run, and most of them were killed after a quarter of a mile burst.

A real fighting animal, to the hunter, of course, is always "magnificent." The leopard, for example—even his "treachery" is praised—or, in Mexico and South America, "that savage tropic terror—the grim jaguar." But hunters reserve special praise for the rhino. In hunting him, of course, one must always be careful that one's natives are up to snuff. Take J. A. Hunter again:

> The first day in this country, the youngest of my scouts was nearly killed. The boy had learned the rudiments of handling a rifle and was eager to try out his new-found

skill. He spotted a rhino sidling along a belt of bush and promptly headed for him. The rhino disappeared in the bush and the scout followed through a partly opened gap in the undergrowth made by the animal's passing. The wind was in the scout's favor, but the rhino must have heard his footsteps on the hard earth. Suddenly he spun around and charged.

The boy had enough presence of mind to leap into the air with his legs apart. This quick action saved him from being rammed in the crotch by the rhino's horns as the beast rushed under him. Rhinos have two horns, one behind the other. The boy cleared the first horn but touched the second. Immediately, the rhino jabbed upward. The scout went up in the air, his unfired rifle whizzing off in another direction. When he hit the ground, he lay there half stunned. I rushed over to him, thinking he was dead, but except for some bruises and losing a certain amount of skin from between his legs, he was unhurt.

When I lifted him up, the boy said apologetically, "Bwana, I did not have time to shoot. That rhino came as fast as a train. He seemed to fill all space and was on me before I could even think of getting my rifle up."

No need to criticize—the "boy" had, after all, remembered to leap into the air with his legs apart. Less fortunate was another "boy" who crossed paths with the most praised of all game animals—the Cape buffalo. "Hell on wheels," Hunter describes him. In any case, Wynant P. Hubbard tells the story of trying to catch the young of these animals for zoos, the book being *Wild Animals: A White Man's Conquest of Jungle Beasts*—surely a catchy title:

"When I was up in Tanganyika before the War my partner and I used to catch buffalo. We got hold of a calf one day in thick stuff. We were dancing around trying to grab its tail when the niggers let out a yell and beat it.

The mother was coming back. I fired at her, but it just made her all the madder. I ran for a tree and climbed. She got my partner. Before I could do anything she hooked him and tossed him about ten yards. Then she went over and knelt on him and danced on him. Every now and then she would leave what was left of Fritz and come over and bash my tree to shake me out. I had to sit up there for two hours and watch that cow trample Fritz into a mass of mud and blood. I'm no good now. If I see a buffalo I shake like a leaf. I can't help it. My nerves are all broken. Elephants, lions. Yes, I'm all right there. But buffalo!"

"What happened to your rifle?" Mackie asked.

"I dropped it trying to climb the tree. Every time I'd start down after it that cursed cow would come for me. Fritz was dead anyway. What could I have done?

"That's the trouble. Catching the calf itself isn't so hard. You might lose a nigger maybe. But the good Lord help you if any of the herd come back to get that calf. It's either kill them or be killed."

"Yes, or climb a tree."

"Climb a tree," snorted Harry. "Supposing there isn't any tree?"

"You're out of luck."

*

The twin gods of the hunter are Ernest Hemingway and Theodore Roosevelt. Of the former, perhaps one of Mr. Hemingway's quotations will suffice: "Certainly there is no hunting like the hunting of man; and those who have hunted armed men long enough and liked it, never really care for anything else thereafter." If this does not suffice, I recall a couple of years ago attending a press conference in which Mrs. Hemingway not only announced a "new" Hemingway manuscript, but also declared there were many more in progress—this some years after Mr. Hemingway's suicide. "There are pounds and pounds of them," she said. She mentioned in particular a long manuscript about a safari in Africa which, she said, "had very amusing stuff." This worried me—in view of her idea of what's amusing. I had just read, for example, a recent interview with Mrs. Hemingway by Judith Martin in the Washington *Post:*

> It's *her* leopard on the study wall. *His* leopard which he gave her one Christmas, is a throw on the back of a chair. "Mine is faded. Ernest's shrank, but his was never as big as mine."
> It's her lion in the hallway, with the bullet hole in its back. "I was going to shoot him in the shoulder but the coward turned around. I had to shoot him in the ass."

Theodore Roosevelt at least could not be charged with humor. Nor can he be faulted for at least some efforts in the field of conservation. But here praise must end. When it came to killing animals, he was close to psychopathic. Many reasons have been given for this, but they are all perhaps best summed up by a close friend who once, late in Roosevelt's life, memorably defended him. "You must always remember," the friend said, "that the President is about six." Perhaps that story would explain the popularity of the children's toy, the "Teddy Roosevelt" iron bank. "Watch Teddy shoot the penny into the bank slot," says the advertisement, "and the 'ole grizzly' pop up and down. Fascinating nostalgia everyone will love."

Roosevelt's famous African safari, out of which came his book *African Game Trails*, was from start to finish a bloodbath. Early in the book he sets the scene:

> I rarely had to take the trouble to stalk anything; the shooting was necessarily at rather long range, but by manoeuvring a little, and never walking straight toward

a beast, I was usually able to get whatever the naturalist wished. Sometimes I shot fairly well, and sometimes badly. On one day, for instance, the entry in my diary ran: "Missed steinbuck, pig, impala and Grant; awful." On another day, it ran in part as follows: "Out with Heller. Hartebeest, 250 yards, facing me; shot through face, broke neck. Zebra, very large, quartering, 160 yards, between neck and shoulder. Buck Grant, 220 yards, walking, behind shoulder. Steinbuck, 180 yards, standing, behind shoulder."

Roosevelt's son Kermit shot seven cheetahs in one day. But not even cheetahs, lions, leopards, buffaloes, elephants, hippos, pigs, impalas, hartebeest and zebra were enough. The party seems to have shot everything but their bearers:

Springhaas live in big burrows, a number of them dwelling together in one community, the holes close to one another, and making what in the West is called a "town" in speaking of prairie dogs. At night, they come out to feed on the grass. They are as heavy as a big jack-rabbit, with short forelegs and long hindlegs and tail, so that they look and on occasion move like miniature kangaroos, although, in addition to making long hops and jumps, they often run almost like an ordinary rat or rabbit. They are pretty creatures, fawn-colored above and white beneath, with the terminal half of the tail very dark. In hunting them, we simply walked over the flats for a couple of hours, flashing the bull's eye lantern on all sides, until we saw the light reflected back by a spring-haas' eyes. Then I would approach to within range, and hold the lantern in my left hand so as to shine both on the sight and on the eyes in front, resting my gun on my left wrist. The number 3 shot, in the Fox double barrel, would always do the business if I held straight enough. There was nothing but the gleam of the eyes to shoot at; and this might suddenly be raised or lowered as the intently watching animal crouched on all fours or raised itself on its hind legs. I shot half a dozen.

Roosevelt seemed to find particular pleasure in assassinating, of all animals, giraffes:

One of the smaller ones began to make off, and both the others shifted their positions slightly, curling their tails. I instantly dropped on my knee, and getting the bee just behind the big bull's shoulder, I fired with the 300-yard sight. I heard the "pack" of the bullet as it struck just where I aimed; and away went all three giraffes at their queer rocking-horse canter. Running forward, I emptied my magazine, firing at the big bull, and also at one of his smaller companions, and then, slipping into the barrel what proved to be a soft-nosed bullet, I fired at the latter again. The giraffe was going straight-away and it was a long shot, at four or five hundred yards; but by good luck the bullet broke its back and down it came. . . . The wounded one lagged behind, but when I got near he put on a spurt, and as I thought I was close enough I leaped off, throwing the reins over the sorrel's head, and opened fire. Down went the big bull, and I thought my task was done. But as I went back to mount the sorrel he struggled to his feet again and disappeared after his companion among the trees which were thicker here, as we had reached the bottom of the valley. So I tore after him again, and in a minute came to a dry watercourse. Scrambling into and out of this I saw the giraffes ahead of me just beginning the ascent of the opposite slope; and touching the horse with the spur we flew after the wounded bull. This time I made up my mind I would get close enough; but Tranquillity did not quite like the look at the thing ahead of him. . . . So I jumped off, throwing the reins over his head, and opened fire once more; and this time the great bull went down for good.

Finally, in Volume Two of *African Game Trails,* we learn that the great "conservationist" did not even spare ostriches on their nests:

> We got them by stumbling on the nest, which contained eleven huge eggs, and was merely a bare spot in the sand, surrounded by grass two feet high; the bird lay crouched, with the neck flat on the ground. When we accidently came across the nest, the cock was on it and I failed to get him as he ran. The next day we returned and dismounted before we reached the near neighborhood of the nest. Then I advanced, cautiously, my rifle at the ready. It seemed impossible that so huge a bird could lie hidden in such scanty cover, but not a sign did we see until, when we were sixty yards off, the hen, which this time was on the nest, rose and I killed her at sixty yards. Even this did not make the cock desert the nest; and on a subsequent day I returned and after missing him badly, I killed him at 85 yards; and glad I was to see the huge, black-and-white bird tumble in the dust.

To "commemorate" that safari—a curious idea in itself—fifty years afterward, in 1959, Theodore Roosevelt's grandson Kermit and his great-grandsons, Kermit, Jr., and Jonathan, made a safari to the same area. Kermit wrote a book about it entitled *A Sentimental Safari.* They were not so sentimental, however, that they didn't do their full share of carrying on the great tradition. This time, as in the first hunt, the excuse was also "specimens" for the museums—as if, after a hundred years of slaughter, the museums themselves weren't stuffed to bursting. In any case, herewith Kermit's account of the "considerable success" of his son Jonathan:

> After losing a couple of hyraxes which, though we thought them hit squarely, had managed to get beyond his grasp into their caves, he had dropped two right in

their tracks, so he had the specimens he needed. Then, as he was walking back toward the track across the center of the rim of rock—I believe the rock walls in which hyraxes had their caves formed the circle of the cone of a long extinct sunken volcano—he had come upon a pair of dik-dik, the smallest of the African antelope, not much bigger than a chihuahua. Dik-dik were also on his list, and a snap shot killed one of the pair. Jonathan had read that dik-dik were among the comparatively few animals that mate for life, and when Terry confirmed this, Jonathan regretted having left half of a happy pair bereft. As Musyemi was loading the animals into the Land Rover, one of the supposedly dead hyraxes revived and attempted to bite him with yellow rodentlike teeth. Musyemi gripped it firmly and hit it just below the base of the skull with the back of his heavy knife. The animal subsided, but ten minutes later, when we were on our way back to camp, the operation had to be repeated. He told us that hyraxes are very tough animals and that this was a pregnant female—these are especially tenacious of life.

Even in Kermit's grandfather's day, such hunting had given rise to criticism—and by no less a personage than Mark Twain himself. Mr. Twain, indeed, made Theodore Roosevelt's hunting an integral part of one of his most famous lectures. Herewith Mark Twain tonight, as reported by eyewitness Samuel Stevens Hood:

"Take this fellow, Harry Orchard, out West," he ingratiatingly began. "Now I like a fellow like that: straightforward, downright honest. He blew up the house of an enemy and then shot to death the only eyewitness of the crime. When interrogated by the police captain after the capture, as to why he had killed the eyewitness, Orchard coolly replied: 'Why, Cap, it stands to reason. I had to shoot the evidence.'

"Now," avowed Mr. Clemens heartily, "I can't help

but like that fellow Orchard. You must hand it to him: he's honest. Cold-blooded, yes; but truthful.

"On the other hand, take Teddy Roosevelt," he continued with a steely glint in his eye. "Just read, if you please, this horrible brutal book about shooting deer and other wild game. Game! Teddy is not content with stalking these poor beasts and mercilessly shooting down the lovely, defenceless creatures from ambush—*from ambush*! (he shouted) with a high powered express rifle. He must go further and tell, with meticulous detail, how he deliberately raised the gun to his shoulder, took careful aim, pulled the trigger, and then—by God!—describes the wave of savage exultation which sweeps through his being as he óbserved the murderous softnosed bullet tear its jagged way through the tender flesh and sees the poor, bleeding, stricken creature stagger, totter, fall to its pitiful death."

These words were shot forth with savage intensity and bitterness. His auditors waited spell-bound, afraid to break the silence with the sound of even a breath. Mark slowly puffed away at the monster calabash pipe and blew out volumes of sulphurous smoke which seemed perfectly attuned to his mood. Then, after a long, ruminative pause, he suddenly barked savagely: "If I had to choose between these two, give me Harry Orchard every time."

*

"Big game buffs of course," writes Russell Barnett Aitken, one of the premier big-game hunters still unmounted,

> have their idols just as do baseball, tennis and soccer fans. In my time, there were four outstanding big game hunters whose feats were hailed around the globe: W. D. M. "Caramojo" Bell, the greatest elephant hunter of them all; Marcus Daly, another case-hardened veteran of the Ivory Trail; Jim Corbett, who tracked down and killed the man-eaters of Kumoon; and J. A. Hunter, guttiest

of the East African professionals. It was my privilege to
have known them all and their boots will be rather hard
to fill.

It won't be for lack of trying. Mr. Aikten himself has even
included in his *Great Game Animals* the giant panda. "A
dedicated hunter," he declares, "will take a chance on frostbite, pneumonia, heart attack and the possibility of a broken
neck in the pursuit of mountain game, whether it be the little
chamois of the European Alps, the Walia ibex of Abyssinia,
or the great corkscrew-horned *Ovis poli* of the Pamir Plateau."
"To get a shot at a tiger," he continues "he will sit patiently in
a leafy *machan* for a dozen grueling hours without moving a
muscle—and do it night after night.

"Frostbite?" Pneumonia? Heart attack? Broken neck?

Perhaps the most remarkable attempt to keep the Big Name
Big Game tradition going was made a few years ago by Peter
Barrett, outdoor editor of *True* Magazine, in his book *Great
True Hunts.* Mr. Barrett brought out a full roster of kings and
princes, Hollywood stars and sports heroes, to show that all
were gamy to the core. Start with Prince Bernhard of the Netherlands, who, along with Prince Philip, is one of the leaders of
the World Wildlife Fund.

> The Prince and his loader worked together like a well-
> drilled team, the Prince firing as soon as the butt of the
> Churchill hit his shoulder, and the loader loading so fast
> his fingers seemed to flicker over the breech momentarily.
> I never saw the Prince miss, and only rarely did he
> have to give a winged bird a second barrel as it came
> skittering down in a long arc.

Move on to King Paul of Greece at Stavros Niarchos' hunting preserve at Spetsopoula:

> The King was swinging and shooting; the gun loader
> was reloading and replacing guns and Halmi was click-

ing his camera as fast as he could, quietly and politely cursing in German, Hungarian and Italian that he didn't have a camera loader along to assist him. The Queen was busy keeping the King informed by shouting strategy.

"Over your left shoulder! Here, comes a big one! Don't shoot that smaller one—it's a hen!"

It's always nice, in hunting, to have the feminine viewpoint. In any case, next turn to one of our own governors, former Governor Quinn of Hawaii, and an after-hunt idyll:

Everyone had connected. But best score—an incredible score for a new hunter, was Quinn's: he had killed seven boars with seven shots.

"How many pigs have we got on this island?" the governor asked Dick Woodward, who's Chief of the Bureau of Game.

"About 60,000. The annual kill averages possibly 6,000—far below the natural increase. We could stand more hunting."

"What a tourist attraction," mused Quinn. "If Ernie Albrecht got word of this to West Coast hunters, I'll bet he could pack some of his off-season Pan American jets."

Someone mentioned that a pig was being roasted over an open fire, and we drifted outside to see it. Other boars were hanging up in one of the meat houses the camp provides for the public. The remaining pigs would be poisoned and set out as bait in the wild-dog eradication program.

Hawaii—the Island Paradise. Moving on to the movie stars in *Great True Hunts,* let us begin with Arthur Godfrey in Mozambique:

Godfrey loaded his big Weatherby. A cock crowed in the village. Minutes dragged by. Suddenly the reeds parted as two big bulls climbed into the open about 125 yards across on a small hillside and kept going.

"The first one!" Walter said hurriedly.

Arthur fired, the buffalo lurched hard, then both dived back into the reeds.

"Damn," said Arthur.

"No, I'm sure you walloped him well. Where'd you aim?"

"Right behind the left shoulder, but he was moving pretty fast and I may have gut shot him."

"We'll have a look. You stay here, and watch in case he doubles back. We can tell from the blood trail if you got into his lungs."

Or take Roy Rogers. "For laughs," as the caption reads, "a kudu-zebra trophy."

They walked with little mincing steps, and somehow gave the impression of hardly touching the ground as they drifted among the trees. Two of the bulls had great, black spiraling horns with two and a half full turns.

"My God," whispered Chico. "Two record bulls!"

"Are you sure?" asked Roy.

"Certain. I'd take the one on the left."

Still we watched. Now that we'd at last stalked these magnificent beasts we had a hunger to just look at them for a bit. Then in one smooth motion, Roy put up his rifle and shot the one on the left. The kudu turned back into the depression, unhurriedly, and disappeared. The other bull jumped at the shot, then seemed to float away. They stopped once to look back into the depression as we got up, then moved off.

"Oh man, look at that!"

The kudu lay dead but had lost none of its glory.

In, obviously, a great cause. Next take Kirk Douglas, and hear him tell what a thrill it was to shoot—of all animals—the leopard:

I was aware now that when I squeezed the trigger I had experienced a thrilled surge of emotion that somehow was vaguely familiar. There had been a warm and elemental satisfaction. Perhaps it was somehow connected with my killing a killer. Certainly I have felt nothing like this when I killed other game. For a moment there was a nagging suggestion, *You've been here before, Kirk.* But that didn't make sense. No matter what or why, the experience left me strangely satisfied, warm and completely relaxed.

Finally, take two sports figures. First, Sam Snead shooting —incredibly—an elephant:

> The big tusker was not in a proper position for the difficult bull's-eye brain shot just in front of the ear. Rather than move and risk "winding" the bull, Sam chose to make the safer heart shot. Mortally wounded, the tusker trumpeted once, spun around, then crumpled as hunter Jenvey automatically fired the crippling leg-breaking shot in case Sam's had not been perfect. Bolting another round into the chamber, Sam quickly applied the *coup de grace* to the downed elephant's brain, then let out a rebel yell that must have scared game for miles around.
>
> "Maaaaan, did you see him go down? Just like he was pole-axed," Sam exulted when he caught his breath. "Wow!"

Mr. Snead, the book tells us, now owns "the most unique golf-bag in the world," which, we are told, is made from his elephant's right rear leg, and has extra pockets and straps of tanned elephant ear. Last but not least, don't overlook Joe Foss, ex-Governor of South Dakota and former Commissioner of the American Football League. He tackled, via airplane, a polar bear.

> "The heck with you guys," Joe said finally, "I'm going to kill the bear, he's turning 'round." He shot and the bear fell, but got up again.

Blood appeared below its left eye.

Foss shot again and ice exploded in front of the bear's head.

"My rifle is shooting cockeyed," Joe said.

Once more he shot and missed the bear.

"Give me your rifle, Tommy."

Now Foss dropped the bear with two shoulder shots (where he'd aimed before) and we breathed easier. The bear lay still as we ran forward. Then we halted 20 feet away.

"He's dead," Tommy said presently. "A fine trophy!"

Jack O'Connor, formerly "gun editor" of *Outdoor Life,* is a present-day hunting expert. In his book *The Art of Hunting Big Game, in North America,* Mr. O'Connor tells you about everything from "stillhunting" to how to "work" a mountain. And, of course, he "knows" animals:

All animals interpret signs of weakness as fear and think they have the upper hand. Stand your ground with a mean range bull and you'll get into trouble. Run and he'll chase you. The first time you ride a horse, belt the hell out of him the first time he decides to poke along at his own gait. Otherwise he'll think you're afraid of him and will make your life miserable.

A bit later, Mr. O'Connor tells you what to do if your horse doesn't want to carry carcasses:

A great many horses are allergic to having a deer put on them. They jump around, making packing the deer difficult, and sometimes they lash out with their hind feet. I cure this by blindfolding a horse with a large bandanna handkerchief, then covering my hand with deer blood and rubbing it over the horse's nose and into its nostrils. If the horse still feels like kicking—and he almost never does—I tie one hind up with a rope to the saddlehorn. When the hunter takes off the blindfold and starts leading the horse to camp he is generally philosophical. I have even seen horses uncomplainingly carry mountain lions and black bears into camp after being blindfolded and given the blood-in-the-nose treatment.

Such a man is obviously well aware of the trials and tribulations of today's hunting. "Drives," for example, he tells us, aren't what they were in the old days because even in Britain "the peasants are getting uppity." Tired, perhaps, of being mistaken for pheasants. But Mr. O'Connor himself is far from uppity. Indeed, when he takes on the question of wounded animals—one ducked by so many hunters, even though the figures are astronomical—he is positively down to earth.

A shot through the body cavity behind the diaphragm made an animal sick and miserable. Animals shot in the liver seem to be in great pain. They are reluctant to move and generally die before long, as the liver is full of blood vessels and they bleed heavily. But the animal wounded only in the abdominal cavity can, if pushed, travel a long way and is often very difficult to recover. On two occasions I have seen animals lose everything back of their diaphragms and yet travel. A big buck mule deer I shot dragged his stomach and intestines along the ground behind him for about 100 yards before he fell. He was dead when I got to him. A desert bighorn ram shot by a friend I was hunting with had his abdomen laid open by a .300 Savage bullet as he ran directly away from the hunter down a canyon. He ran out on a flat and when he jumped a barrel cactus the protruding stomach caught in the thorns and was jerked out. The ram ran between a quarter and a half mile before he fell dead.

Make no mistake. Mr. O'Connor's book is full of helpful hints. "It is dangerous," he tells us, "to try to cut the throat of an animal that is still living." To *try*, mind you. But always Mr. O'Connor is a lover of beauty. In one of the photographs accompanying one of his articles in *Outdoor Life,* he is pictured, a bald man with glasses, sitting on top of a kudu he has just shot. The caption reads, "Kudu I took after a pretty stalk."

*

"The rewards of hunting are physical, emotional and in many cases spiritual." So states the National Shooting Sports Foundation, an organization that may not shoot sports foundations but apparently does shoot almost everything else. And the spirituality bit looms large in hunting literature. In a University of Arizona booklet entitled *Values of Hunting and Fishing in Arizona*—a typical promotion effort—one hunter is quoted: "It makes me almost religious when I'm sitting on a mountain waiting for a deer sometimes. I almost feel like praying." At the 1973 North American Wildlife Conference, 5,540 "sportsmen" were asked to rank their hunting "satisfaction." And the very first was "being close to Nature." Other "satisfactions" were, in order, "escapism," "companionship," "shooting," "hunting skills," "reading and talking about hunting," "display of trophies," "actual game harvest," and finally "enjoyment of equipment."

Leaving the latter three thrills for a moment, there is no question that "reading and talking about hunting," like hunting itself, is big business. And, as Robert T. Allen notes in *Give Our Animals an Even Break,* the game doesn't have to be big to give the big thrill. Here's Gil Faust, for example, in *Sports Afield*: "The cross hairs quartered the little chuck's chest . . . my finger tightened . . . I saw the chuck explode in the scope as though it had swallowed a grenade." Frank DeHaas in *Guns* began, "Dad, what can I shoot? You gave me a rifle, when can I use it?" Dad's answer was that he could shoot turtles, water snakes, pocket gophers, ground squirrels, crows, jack-rabbits, blackbirds, woodchucks, prairie dogs, foxes (Dad especially recommended picking off young foxes as they played around the den), English sparrows, starlings, great horned owls, magpies, jays and crows (the sport, Dad said, could be had when the young were just old enough to fly and he added that he had nothing against shooting them off the nest).

"That's one little boy," commented Allen, "I wouldn't want to turn my back on."

All the gunmen's magazines do their best to carry on the "great" hunting tradition and to tell you—even nowadays—how dangerous it still is and what a hero you still are. " 'Okay,' " one article begins, " 'there's your Alaska trophy brown bear,' I said to Bill Baker, my current hunter, when we spotted the brown giant and his mate in a snowlined drift 120 yards above us. 'Anchor him, boy.' "

" 'Here comes your Alaska grizzly, boy,' " begins another article in another magazine, "I said to young Dale Evarts, the newest guest at Denna Lake Lodge, as the big, high-humped bear charged into view. 'Harvest!' "

Second sentences are apparently allowed to vary, but not by much. Poundage is almost always emphasized. "1,000 POUNDS OF TROUBLE" is one title. In "THOSE KILLER TRAMP TIGRES" the author writes, "A handsome, heavy-shouldered brute . . . I gave him 240 pounds." In "SAGA OF A HUNTING CAYUSE" the victim is "A mahogany-colored specimen, hog-shouldered," but the line is almost the same, "I gave him 500 pounds."

Bears are a favorite of the hunters' hero syndrome. "BELIEVE IT! BLACK BEARS ATTACK!" one article is entitled. "Angry charging bears convince me . . . shouldering out of some wolf willows, he gave a hoarse whowf-whowf and popped his

jaws." "THE LOOKOUT GRIZZLY" is another title, one with the
subtitle, "A FURIOUS SOW CHARGES US AND WE'RE TRAPPED
WITH NO EXIT." "I WAS MAULED BY A BROWN BEAR" is still
another; this one is subtitled "AN ALASKAN GUIDE, WITH 150
BROWN AND POLAR BEARS TO HIS CREDIT, FINDS HIMSELF FLAT
ON HIS BACK WITH A WOUNDED, ENRAGED BROWNIE CHEWING
ON HIS FACE AND HIS CLIENT UNABLE TO GET A CLEAR SHOT."
Well, some days are like that. In any case, bears are by no
means the only danger. In fact, it soon becomes evident from
reading these magazines that whatever the hunter wants to
assassinate is a fearful foe indeed. Of course, when it comes to
the deer family, the proving of the danger is more difficult—
but it's not for want of trying. "I WANTED IT WILD" reads one
title. "I LEARNED HARSH FACTS FROM MY FIRST MOOSE HUNT—
BUT WHAT A SEQUEL!" "EVEN YOUR ODDS FOR ELK" is another
—a spotting scope is suggested for "trophy action." "NEVER
UNDERESTIMATE THE MULEY" is still another. "THE AVERAGE
MULE DEER BUCK," goes the subtitle, "HAS SOME HAZARDOUS
HABITS THAT WOULD MAKE THE MOST FOOLHARDY WHITETAIL
TURN PREMATURELY GREY." Dangerous, apparently, to other
deer, if not to you. But even whitetails can be made, in these
magazines, to appear ferocious. "NOW YOU'RE HUNTING SUPER
DEER," reads one of these. "EACH YEAR THE BUCKS ARE GET-
TING SMARTER. HOW CAN THE HUNTER KEEP PACE?"

It wrings your heart, all right. However, one way that is
suggested is to walk differently. "There's a definite difference,"
the author states firmly, "in the manner in which a bear or
another deer breaks a twig as opposed to the way man does it.
A man walks with a purposeful, rhythmical gait which gives
a clear alarm. Try to cultivate a quiet, uneven gait."

Be a man, in other words, who walks like a bear. But
remember, of course, that the deer has tremendous advantages

over you—such as, for example, its vision. "Those big brown eyes," the articles goes on, "have a light-gathering ability that makes you blind by comparison."

Just little you—against the big, all-seeing horned monster. But deer aren't the only worthy adversaries—there are also turkeys. "MY OLD KENTUCKY GOBBLER" is a title here. "THESE GIANT GOBBLERS," runs the subtitle, "HAVE STEADILY OUT-WITTED HUNTERS FOR 200 YEARS, AND THEY'RE STILL AT IT." A wild turkey, we learn, is the only animal that can distinguish a man sitting motionless on a stump. A terrifying thought for the little man out there indeed. And you must watch out, of course, for other birds. "MONARCH OF THE WESTERN SKIES" is the title of an article on how to kill the "Great Canada Honker." "THE HONKER," the subtitle tells us, "IS A WILY BIRD." Even grouse, in these articles, can grow to—and we quote— "BROWN BOMBERS."

If you're not already frightened to death, you must also apparently keep an eagle eye out for raccoons. "MORE COON THAN WE COULD HANDLE," says one title—and "I RAN INTO ONE THAT WAS SHEER DYNAMITE." Or rabbits. They apparently can be "super," too. "RABBITS DON'T BLINK" says another title— "MAKE NO MISTAKE, THE COTTONTAIL IS NOT A DUMB BUNNY." And then we have "RABBITS THE HARD WAY," by, of all people, a John W. Rockefeller:

> For the "nonchalant approach" you just pick a point a bit off to the side of your intended victim, and go strolling toward him. Do not stop or change direction, or the bunny will hit the panic button and take off. Just walk along as though you hadn't a thought in your head, as though you didn't even know there was a bunny in the world. Then, at your point of closest approach, you suddenly wheel around, raise your gun quickly and get your shot. Won't he be surprised?

Otherwise, apparently, *he* might surprise *you*. The important thing, evidently, is not to underestimate your furry terror. Harold Blaisdell, in a 1974 *True* Magazine, finds the rabbit "WINTER'S SPORTIEST HUNTING," and he should know, because he has, as he modestly puts it, faced "such challenges as exploding grouse, veering woodcock, and mile-a-minute black ducks." And then Mr. Blaisdell goes on with an experience with his dog Sarah which was, evidently, nip and tuck:

> The magazine of my autoload holds 15 long-rifle cartridges. When I went to unload before snapping the lead to Sarah's collar, I discovered that the rifle was empty! When a plain old snowshoe hare can come that close to taking you for all that you have in the pot, who needs tigers?

A snowshoe *hare*! Last but not least one of these magazines comes to grips with the perils of going after—hold everything now—the prairie dog. One tough bozo, you'll learn. Writes Don L. Flores in " PRAIRIE DOG SHOOT":

> I am a 24-year-old college instructor. . . . We agreed that we would devote a day or two to gunning the large prairie-dog towns scattered throughout western Oklahoma. Having been something of a prairie-dog hunter for several years, I knew we had tough shooting ahead. . . .
> In addition to our rifles and indispensable binoculars, we broke out three bench-rest saddlebags, a bipod and a light camera tripod.

What, no quadpod? The article proceeds, with one particularly memorable eyeball-to-eyeball confrontation:

> This particular prairie dog was one of those adolescents that just barely peek out from a burrow and yap about your shooting ability. The range wasn't much over 60 yards, but all I could see was an eye peeking out of the hole. I imagine the vertical target area was about a

quarter of an inch. At the shot, dirt erupted from the mount and the prairie dog stopped yapping for good.

Taught his lesson by a college instructor.

But of course some animals are so vicious, or perhaps so viciously difficult to kill, that the poor hunter needs help. Here all the sporting magazines courageously rise to the challenge. Page after page of their issues are devoted to calls, lures, baits and scents. And, if you can't afford the mechanical or even electronic masterpieces, you can at least learn, like the wise old hunters of yore, to roll your own. The realistic "mouse squeak," so effective for "varmints," we learn, for example, is done so simply it's amazing—just "by kissing the back of one's hand." You must practice, though, over and over. Only then can you get to be an "expert." It's certainly a lovely picture. A fieldful of hunters, all kissing the backs of their hands. Hands, we repeat.

Joining the "varmint callers," however, writes Lupi Saldana, in the Los Angeles *Times,* can be expensive:

> Equipment includes: a jeep type vehicle with a platform built in the rear section by cutting off part of the top: a rifle, anything from a 22-250 to a 300 H&H; rifle holders; a tape deck and loudspeaker to use for recorded calls; Weems handcalls for those . . . who prefer to do their own calling, a camouflage suit; two-light spotlight; floodlight; extra batteries and an atomizer filled with rabbit scent that is discharged to decoy the predators when they get downwind from hunters.
>
> The tapes include such calls, or "songs," as young jackrabbit, adult jackrabbit, yellow hammer woodpecker, flicker, cotton tail, rabbit and deer.

And calls aren't just for "varmints." In *Great True Hunts,* there is the story of Dale Lee, one of the two remaining of the five Lee brothers who, the book tells us, are "the outstanding hound-and-cat men in North America." Dale Lee built his own jaguar call—a *bromadura*, or roarer, a large gourd cut open again, covered with a sheet of rawhide, to which was attached a thong rubbed with resin. By pulling the thong between his thumb and forefinger, Mr. Lee can, the book tells us, "make a grunting roar which sounds more like a jaguar than another jaguar":

> At one time, in the Bravo Swamps, when Dale and his brother Clell were hunting in a native dugout canoe, a jaguar answered the call so enthusiastically that the cat swam out and threatened to climb into the canoe with them. They beat him off with a wooden paddle.

An advertisement in *Field & Stream* for "buck scent" reads, "One whiff and your trophy buck will be charging in." "BUGLE YOUR ELK IN CLOSE," reads an article in the same magazine. In this Dave Harbour tells us that "good recordings" are available for "both a mature and a young elk" from Electronic Game Calls, Inc. It's only a matter of time, obviously, before one can do the whole thing without the necessity of leaving the fellowship of your camp at all.

Bert Popowski, the King of the Crow Killers—he has killed over 100,000 of them—estimates that there are a million "calls" of various types made and sold every calendar year. In his book, *Calling All Game*, he puts us on notice, however, that squirrels can be very wary. "Once they have been worked over by call and gun," he writes, "their curiosity is vastly tempered with caution." One of Mr. Popowski's friends, a man named Bill Donovan, does not, Mr. Popowski points out, even use squirrel dogs to hunt these wary animals but instead prefers his "squirrel cat"—who, we learn, is an ordinary house cat named Comanche:

> "About four years ago, I decided that Comanche ought to be able to help me bringing in a mess of squir-

rels. So I put him in a burlap sack and carried him out
to the woods and turned him loose. He didn't like that
ride in the sack; it not only ruffled his dignity but set a
good share of his hair on end. So the first thing he did
was to get far enough away from me so I couldn't catch
him, then sat down on a log and started to lick his fur
into some semblance of order.

"I don't believe he'd been at the job for ten seconds
before a squirrel spied him. And ten seconds later, there
were four of them, calling down the wrath of all squirrel-
dom on his feline form. Comanche merely glared at his
tormentors and went on straightening his rumpled fur.

"But when I shot one of those squirrels through the
head with a .22 scope-sighted rifle, Comanche was on it
almost as soon as it hit the ground. Did those other squirrels go back into hiding? Not so you'd notice it.

"They literally exploded at the big tom cat handling
one of their kind. I shot the other three, on easier shots
than I've ever had in squirrel hunting, took the ones
Comanche had picked up away from him, and led off
farther into the woods. Comanche followed, the fresh
blood of that one squirrel on his whiskers.

"We got three more at that second stand. . . ."

And, if a cat is so terrific as a lure for squirrels, why, a doe
in heat for bucks is surely buck soup. Mr. Popowski quotes
Bill O'Rourke of Gaylord, Michigan, who, he says, "has probably killed as many deer as any hunter of my acquaintance."

"The herd was in thick, low cedar, where I couldn't
see them too well. That doe was my decoy for all three
bucks. I shot a 5-pointer through the shoulders as he
mounted the doe. I was using a little .250 Savage, the
wind was blowing hard and the herd just milled around
after the first shot. Pretty soon a thin-antlered 4-pointer
tried his luck and I shot him. Then a husky spike got interested, and I got him too."

And, finally, there is in almost all of these magazines a column of helpful hunting hints. It's difficult to pick a favorite here, but one candidate would surely be, from "Tap's Tips," the following:

> Some hunters tie off the anus and bladder when they dress a deer, and some don't. If you do, take some wire "twisters" with you, and use them. You will find they are much handier for this purpose than a piece of string or boot lacing.

And then, of course, there's the danger of forgetting how much you've shot. Take the following from *Field & Stream*:

> Can't remember how many game birds of what kinds you shoot each year? Save a tail feather from each bird as a tally. At season's end, arrange a "bouquet" of them in a small vase filled with sand, for a souvenir of the hunting season.

To tide you over, with the beauty of it all, until next year.

*

Ludicrous as is the present-day promotion of hunting, its excesses in the past alone would have occasioned it to die— you will excuse the expression—a natural death. It would have, that is, had it not been for the fact that the hunter, seeing there would soon be nothing left to kill, seized upon the new-fangled idea of "conservation" with a vengeance. Soon they had such a stranglehold on so much of the movement that the word itself was turned from the idea of protecting and saving the animals to the idea of raising them and using them—for killing. The idea of wildlife "management"—for man, of course—was born. Animals were to be "harvested." They were to be a "crop"—like corn.

The word "conservation" is a twentieth-century word, dating

only as far back as 1907, when Gifford Pinchot, riding in Washington, D.C.'s Rock Creek Park, first determined, as he wrote in his autobiography, "that there was no single word to describe the interrelationship of forests, soils, water, fish, wildlife, etc." Later, either he or an associate of his in the Forest Service, Overton Price—they never could remember which—suggested the word, one which, says historian James Trefethen, was derived from the word "conservator"—as used by the British Civil Service for one of its colonial offices in India.

In the old days, all animals "belonged" to the king. Since the United States decided not to have a king, all animals "belonged," as it were, to no one. And then, since our Constitution made no specific provision, and since all matters not specific to the Federal Government reverted to the states, the animals, still not belonging to anyone, were left, legally, to the tender mercies of the state governments—where they still remain, except that, of course, the hunters soon saw to it that they got control of all state governments; at least as far as wildlife was concerned.

Not that it would matter much if the animals belonged to the Federal Government. The Federal Government is riddled—again, please excuse—with pro-hunters. Some years ago, it will be recalled, the then Vice President Lyndon Johnson attempted to hold President Kennedy up to ridicule because the latter, on a visit to Johnson's Texas ranch, did not want to shoot a deer. And President Nixon, choosing a gift for Soviet chief Leonid Brezhnev, chose, of all gifts, an elaborately engraved gun, inscribed in gold with the Russian bear and the American eagle, as well as a plaque reading, on top, "TO HIS EXCELLENCY, LEONID BREZHNEV, FROM THE SPORTSMEN OF AMERICA," and, underneath, "FROM SPORTSMAN TO SPORTS-

MAN IN PEACE AND TRADE." Man to man, in other words, and son of a gun to son of a gun.

The United States Fish and Wildlife Service—the "service," presumably, being the good they do killing animals—is the official name of the U.S. Government's department which concerns itself with wildlife. Under this is the bureau that does its work—and thus has the graciousness to add the word "Sport" to its title—the Bureau of Sport Fisheries and Wildlife. Recently, and for many years, the director of the Bureau of Sport Fisheries and Wildlife was Dr. John Gottschalk, and few men ever "served" hunters more solicitously. Witness a typical Gottschalk statement:

> Hunting is a sport often tedious, always demanding of exertion, but nevertheless exciting and pleasurable. It is not all "fun" to pluck geese or haul the carcass of a 150-lb. deer through brush. . . . The waterfowl gunner is, more often than not, cold in autumn's early morning marsh and frustrated because the greenhorns in the neighboring pit have been shooting at high-flying fowl. A pheasant hunter plods on feet aching from miles of fields and borders. The quail shooter may be hot and itchy in the warm southern afternoon or shivering on a frost-rimmed landscape. A rabbit hunter growls at the weight of six cottontails while looking for his lost beagle. The deer slayer snarls in frustration after two days of no whitetail. A dove hunter gets fingertips full of burrs and the squirrel hunter had a crick in his neck from looking at treetops. . . . And all of them think the price in pain—and cash—is little enough to pay for their favorite pastime.

Pamphlet after pamphlet and leaflet after leaflet pour from the U.S. Fish and Wildlife Service, which is part of the Department of the Interior, telling of, if not the virtues of hunting, at least the nonvirtues of nonhunting. When you write to the Government, for example, protesting a particularly vicious and cruel hunt, you will get back a leaflet entitled *Today's Threat to Our Nation's Wildlife.* It begins as follows:

> The U.S. Fish and Wildlife Service receives several thousands of letters a year expressing a deepening concern for the future of wildlife. These letters hold two widely divergent views: the hunting of animals versus complete protectionism. The vast majority of letters ask about endangered species of wildlife and very strongly favor more animal protection. However, much of the sentiment against hunting is based on misinformation.

Then it goes on:

> Whether you hunt wild animals or wear their pelts is a matter of personal choice. Legal hunting is not a threat to any species in this country.

No mention, of course, of the illegal. Then:

> The danger today is that these two groups will get so emotional arguing for or against hunting that they'll not unite against the real threats to wildlife destruction— *pollution* and habitat destruction.

Join in this crusade, the leaflet asks, and forget about why you wrote in the first place. And, in a spirit of brotherhood with the hunter, the leaflet concludes:

> So now we have a new, valid wildlife constituency. Hunters, fishermen and citizen wildlife organizations have been on the battleline a long time, and most of the species they love and use are not in trouble—yet. Now many millions more of our people are concerned, but through lack of information wrongly blame hunting interests for wildlife's plight. This is not the time for those who love wild things to be attacking each other, but to join together in putting forward bold new programs.

Even Nathaniel Reed, Assistant Secretary of the Interior, and a man who has probably done more for animals than most government figures in recent years, was by no means up to taking on the hunters. Indeed, accepting an award for President Nixon at the annual convention of Game Coin—a group of international big-game hunters—in San Antonio, Mr. Reed wet out of his way to pay tribute to the group. "In considering what is humane," Mr. Reed asked, "is it worse to kill a selected animal cleanly as a hunter—or to cover it with oil, drain its habitat so it can't reproduce or subtly poison it with chemicals over a period of years?"

The hunting question, indeed, was quickly begged. Then, obliquely at least, praised. "Harry Tennison," Mr. Reed went on, speaking of the president of Game Coin, "referred to the hunting areas of the world as the 'cathedrals where we worship.' I agree." One wonders whether Secretary Reed would also have agreed with the way one listener interpreted the minister's invocation at the beginning of the meeting, "O Lord, in Thy goodness, grant us more game animals. . . ."

As for the United States Congress, here perhaps the man who in recent years has been responsible for more pro-animal legislation than any other is Representative John Dingell (R., Michigan). Yet any suggestion that anyone is anti-hunting is enough to make Representative Dingell's blood boil. In the spring of 1972, he was keynote speaker at the National Conference of SAM, the Sportsman's Alliance of Michigan, and sharing the dais with Representative Dingell were such luminaries as the president of the National Shooting Sports Foundation, the field representative of the National Association to Keep and Bear Arms, the Trout King of Michigan and the national commander of something called the North-South Skirmish Association. In such company, Mr. Dingell, who is himself on the board of directors of the National Rifle Association, promptly delivered his credentials:

> I would like to assure you of our hope that we have of continuing our use of firearms, of hunting, our collecting and shooting and all the other activities that mean so much to all of us, will continue unimpaired and unhampered. I'd like to offer you assurance that these things can be passed from generations of Americans yet to come, and that you might someday pass your gun to your son, and that he in turn might pass his gun. . . .

This, mind you, from the man most humanitarians have, sooner or later, to face to get any hearings, let alone any action, on wildlife legislation.

＊

The story of the fight to save America's last wild horses, the wild mustangs, is perhaps the best example of the difficulty of trying to protect any animal against the combined forces of the governments, both Federal and state, and the hunters. In the movie *The Misfits,* Clark Gable's last, and one of the last of Marilyn Monroe's, there were memorable scenes of the savagery of mustang hunting. A similar scene, however, was witnessed in person one day by a woman named Velma Johnston, a secretary in a Nevada office. It made an indelible impression on Ms. Johnston, and, after long and hard work collecting firsthand material, she took her case to the Nevada legislature. Finally, this legislature passed a bill—one that outlawed the running down of wild horses or burros, at least by airplane and other unfair means. But even this small victory was won only barely and even jokingly. The legislators dubbed Ms. Johnston "Wild Horse Annie," and one of them openly boasted she didn't even know that the Federal Government, not Nevada, owned 85 percent of Nevada and practically all of its mustang-hunting land.

Joke they did, but almost before the ink was dry on the state bill, Ms. Johnston was in Washington, D.C., cornering every Senator and Congressman she could find. "Look," she would tell them, "the poor people of Nevada have themselves tried to protect their mustangs, even though they know they own only fifteen percent of their land. Now they're asking you to protect the rest." In short order, the last laugh was hers. Wild Horse Annie had her law.

But still the wild horses and burros were not really protected. The law was in reality just a no-chasing law. The mustangs could still be chased to private land, and no one could prove where the chase had started. They obviously needed further protection, but such was the hold of the hunter-management people that more protection looked impossible to achieve; the Federal Government did not even have a category for such an animal. The Federal Government had, in fact, just four categories of animals: (1) predators, like the wolf and mountain lion, virtually all of which have been hunted or trapped to near extinction; (2) target—i.e., "game"—animals, deer, antelope, etc., which are hunted in regular seasons; (3) "varmints"—coyotes, foxes, raccoons, skunks, etc., which are killed all year 'round, by day and night, by hunting, trapping, poisoning and every other way; and finally (4) endangered species—animals whose whole population is so low that, under certain conditions, they are protected.

The mustang, of course, did not fit under any of these. He was certainly not a predator, nor a target animal—even the hunters, apparently, blanched at shooting horses. Nor were they, even by the hunters' lingo, "varmints." That left only an endangered species, but even this was an impossibility.

The Government had "counted," they said, seventeen thousand wild horses. That was too many for an endangered species. And, even if it weren't, the "Governmentologists" figured out, the wild horse and the wild burro were, after all, just wild brothers of the domestic horse and donkey and surely there were millions of those.

The hunters not only did not help in the fight for the protection of the mustang—they fought it every step of the way. Hunters may not like shooting them but, it seemed, the wild horses as well as wild burros got in the way—or, rather, in the way where feeding was concerned, of some of the hunters' favorite targets, like bighorn sheep. But, though the wild horses and burros may have gotten in the way, for once the hunters did not have their way. Another lone woman champion had appeared—Miss Hope Ryden. Her book, *America's Last Wild Horses,* was even written about on the front page of the *New York Times.* Once again a bill was put into Congress, only this time it was a landmark bill. Because, for the first time, this bill created a brand-new category for wild animals. The wild horse did not have to be predator or varmint, target or endangered species. Instead he was declared, in ringing language, an "aesthetic heritage and national resource."

A class of nine-year-old schoolchildren in Roseburg, Oregon, under the direction of their teacher, Miss Joan Bolsinger, wrote to Washington. Then children in other states also wrote. First there was a trickle, then a river, finally a flood—the largest amount of mail from children in Congressional history. The children went to Washington, too, and personally visited with the children of Senators and Congressmen since it is a bold legislator who will vote against his children's wishes.

*

On December 15, 1971, Congress passed the Wild and Free-Roaming Horses and Burros Act. "Be it enacted," the act read, "that Congress finds and declares that wild free-roaming horses and burros are living symbols of the historic and pioneer spirit of the West, that they contribute to the diversity of life forms within the Nation and enrich the lives of the American people," etc., etc.

But animal workers had long learned that passing an animal bill and enforcing it are two very different things indeed. Scarcely a year after the passage of the act there occurred in March 1973 one of the most brutal wild horse roundups in history. Called the "Howe Massacre"—it took place near Howe, Idaho—it was particularly heinous because it was, according to the Interior Department's own "status sheet" on the roundup, actually "encouraged" by Bureau of Land Management employees in Idaho field offices. George Wilson told the story in *Defenders of Wildlife News*:

> Here was the sequence of events, according to Mrs. William L. Blue, vice-president of the American Horse Protection Association and one of those who went to Idaho to investigate the roundup: A group of Howe, Idaho, ranchers—at the urging of Bureau of Land Management officials—pursued a herd of wild horses by helicopter and snowmobile in the hills outside Howe. Then the ranchers went into the public land on horseback to drive the herd into a corral built on the edge of a cliff. They sewed hog rings into the noses of the 50 to 60 captured horses, with the idea this would impede breathing and make the panicked horses easier to handle. Seven wild horses and one aborted foal—in desperate efforts to escape their captors—plunged over the cliff to their deaths. . . .
>
> "A rancher said a cougar had scared the horses into

jumping over the cliff," Mrs. Blue said. "I asked him: 'Is that the same cougar which sewed in the hog rings?' "*

Another thing animal workers have learned is that, if the Federal Government is hardly a reliable friend, the State Governments are usually animals' mortal enemies. Take, for example, a pamphlet put out by the New York State Department of *Conservation*—italics ours. First there is a "Governor's Message"—"New York State has hunting lands as fine as can be found anywhere. . . . Each year the sportsman can plan for many pleasant and productive days afield." On, presumably, the production line. After the "Governor's Message," there follows a "Commissioner's Message." "In the out of doors," this reads, "few recreational interests are so stimulating as being afield during the autumn hunting season." Particularly stimulating, obviously, when one's own property is under fire. In any case, there follows an "Introduction":

> Hunting, which historically was done out of necessity, is now, in addition to being a traditional American sport, part and parcel of sound game management. The harvesting of surplus game is good conservation. Since wildlife almost always produces more young than the habitat can support, the surplus is lost by death in some manner, including starvation, predation or disease, and thus is wasted. Good conservation and waste are incompatible. Ideally the hunter takes only what would be lost anyway

* As we go to press, there are many suits and countersuits over the "Howe Massacre" still pending. As for the horses themselves, an estimated forty of them survived the massacre and were trucked to the Central Nebraska Packing Plant in North Platte, Nebraska. Here they were supposed to be slaughtered for dog meat at six to eight cents per pound on the hoof. However, due.to the countrywide furor over the massacre, at the last moment the horses were freed. There was just one problem. Of the forty who started the 850-mile truck trek to North Platte there were just eighteen, including one colt born in captivity, who survived it.

and the gun can be much more humane than slow death by starvation or disease.

Moreover, hunting plays a very important part in today's outdoor recreation picture. It is more popular than ever among men and also women of varying ages and is especially important to our youth. With available· leisure time increasing steadily, it is important to teach our youngsters how to use this time to keep themselves healthy and happy. Hunting is an excellent way for them to keep physically fit and at the same time develop an awareness of the natural world around them and the need for the conservation of natural resources.

These paragraphs are almost incredible. First stating it is "much more humane"—without, of course, any mention of the millions of animals wounded each year—the argument then moves on to outright lies. In the 1960s, hunting, despite frantic promotion, almost steadily declined—and this in *total* numbers despite steadily increasing population figures. In actual fact, the total number of hunters, as compared to the total population, is an extremely small fraction. Far less, in fact, than 10 percent. In California, for example, it is 3.4 percent. And, in a recent extensive survey by the Outdoor Recreation Resource Review Commission, headed by Laurance Rockefeller, hunting constituted, of the outdoor activity of Americans, exactly 1.87 percent.

But, to continue with the hunters' control of the State governments, take the mere matter of the name of the departments through which such control is exercised—the state "Fish and Game" departments. Who decreed that all animals—and these fish and game departments do indeed control all wild animals —come under the head of "game"? Not long ago, at a dinner in California, I introduced Margaret Owings, the remarkable humanitarian who is president of Friends of the Sea Otter. Her speech which followed was a memorable one, and deserves careful study by anyone attempting to take on the hunters' control of the States:

> My introduction to wildlife management took place along the border of the Los Padres National Forest, California, in high ridge country laced only by a fire-road. It was the early fifties when I was hiking along an animal trail with my dog. A government vehicle appeared and braked to a stop to warn me that I had better pick up my dog since traps and cyanide guns had just been set out. Quite naturally, I asked the man what they were after. The answer was "predators" because they had just introduced a dozen wild turkeys into the area and wanted to clear the region of their natural enemies. I didn't need an education in science to recognize that the protection of exotic game targets for the sportsmen through attrition against predators upon which the natural system depended, was wrong. From that moment on, I took a new look. I paid attention to government agencies and their bureaus and the pressures that directed their activities.
>
> Administrators of the natural resources, I found, usually claim that their decisions are in the public interest. This "public interest," however, is subject to opinions based on self-interest and reflects dominant groups.
>
> Who are the dominant groups that direct the administration of wildlife in California? Since few in the Department of Fish & Game are charged with maintaining wildlife for the enjoyment of citizens who do not care to kill, the dominant groups to receive attention are the Associated Sportsmen and the California Wildlife Federation —the hunting public.
>
> Under the guise of "animal lovers," the National Wildlife Federation across the country is backed by the rifle companies. This is the organization that sends out the wildlife stamps—the rabbit in the snow, the mountain lion on a tree limb, the bear in the woods. Their lobbyists

attend all legislative hearings dealing with wildlife. They are alert and shrewd—intent upon keeping the very animals pictured on their wildlife stamps as targets for their gun-carrying membership.

Though the public owns the game, the Department of Fish & Game, supported mainly by funds which accrue from hunting and fishing licenses, duck stamps, wetlands stamps, and the Pittman-Robertson tax, serves primarily to enhance this game for some 763,284 hunters and 2,323,847 fisherman whose fees pay the bills.

Thus, because they pay the bills, we repeatedly hear that "hunters are the true conservationists." Yes, the hunter pays a privilege tax for the right to "take" the life of wildlife that belongs to all of us. Thus, approximately three million hunters and fishermen, out of some 20 million citizens in the State, believe they are entitled to direct the wildlife program, sending their lobbyists up to the legislature and penetrating in depth the Administration of the Department of Fish & Game. Ray Arnett, California's Director of Fish & Game, serves also as Vice President of the National Wildlife Federation. His attitude toward the citizens who value wildlife alive is epitomized in this comment reported last month in the sports magazine, "Outdoor Life": "If they [the public] don't enjoy hunting it, fine—but let me and my sporting friends who do enjoy it alone." This man is the public's steward for wildlife in California.

Mr. Arnett is worthy of one other small mention. For out of his office came the immortal answer as to why it wouldn't stop the killing of California's few remaining mountain lions. "We have to kill them," someone protested, "to count them." The human population can, one supposes, count itself lucky that whoever said that does not head the census bureau. In point of fact, however, the California mountain-lion fight was close to a textbook picture of Fish and Game operations. After a prolonged struggle, the California legislature finally passed a moratorium on the hunting of these lions. But it was bitterly opposed by Fish and Game and they were able to add a last-minute rider that the mountain lion could be, if not hunted, at least "chased" for "scientific reasons." Then, at a meeting which was scheduled in the out-of-the-way spot of Bishop, California—one made purposely difficult for humanitarians to attend—they voted to extend the "scientific reasons" to permit hunters to run down mountain lions with dogs—in other words, to tree them but not kill them. You can even chase pregnant mountain lions; the only thing you cannot do is "knowingly" pursue an "immature" lion, i.e., one less than one year old.

One way the States have of maintaining "right thinking" about hunting is to begin at the very beginning—with the children in school. In the Dexter High School, of Ann Arbor, Michigan, for example, the school handbook lists only four reasons for "excused absences": (1) sickness or death in the family, (2) a family "emergency," (3) a doctor's or dental appointment, and, (4) "hunting season." In the doctor's and dental appointments, however, a note says, "An excused absence will be given "only in extreme emergencies"—yet the hunting-season reason seems to welcome excused absences, and a note under "Hunting" mentions the fact that it may be for more than one day. "A student may be excused for a longer period to accompany his parents on a hunting trip . . . providing he is passing all his subjects."

The hunters do not even take a chance at the college level —as witness the following letter from Jan B. Gundlach of Ypsilanti, Michigan:

> I have just completed a six week course in the physical education department at Eastern Michigan University called "Recreation Shooting." . . .
> We were shown a movie, "Sure as Shootin'," about a

man and his son who go on a camping/hunting weekend in search, I presume, of the son's manhood through killing some woodland animal. The father pointed out to his son that although some people feel "sad" that animals are hunted, they don't realize that hunting is a good conservation practice and everyone, everything is much better in the end. . . . There was, of course, no mention of the possibility of wounding an animal or how to deal with that situation. Nor was there a visual recording of the dying animal. The father and son spotted a group of deer; they both fired but the son was given credit and they gleefully ran to the prize. It was, needless to say, a beautiful, large, six-eight point buck. The film did not show the deer falling to the ground. . . .*

And, finally, after all this "right thinking" in schools and colleges, there are the actual "conservation" trade schools. "IF YOU LIKE TO HUNT AND FISH," reads the come-on for the North American School of Conservation, "CONSIDER THESE OPPORTUNITIES." It is, the school tells you, "A CAREER OF THRILLS AND ADVENTURE."

Greet each day knowing thrills and excitement await you. Experience scalp-tingling adventure you will never forget, whether helping to fight forest fires, hunting predators, rescuing lost campers or any other of the day after day experiences so often common to Conservation workers.

And, lest you fail to grasp the he-man he-hunter message, the school helpfully encloses a kind of hee-haw article which, they

---

* In Michigan in November, 1973, a "Michigan Wildlife" TV program was shown. A group of hunters watching it in the TV studio were worried when a sequence appeared in which deer, helpless in three feet of snow, were gunned down by snowmobile hunters. One of the watchers was worried about Michigan's Department of Natural Resources. "Wait until the DNR hears about this," he said. In the very next sequence the camera zoomed in on the shoulder badge of one of the men obviously running the hunt. There, unmistakably, was the insignia "DNR."

tell you, is "reprinted courtesy of *Sportsman and Guns* Magazine":

> No matter how you slice it, there are three kinds of working stiffs. The first species bends his brain six days a week behind a desk in the city and inhales nothing but air conditioning. The closest he ever gets to the outdoors, is a Sunday visit to the local zoo's hippo cage with a string of brats strapped to his arm.
>
> The second kind of guy has it a little easier. He flies his desk maybe five days a week instead of six, and has the kind of wife who doesn't mind letting him punch out once in a while on weekends so he can haul a few trout out of the water in his favorite fishing spot.
>
> But it's the third type who really has it knocked up. He spends no days a week behind a typewriter. He doesn't know a time clock from a duck-billed platypus and he doesn't have to sneak off to the woods like a criminal. *He actually lives and works in the outdoors.*
>
> You'd think this kind of guy would be tickled to work for pennies and keep his mouth shut. But the amazing part about outdoor jobs is that in many cases they actually pay off in gunny sacks of money.

Gunny sacks, indeed. Then the pamphlet proceeds: "Out in the Western States," it declares, "the Bureau of Land Management takes on bunches of guys." To go after, we presume, coveys. In any case, the section under "Hunting and Fishing Guides" is particularly revealing:

> A-1 for the outdoor guy who'd like to step into this lucrative job is that he should know at least one hunting or fishing area like the back of his hand. . . .
>
> If you don't feel like guiding the year away part-time guiding is a good way to earn a quick buck and get at least a couple of months in the outdoors. Many guides spend at least half the year at their regular jobs, such as farming and horsewrestling.

Or, possibly, dogboxing. In any case, the pamphlet also has a moving section on your great chance to get a job with your ever animal-loving Government:

> Government's Fish and Wildlife Service is really beating its brains out trying to scare up enough animal trappers. Most of these fresh-air jobs are in the Western States and a man has got to be willing to clock at least half a dozen hours a day at muscle-tiring labor in all kinds of weather. But above all, he's got to be willing to live alone in the wilderness and like it.
>
> Trapping agents spend most of their time trapping, hunting, poisoning and generally putting the skids to coyotes, bobcats, wolves and predatory bears. Trappers have to keep up traps, maintain a field camp and turn over all skins and pelts of any value to Uncle Sam. Quite a bit of their time is spent in charge of crews hunting down prairie dogs, ground squirrels, pocket gophers and jackrabbits.

From such a school pours forth a veritable army of "gunmen"—in official positions—all of whom, having been "trained" by such pamphlets, which advise the clobbering of even such rare and endangered animals as bobcats and wolves, will then have the job of "controlling" hunting. And it is this sort of army which works day and night not only on such "issues" as the subsidizing of farmers to permit hunting on their lands, but also on such legislation as that for "National Hunting and Fishing Day." This "Day," the brainchild of the National Shooting Sports Foundation and supported by such high-minded groups as the National Rifle Association, the National Sporting Goods Association, the National Reloading Manufacturers Association, and the National Muzzle-Loading Rifle Association, was established in a joint resolution passed unanimously by Congress on June 24, 1971, and contained the wording: "Whereas there are few pursuits providing a better chance for healthy exercise, peaceful solitude and appreciation of the great outdoors than hunting . . ."

In observance of this day, held each September, each of the country's thousands of gun clubs receives a large packet of instructions telling its members how to set up everything from "skill centers" to "parking, communications, concession and cashier chiefs." "When a youngster first takes an interest in shooting," this packet says, "learning to shoot is both means and end—he wants to hit targets, perhaps later hunt." And not even the women are overlooked:

> It's critical to the success of your entire program, both for conservation exhibits and skill centers, that you assign squad leaders or hospitality crews. Their purpose is to ensure that all of your guests see everything and try almost everything. As you know from past experience, many adults will bring their youngsters out and see that they get started; then the adults will cluster in the shade and talk. That's when you squad leaders go to work. They should walk over and invite the housewives to try their hand at shooting. . . . There may be some reluctance on the part of a 40-year-old housewife to try shooting for the first time in her life. But with humor and patience, coax her over for instruction. She is sure to enjoy it after a few instructions. She is sure to enjoy it after a few bulls-eyes.*

✳

Even the hunters' stranglehold on Federal and State governing bodies, however, pales before their hold on virtually all the

---

* Not content with running everything seemingly entirely for the benefit of hunters, State Conservation Departments also make it almost impossible for a Good Samaritan even to rescue a wild animal. Mrs. Era Zistel, in the NEW YORK SUNDAY NEWS MAGAZINE, told of trying to interest a New York State conservation officer in the plight of a starving, terribly emaci-

major "conservation" and "wildlife" societies. Indeed, with the exception of Defenders of Wildlife, there is hardly a single such society with the word "wildlife" in it which is not hunter dominated. And even Defenders, fine as its work has been against roadside zoos, poisoning, and so on, takes no official stand on hunting. The other large organizations in this field vary only between being hunter dominated and totally hunter —the best example of the latter being the Boone and Crockett Club. The first in the field—in more ways than one—this organization is now primarily known for its registration of trophies. Founded by Theodore Roosevelt, the club in its original constitution left no doubt where it stood. "The Number One object of the club," this stated, "is to promote manly sport with a rifle." And, stated Article III, "no one shall be eligible for membership who shall not have killed with the rifle in fair chase, by still-hunting or otherwise, at least one individual of one of the various kinds of American large game." Later this qualification was amended to read, "one adult male individual of each of three of the various species of American large game," to which was also added, "provided, however, that,

---

ated three-legged fawn. The conservation officer said it was "against the policy of the Department to interfere." The officer agreed with Mrs. Zistel the fawn would probably expire if she was not taken from the woods and helped but stated that she also might, before expiring, give birth. "Then," he said, "if there is only one fawn, we at least have a replacement. If she has two, we'd be one deer ahead." To provide, Mrs. Zistel noted, additional sport for hunters in the fall. Mrs. Zistel went on from this experience to a careful study of other "conservation" laws. She discovered that any land-owner who objects to the presence of wildlife on his property can simply declare it a nuisance and, if it is in the "unprotected" category, dispose of it in any manner. If it is in the "protected" category the landowner has even greater latitude—he may "take" skunks, racoons, squirrels, owls, hawks, hare, rabbits, bear and beaver "in any manner notwithstanding any other provision of the law" except that he must not allow his dog to dig skunks out of holes or to use ferrets to get rid of rabbits. One man refused to abide by such archaic laws. Rather than give up an injured racoon, Jim Westra of "Animal Kingdom," Grand Rapids, Michigan, went to jail.

if the executive committee deems any candidate otherwise exceptionally qualified for regular membership, it may substitute, in place of two of the three requisite species of American large game, the adult male individual of two species of the big game of other lands."

The Boone and Crockett not only dominated other societies in the early days, its membership actually overlapped almost all of them, from the Campfire Club and the Wilderness Society to the later Izaak Walton League and Ducks unlimited. Indeed, the kinship of all the big shots within these clubs was evidenced from their very beginning. J. Coleman Drayton, for example, facetiously suggested, at the founding of the Boone and Crockett Club, that it be called "the Swappers"—for the times to come, he pointed out, when "we got old and swapped stories, true or otherwise." This, the club official history sternly records, "nearly aroused Roosevelt's famous temper." In the same sort of spirit, at the formation meeting of Ducks Unlimited, one member suggested the name Ducks Limited. "Limited, hell!" exclaimed another member. "What we're talking about is ducks unlimited." And, sure as shooting, the new club had its name.

But the Boone and Crockett Club did far more than dominate other societies. As its official history notes proudly, "The Chief Forester of the United States has traditionally been a member of the Club, as have the heads of the Park Service and of the U.S. Fish and Wildlife Service." And, as if this were not enough, the club also allied itself early on with something called the American Game Protection and Propagation Association. Here at last was a name which was accurate—a true, raise 'em and kill 'em society and, even more important to the future of "conservation" by "management" standards, the AGPPA was actually underwritten by the leading sporting arms and ammunition manufacturer. Following this alliance, on April 24, 1935, at the Waldorf-Astoria Hotel, New York, representatives of Hercules Powder, Remington Arms and DuPont agreed to subscribe the funds which led to the birth of the American Wildlife Institute—later the Wildlife Management Institute—and the National Wildlife Federation. That these societies have ever since sided with the "sportsmen" against the animals—at least where hunting is concerned —is not surprising. They are, in a sense, paying their "dues" —by speaking up on any and all occasions where gun control is concerned. "The supreme demonic defense from this group," declares Robert Sherrill in *The Saturday Night Special,* "always comes in the person and voice of Thomas L. Kimball, executive director of the National Wildlife Federation, who becomes quite incensed when any laws are proposed that, by discouraging the ownership of guns, might discourage hunting."

And it was this same Kimball, Carl Bakal recalls in *The Right to Bear Arms,* who less than a month after the assassination of President Kennedy leaped, in a manner, into the breach before a Senate Committee hearing. "Will," he asked, "the enactment of laws controlling the sale and possession of firearms, short of complete and effective disarmament of the citizenry, prevent the brutality and senseless murder committed by the assassin? Insofar as the National Wildlife Federation is concerned, the answer is a forceful and resounding 'No' to both questions."

Mr. Kimball aside, the case of the National Wildlife Federation is a peculiar one indeed. On the one hand, they seemingly promote love of wildlife through everything from stamps to sugar packages. On the other hand, when any issue involves hunting or their idea of "management" they are sternly against the humanitarians. On the one hand, they promote, among their children members, a nature-and-animal-loving fellow named Ranger Rick—the man who also gives his name to their children's "nature" magazine, which they gamely manage to get into all the school libraries. On the other hand, in no time at all it seems, Ranger Rick becomes Deadeye Dick. How this is done, in one easy lesson, is evident from Adventure No. 70 in *Ranger Rick* Magazine for February, 1974. The article was written by J. A. Brownridge, a man who, though vice-chairman and administrative vice-president of the National Wildlife Federation, still manages to have time to turn out children's fiction.

> "Wow! Have the deer always had this much trouble in winter?" asked Ollie, looking worried.
> "No, Ollie," said Rick. "Many years ago much of this part of the country was covered with old, deep forests. The trees grew large and tall and there were fewer bushes and small trees with low branches. There was less deer food than there is today, but the deer population was in better balance with the food supply. There were plenty of wolves and cougars around to help keep down the number of deer."
> "Then came trouble," said Herman.
> "Was it man?" interrupted Ollie.
> "Right," said Rick. "Man began cutting down the large trees. Small trees and bushes sprang up. Over the years the deer's food supply grew. This allowed the numbers of deer to grow larger. At the same time man killed off or chased away the wolves and cougars. Now that there are so many deer, just one severe winter can cause many of them to starve."
> "Boy, these coyotes have a bigger job than they can handle," added Ollie.
> "Right again, Ollie," said Rick, "and in many parts of the country the coyotes are the only predators large enough to hunt deer."

"Can't anything be done?" asked Ollie.

"I talked to Ranger Tom about it the other day," said Rick. "He told me that many people believe that to solve the problem man must take the place of predators. He said people call it *game management*."

"Game management? This doesn't sound much like a game to me!" said Ollie.

"No, no, Ollie," said Rick. "Game is a word used for animals which are legally hunted by man. Game management means controlling the numbers of these animals. This can be done by hunting them according to certain rules and regulations."

"How do the game managers know how many deer should be killed?" asked Ollie.

"Ranger Tom said that most states have biologists who carefully study the deer in their habitat. If they think the deer are multiplying too fast, they may suggest that they sell more doe hunting licenses."

It's always tough, apparently, to sell even the Ranger Rick kids on killing does. But the National Wildlife Federation wants to make certain that its young readers will grow up to march hand in hand with the hunters into any legislative hearing involving hunting restrictions. In the matter, for example, of New York's widely praised Mason Bill, prohibiting the import of endangered species, the federation declared glumly, "The language of the Mason Bill is such that some species not endangered have been included. Apparently the decision to add species is being done on the basis of incomplete knowledge, the lack of knowledge or upon an emotional approach." Nothing, in National Wildlife's view, is worse than an emotional approach. If, for example, you write to ask them how they stand on hunting, you will probably get back a "Statement of Conservation Policy" called "This We Believe." It is a truly remarkable document—seven single-spaced pages of small type on every angle of "conservation" from "Natural Stream Values" to "National Parks and Monuments." But somehow, not once is the word "hunting" mentioned. This, mind you, from an organization which, along with the National Rifle Association, sponsors National Hunting and Fishing Day and which also stated in a letter from the executive director to the *New York Times* that—and we quote—"The principal wildlife restoration accomplishments in America today have resulted from licensed hunters."

Another major organization with a gun-ho hunter hang-up is, curiously, the World Wildlife Fund. Here the reigning royalty, Prince Bernhard of the Netherlands and Prince Philip of Britain are both suspect to animal people—and for good reason. Prince Bernhard, whom we met before in *Great True Hunts*, not long ago shot so many birds in Italy that he ran afoul of even the Italian Government—one not notably averse to shooting pretty nearly everything. He was also, according to the London *Times*, accused by a Belgian animal-protection society of hunting pheasants "in conditions near to massacre." As for Prince Philip, he has been called "one of the world's leading tiger hunters." And on the same day that he sent personal letters to rich Britons asking for Wildlife Fund donations he set out, with friends, on a five-week pheasant shoot. In the previous season's shoot, the Prince, with the help of his friends, had, said the *Sunday Mirror*, "blasted a staggering total of 15,500 birds."

The World Wildlife Fund's pro-hunting proclivities have also brought forth protests in this country. For many years, its president—now honorary president—was C. R. "Pink" Gutermuth—a man who is president of, of all organizations, the National Rifle Association. "This gives him," Lewis Regenstein, executive vice-president of The Fund for Animals, was quoted in the *Wall Street Journal* as saying, "a shoot-em-up philosophy that is perforce at odds with what a conservation group ought to stand for." Replied Gutermuth, "If Regenstein and people like him are going on writing things about me that hurt the World Wildlife Fund, I'm going to graciously resign, go to Florida and go hunting." The World Wildlife Fund next elected as its U.S. president Francis L. Kellogg, a retired mining executive whose big-game hunting trips to Africa and other places have been widely publicized for years. Mr. Kellogg has not been in office for long, and it is not yet clear how he proposes to tell the natives of Africa to stop killing animals for food and profit so that he and his friends can kill them for fun and games.

If the "wildlife" societies are, obviously, in favor of wild death, what, it may well be asked, about the SPCA? Many people indeed labor under the belief that the "American" SPCA stops cruelty in hunting. It does not—for two very good reasons. The first is that, although the New York SPCA calls itself the "American" SPCA, it operates in New York only. The second reason is that, although many independent SPCAs around the country do attack hunting cruelty, the New York SPCA takes no stand on hunting at all, and indeed the only national organization of which it is a member, the American Humane Association, has long been pro-hunting. In a 1972 speech to Game Coin, Richard Denney, Wildlife Consultant to the American Humane Association, first made fun of anti-hunting sentiments, then attempted to prove they were psychologically suspect, then stated proudly that his organization had "issued a position statement on hunting which recognizes that the licensed sportsman is the only practical game population reduction tool currently available on a broad scale to the State conservation agencies."

Finally, what about the so-called "good" conservation organizations—the ones everybody supposedly trusts for good
works? These would include the Sierra Club, the National
Audubon Society, the Wilderness Society, the National Geographic Society, the New York Zoological Society and the
American Forestry Association—and perhaps even The Wildlife Society and the Izaak Walton League of America. Where
are all these when the hunting chips are down? The answer is, unfortunately, if not actually out hunting, at least out to lunch. In a
recent article in *National Wildlife* Magazine entitled "Hunters
and Conservationists Share Goals" and published by your
old if questionable friends, the National Wildlife Federation,
all these organizations, with the exception of the Geographic
and the Zoological societies, bestowed their blessing on hunters. Taking them in reverse order, the Izaak Walton League
declared, "Hunting should be considered a valuable management tool," while The Wildlife Society not only went on to
"recognize sport hunting as one legitimate and desirable use
of wildlife resources" but also added the odd statement that it
"strongly favored preservation of the original human elements
of the hunt." The American Forestry Association also believed
in hunting as "a tool of management by owners of large
forest and range holdings," and then added, "It is of increasing
value because of its importance to a growing, mobile human
population seeking recreation."

As for the two organizations not quoted in the article, the
National Geographic Society and the New York Zoological
Society, these two would have officially little quarrel with it.
The New York Zoological Society, better known as the Bronx
Zoo, not only owes its existence to the Boone and Crockett
Club but also has never officially opposed sport hunting,
except of endangered species. "We just can't say we're against

it," an officer told this writer, "and I can't be quoted on the subject at all." One reason for this bashfulness is that ever since 1906 the Zoological Society has housed what has been called "the largest aggregation of superior big-game trophies to be seen in one place in the world." By 1922, this aggregation, called the "National Collection of Heads and Horns," had grown so large that the zoo had to erect a special building to house it. Today, to the credit of the zoo, these "Heads and Horns" are so played down by the authorities that the collection is not even open to the public. Two of the halls in the building which houses it are now being used as an "education department"—and at least part of this education consists of the fact that all the heads are covered up.

The National Geographic Society is perhaps the most outstanding example of an enormously rich and powerful society which does nothing to stop hunting abuse, let alone hunting in general. The articles in its magazine are generally pro-animal —so are its films on television. But who can name a time when it has spent a penny in a pro-animal fight which involved head-on confrontation with the hunters. Indeed, as recently as February, 1972, Allan C. Fisher, Jr., went all out for hunting. "I do not know," he wrote, "a single conservation expert who decries controlled, licensed hunting." Presumably, he knows one now.

The National Audubon Society in the aforementioned *National Wildlife* article was perhaps the strongest pro-hunting of all—something that must have appalled the countless "little old ladies in tennis shoes" who have for so long been the bulwark of what is—with the exception of hunting—a fine conservation organization. "The National Audubon Society," the statement read, "since its origin at the turn of the century, has never been opposed to the hunting of game species. . . . We have made this clear repeatedly in official statements and

policies and it remains Audubon policy." Which is certainly
clear enough. However, from time to time, the society's *Audubon Magazine* also enters the fray—on, usually, the hunter's
side. An article in the January, 1972, *Audubon*, for example,
was written by Ed Zern an "outdoor" writer whose articles
since 1958 have also appeared in *Field & Stream*. Mr. Zern's
words must have shocked at least some Audubon contributors.
In any case, not content with calling a neighbor "well-meaning,
kind-hearted, anti-hunting, and nitwitted," because she "rescued six mallard ducklings," he writes that when he's hunting
he feels—and we quote—"a oneness with nature that I never
feel except when hunting, and that no non-hunter, much less
an anti-hunter, can possibly experience." And he also declares, "If I were to leave the gun at home, or to bring it without the intention of using it, I'd be in that marsh as a spectator,
or a peeping Tom, or a bystander."

Peeping—if the expression may be pardoned—farther back
into Audubon Society history, it is not difficult to find other
shockers. John James Audubon himself, the man for whom the
society was named and whom it presumably delights to honor,
was also a man who not only delighted to shoot animals but
also birds—in fact pretty nearly anything that moved. His two-volume *Journals* are literally filled with the joy of killing:

> August 2. Started at half-past seven this morning; saw
> several Yellow-legs (Godwits), and some young Blue-winged Teal in the pond in the first prairie. Shot two
> Curlews; saw two very fine male Elks; they were lying
> down quite near us, under a bank when they got wind
> of us. The Sharp-tailed Grouse are first-rate eating now,
> as they feed entirely on grasshoppers, and berries of
> different kinds. Owen climbed a tree to a White-headed
> Eagle's nest, and drove a young one out, which fell to
> the ground and was caught alive and brought to the fort.
> Is it not very remarkable that Eagles of this species

should have their young in the nest at this late season, when in the Floridas I have shot them of the same size in February? Shot at a wolf which being wounded went off about one hundred yards and yelled like a dog; a very remarkable instance, as all we have killed or wounded, and they have been many, rarely make any sound.

It is not surprising that wolves made no sound when Audubon was around. For, when in his *Journals* he isn't out shooting, he is enjoying trapping, snaring, "baiting," pitting and virtually every other form of cruelty. In another place in his *Journals* he makes "capital sport" with a farmer who has "pitted" a wolf:

I peeped in and saw the Wolves, two black and the other brindled, all of goodly size, sure enough. They lay flat on the earth, their ears laid close over the head, their eyes indicating more fear than anger. "But how are we to get them out?" "How, sir?" said the farmer, "why, by going down to be sure, and hamstringing them." Being a novice in these matters, I begged to be merely a looker-on. "With all my heart," quoth the farmer, "stand here and look at me through the brush." Whereupon he glided down, taking with him his axe and knife, and leaving his rifle in my care. I was not a little surprised to see the cowardice of the Wolves. He pulled out successively their hind legs, and with a side stroke of the knife cut the principal tendon above the joint, exhibiting as little fear as if he had been marking lambs.

"Lo!" exclaimed the farmer, when he had got out, "we have forgotten the rope; I'll go after it." Off he went, according, with as much alacrity as any youngster could show. In a short time he returned out of breath, and wiping his forehead with the back of his hand. "Now for it." I was desired to raise and hold the platform on its central balance, whilst he, with all the dexterity of an Indian, threw a noose over the neck of one of the Wolves.

We hauled it up motionless with fright, as if dead, its disabled legs swinging to and fro, its jaws wide open, and the gurgle in its throat alone indicating that it was alive. Letting him drop on the ground, the farmer loosened the rope by means of a stick and left him to the dogs, all of which set upon him with great fury and worried him to death. The second was dealt with in the same manner; but the third, which was probably the oldest, as it was the blackest, showed some spirit the moment it was left loose to the mercy of the curs. This Wolf, which we afterwards found to be a female, scuffled along on its forelegs at a surprising rate, giving a snap every now and then to the nearest dog.

Everything from cougars to prairie dogs—and, of course, raccoons—get virtually the same treatment. But Audubon had particular fun one day with bears. After getting two cubs—"they were cubs of no great size and being already half dead, we left them to the dogs"—he and his party turned their attention to the mother bear:

> We were anxious to procure as much sport as possible, and having observed one of the Bears, which from its size we conjectured to be the mother, ordered the negroes to cut down a tree on which it was perched, when it was intended the dogs should have a tug with it, while we should support them, and assist from preventing the bear from escaping by wounding it in one of the hind-legs. The surrounding woods now echoed to the blows of the axmen. The tree was large and tough, having been girded more than two years, and the operation of felling it seemed extremely tedious. However, it began to vibrate at each stroke; a few inches alone now supported it; and in a short time it came crashing to the ground, in so awful a manner that Bruin must doubtless have felt the shock as severe as we should feel a shake of the globe produced by the sudden collision of the comet.

The dogs rushed to the charge and harassed the Bear on all sides. We had remounted and now surrounded the poor animal. As its life depended upon its courage and strength, it exercised both in the most energetic manner. Now and then it seized a dog, and killed him by a single stroke. At another time, a well-administered blow of one of its fore-legs sent an assailant yelping off so piteously that he might be looked upon as *hors de combat.* A cur had daringly ventured to seize the Bear by the snout, and was seen hanging on to it, covered with blood, whilst a dozen or more scrambled over its back. Now and then the infuriated animal was seen to cast a revengeful glance at some of the party, and we had already determined to despatch it when, to our astonishment, it suddenly shook off all the dogs and, before we could fire, charged upon one of the negroes, who was mounted on a pied horse. The Bear seized the steed with teeth and claws, and clung to its breast. The terrified horse snorted and plunged. The rider, an athletic young man and a capital horseman, kept his seat, although only saddled on a sheep's skin tightly girthed, and requested his master not to fire at the Bear. Notwithstanding his coolness and courage, our anxiety for his safety was raised to the highest pitch, especially when in a moment we saw rider and horse come to the ground together; but we were instantly relieved on witnessing the masterly manner in which Scipio despatched his adversary by laying open his skull with a single, well-directed blow of his axe, when a deep growl announced the death of the Bear, and the valorous negro sprung to his feet unhurt.

So much for John James Audubon. It is hardly surprising that the society that was named for him has not been of large service when it comes to confronting hunters. It may, however, surprise some of its members.

Last but not least, we come to the famed Sierra Club. Once again the official policy, as evidenced by the *National Wildlife* article, is crystal clear: "The Sierra Club is not opposed to sport hunting outside of appropriate sanctuaries such as national parks." Not content with this, more than once this club has seen fit to replace chapter heads for anti-hunting positions. Indeed, Dr. Cyril Toker, one of the strongest anti-sport hunters, was in 1971 relieved of his duties as head of the Wildlife Committee of the Atlantic Chapter for just such a position.

Going back into Sierra Club history, however, offers a sharp contrast with Audubon Society history. Not only was the founder of the Sierra Club, the great John Muir, unlike Audubon, no hunter, he was that rare combination of the country's first great conservationist and at the same time the strongest anti-hunter of the nineteenth century. For the Sierra Club to "buy"—in all senses of the word—sport hunting, it had to turn its back on the very cornerstone of its founder's philosophy. Here was a man who, from 1834 to 1914, covered most of America's wilderness, as well as Canada's, alone, on foot and unarmed. Carrying only a sackful of stale bread and cheese, by himself for weeks at a time, he neither harmed nor, in turn, was he ever harmed by, any animal. "Making some bird or beast go lame the rest of its life," John Muir once said, "is a sore thing on one's conscience, at least nothing to boast of, and it has no religion in it." And he also said,

> In nothing does man, with his grand notions of heaven and charity, show forth his innate, lowbred, wild animalism more clearly than in his treatment of his brother beasts. From the shepherd with his lambs to the red-handed hunter, it is the same; no recognition of rights— only murder in one way or another.

And, too, this was the man of whom his biographer, Edwin Way Teale, wrote as follows:

> He never carried a gun. Travelling alone and far from every other human being for weeks at a time, he never was harmed by bear or rattlesnake, never was seriously

injured in an accident. . . . In this world, where men are afraid they will catch cold, afraid they will be eaten by bears or bitten by snakes or touch poison ivy or fall over a log, John Muir, faring forth into the wilderness unarmed and alone, was the man unafraid. He was unafraid of danger, of hardship, of wildness, of being alone, of facing death. He was unafraid of public opinion, he was unafraid of work and poverty and hunger. He knew them all and he remained unafraid.

One wishes the club Muir founded could have continued this tradition. Or at least could reread, on occasion, Muir's *Journal.* One section of this journal was written in 1899 on Kodiak Island. The night before, to Muir's camp had come members of the famed Harriman hunting party. The latter talked late and long that night of their successful day's hunting. The next morning in his *Journal* Muir wrote just eleven words: "Harriman returned last night after killing two bears—mother and child."

*

In spite of the hunters' control of Federal and State Fish and Game departments and other local authorities, their dominance over virtually all of the largest "conservation" and "wildlife" societies—not to mention their august position in language (i.e., "sure as shooting," "a square shooter," "loaded for bear," etc.)—the hunters, nonetheless, have a persecution complex which is truly remarkable. Their organized enemies—i.e., the primarily wildlife national societies which oppose them—number fewer than the fingers of their hands, and only two of these, The Fund for Animals and Defenders of Wildlife (the latter still not officially opposed), have been able to build really solid support. Nonetheless, the least implication anywhere that hunters are not the worthiest souls to inhabit the earth since the Apostles drives them into virtual paroxysms of self-pity. A couple of years ago, for example, the hunters' patron saint, the National Rifle Association, sent out an extraordinary advertisement for itself. This advertisement showed the black silhouetted figures of a father and son in front of a fire. The headline read, "DADDY, WHAT WAS A HUNTER?" Underneath this scene, which was evidently supposed to be truly ghastly in its horror, were the lines:

YOU ARE IN DANGER!

Picture yourself sitting in front of a cheerful fire, telling your children or grandchildren about . . . the year hunters became extinct.

Make no mistake. It could happen—because there's a huge wave of anti-hunting sentiment building on the horizon, right behind the anti-gun wave that has already come booming in.

Boom indeed. In any case, a couple of paragraphs later, the advertisement bangs out the message:

That's why I invite you now—*in your own best interests*—to become a member of the National Rifle Association and support NRA's nationwide information programs that give the public *facts about the contribution of hunters* to conservation and sound game management.

You'll be joining an organization that has fought for and taught sound conservation and game management . . . trained over *five million* safe hunters . . . has annually published the "Hunter Casualty Report" . . .

Always good reading, of course. In any case, the NRA hits hard on accidents—to hunters, that is—in other advertisements. The 1973 NRA *Hunting Annual*, for example, showed an extremely grim-looking camouflaged-cap fellow pointing

directly at you, with the headline "ONLY YOU CAN SAVE HUNT-
ING . . ." And underneath this was:

> Today hunting is safer than ever. The National Safety
> Council reports a 7.4% decrease in hunting accidents in
> the past decade. The Metropolitan Life Insurance Com-
> pany points out hunting is safer than swimming or fishing.
> BUT . . . Some people aren't interested in facts. They
> want hunting stopped *forever*. Here's what they're repeat-
> ing often enough so the public is starting to believe them.
> (Write NRA for list of sources.)
> "The yearly death and accident rate among hunters
> and innocent civilians indicates that hunting should be
> outlawed."
> "The only herd that needs trimming is the herd of
> hunters."
> "Hunters are generally a destructive, dangerous lot who
> have made a mess of our wildlife resources."
> How can you, as a sportsman, fight this kind of talk?
> Best way is by joining NRA now. Become an NRA mem-
> ber and give us more muscle in our continuing efforts to
> tell and sell the truth about hunting and firearms. It's time
> you stood up for the hunting and shooting heritage you,
> as an American, believe in.

As an *American*, of course. The National Rifle Association
has been called by the *Wall Street Journal* the kingpin of the
alliance of hunters, target shooters and gun manufacturers.
In fact, in their NRA "Hunters' Code of Ethics" they state,
"I will support conservation efforts which assure *good hunting*."
Just why, however, they remain a tax-exempt nonlobbying
organization, when to the outsider it seems virtually all they do
is lobby, has long baffled observers. NRA officials, however, claim that only about $100,000 of NRA's annual $7.7-
million budget goes for such activities. "Our members do the
legislative work for us," says Jack Basil, director of NRA's

"Legislative Service." "All we do is keep our members advised about what is going on." Among NRA's "members," the *Wall Street Journal* also pointed out, were at least "35 Congressmen," and if this did not suffice, the article also added, the NRA "once boasted that an appeal to members could produce half a million letters to Congressmen within 72 hours."

One would presume such awesome power would be enough to finish off in short order such tiny little enemies as the animal societies. Apparently, however, it is not, because the article pointed out that even the NRA admitted opposition to hunting was growing. What the article did not say and what is this writer's personal opinion is that the NRA, for all its loud talk, does not care very much about its vaunted "right to bear arms" cry—at least when this cry concerns your right to defend your home, your castle, your outhouse or whatever. After all, you in your home with a rifle, a shotgun, a pistol or, for that matter, a howitzer, do not represent, for them, a very important investment. You only have, presumably, one of whatever you've got and you only shoot it off once per prowler. What the NRA cares desperately about is selling guns for "sport"—i.e., to pot everything that moves in the woods and fields and everywhere else. That is where the money is—in new guns, new equipment, endless supplies of guns and ammo, etc., etc., from the sale of all of which, of course, it draws its support.

In any case, hand in glove with the National Rifle Association's advertisements go equally desperate appeals to contribute to the National Shooting Sports Foundation. One of these had a large headline, "NEXT TIME SOMEBODY PUTS THE KNOCK ON HUNTERS, TELL HIM THIS":

> Tell him that hunters do more for conservation than the rest of the population combined.

It's the hunter and fisherman who ante up $140 million a year for the support of State Fish and Game Departments. All 50 of them.

The same advertisements included another headline, "GIVE YOUR FRIEND A DOSE OF THE BIRDS AND BEES":

Tell him the real facts of wildlife. He probably doesn't know that changing farming and forestry practices have more effect on wildlife populations than hunting has.

He probably doesn't realize that dove and quail have a 75% annual mortality whether they are hunted or not. If the hunter did not crop the surplus each year, nature would.

Then stop him cold with a hot statistic: Because of scientific game management, paid for by hunters, many species such as the white-tailed deer are more numerous today than when the Indians were doing all the hunting!

In fact, hunters have actually *added* species. The ring-necked pheasant, for example, has been around so long that most people think he's a native. What they don't know is that hunters *paid* to import and propagate these birds. Now we have more than 60 million ring-necks.

And, presumably, sixty million rednecks too. But the National Shooting Sports Foundation does more than just write —on stationery which has, printed at the top, "Take a Boy Hunting." The Foundation also shoots from the lip—as evidenced by a 1973 speech to Michigan "sportsmen" by the foundation's president, Warren Page, formerly Shooting Editor of *Field & Stream*:

Good morning, fellow murderers. I don't care if anyone disagrees, I'm sure that you're all aware of the fact that every one of us at some time or another, usually quite frequently, has been damned as a murderer. I was hysterically called an outright murderer by a faculty wife from Iowa State University, all because she had just read

a piece I did about shooting a lion in Africa. That shooting was remarkable only because she could scream louder
than most females. The irony of the whole situation was
that Iowa State is the university which was the birthplace
of wildlife management training in this country. It was set
up originally back around W.W. I. For over 25 years I've
been involved in shooting and hunting and all the latest
conservation activities and I say to you now with all possible emphasis that we of the hunting and shooting community are considered immoral murderers by vastly too
high a percentage of our fellow citizens. Certainly this is
true in the U.S. Elsewhere the hunter is not damned with
the bloody hand of guilt. In fact, in European countries
the hunter stands as a figure of respect and is socially
most acceptable, he's a personage of consequence even
though he does not get up one tenth the cash to be put
towards conservation efforts as you and I do. In Africa
both the visiting safaris and the professional hunter
qualify as decent human beings. You've all heard about
the Victorberg shooting in Italy but that's just a local
phenomenon among the spaghetti benders. Essentially
it's only the serious hunter of the U.S. who is under
strong and conspirated and deliberate and planned attack
and the causes of our ridicule are brutally simple. Every
one of them, unfortunately, emotional. It's very difficult
to answer by a rational approach. For one thing, in this
country we have undergone an entire generation of brain-
washing. Not only our kids but our wives, our brothers,
our mothers, our cousins, our brothers-in-law have for 25
years been subjected to constant film and TV presenta-
tions of the Disney myth. In the Wonderful World of
Disney animals are cuter than people. Wolves spend their
time playing like kittens. The lion and the lamb love one
another and only man is the bastard in the black hat . . .
whose chief aim is the spilling of Bambi's blood. Now
this is the Bambi Syndrome. The Disney films may not
have started out that way, but once it became clear that

sentimentality and outright anthropomorphism would make money, that's the way the films went. And as time went by it was inevitable that TV, with such outright nature fakers as Ivan Tors with his *Daktari* and its imitations, by such unctuous hypocrites as the ex-zoo chairman of St. Louis who chases animals all over Africa with a Land-Rover in order to get the action for cameras, such even more unctuous hypocrites as what wavy-haired gent who sells cat food, Bill Burrud, plus a whole legion of imitators, would take up the Disney approach. They deliberately misinform viewers of basic biological facts.

*

In recent years the hunters' all-time *bête noire*—to use an anti-animal expression—was the television documentary *Say Goodbye*, produced by David Wolper and shown on the NBC network in 1972. Although it was a documentary specifically made to dramatize the plight of endangered animals, and although it actually showed so many predator kills that it was offensive to many humanitarians, the film did include, out of a 53-minute, 3,943-word total, one polar-bear-hunting sequence of exactly 4 minutes and 73 words. This showed a mother polar bear shot in front of her two cubs—and it so infuriated the hunting fraternity that they become apoplectic whenever *Say Goodbye* is mentioned. The hunters concentrated their fury on the fact that the bear "kill" sequence was accomplished by a tranquilizer gun; although the fact is that this kind of simulated sequence is widely used in documentaries of the sort (after all, the only other alternative would be actually to kill the animal) this made no difference. Nor did it make any difference to the hunters that Wolper could have used existing footage on the actual killing of hundreds of mothers in front of their cubs. This, it now becomes clear, he should have done. As Mr. Wolper himself now puts it, "With the benefit of 20-20 hindsight, we would probably not have produced the sequence in the same manner." All in all, if it was ill advised of Mr. Wolper, the hunter-stimulated overaction was incredibly much more ill advised. Although equally cruel hunting activities go on by the thousands every single day of the hunting season—and out of season too—the hunters of course ignored these matters and instead fastened on the single tranquilizer sequence with such overkill that it only served to demonstrate conclusively the old story of one who protests too loudly. At first the letters to the Quaker Oats Company, the sponsors of the film, poured in and they were virtually all favorable—thousands upon thousands of them. There were actually over 75,000, and this writer personally went through close to half of them and found only about twenty against the documentary—i.e., in favor of the hunters. Then, when the hunter and guns and ammo organizations went to work, a flood of anti–*Say Goodbye* letters dutifully arrived. In all, however, they were in number less than a third of the favorable letters.

But still the hunters were not finished. Wallace Noerenberg, Commissioner of the Alaska Department of Fish and Game, branded the film "hokum!" Alaska's Governor, William Egan, called it "reprehensible distortion of truth," and three suits against Wolper Productions were brought in Alaska's courts —one by a game biologist with the Fish and Game Department, another by an Anchorage doctor who charged that some of the footage was taken by him on a bear hunt and had been distorted, and a third by another Anchorage man who said the film depicted him violating Alaskan game laws. At one point, it even looked as if Mr. Wolper would be subpoenaed to appear before a Congressional committee. Wolper promptly agreed with one proviso—that he be able to show the committee his complete compilation of hunting film. In short order, the hunters' urge to have Wolper appear seemed to die a quick and unnatural death. They had little stomach, it seemed, for the whole truth. And they were so right. This writer has seen Wolper's total hunting collection—in fact, it took two full· days to view it—and he can say unequivocally that all those films together make the polar-bear death in *Say Goodbye* look like Dr. Doolittle.

In the years that have passed since *Say Goodbye*, the hunters and their attendant guns and ammo people have concentrated their efforts on trying to keep prints of the documentary out of the hands of local TV stations, libraries and schools. "The film," declared the National Shooting Sports Foundation, "includes three major objectionable segments which have been strongly criticized by nearly all the major conservation organizations"—which is an extraordinary statement since the documentary has not been criticized at all, let alone strongly, by a single "conservation" organization which is not hunter dominated. "Sportsmen," the Shooting Sports continued, "should contact local TV stations, libraries and schools in their areas" and (a) "urge that these organizations not obtain copies of the film if they have not already done so," and (b) "if they already have the film . . . it is suggested that the following segments be edited":

> I. The first segment that should be edited involves the clubbing of fur seals. It is suggested that the last 50 or so seconds of this segment be totally removed.
> II. The second segment that has been criticized is one that highly dramatized the shooting of prairie dogs. It is also suggested that the last 50 or so seconds of this segment be removed totally.
> III. The third and most objectionable segment is the now infamous polar bear sequence. It is suggested that

the entire last minute of this sequence be removed. The polar bear segment can be further improved by including the following messages in the film: "The polar bear scenes were dramatized for 'Say Goodbye.' A tranquilizer dart was used to simulate this episode."

During the polar bear sequence, a slide can be super-imposed which reads, "Polar bear shot with tranquilizer." At the end of the scene a slide and announcer should say "Today polar bears are a protected species under the Marine Mammals Act of 1972."

A fourth segment showing a closeup of a giraffe being skinned and flesh being taken—apparently for eating right on the spot—may also be removed.

But without, evidently, mention that virtually every hunter organization from the NRA on up fought the Marine Mammals Act of 1972—weak as it is—every single, solitary step of the way. And, in fact, the fight is still going on. Facts like these are, apparently, not hunter "facts" and therefore are not worth mention. "HUNTERS, BEWARE!" ran the scare headline in *Outdoor Life*, which in 1972 published a three-part article entitled "The Big Lie" by a man named Ben East. "TV fakery and outright falsehood," said the subhead, "have fired a conflagration of anti-hunting hysteria. If we don't act now, we can 'Say Goodbye' to the sport of hunting." It did not occur to Mr. East or at least his headline writer that "the conflagration of anti-hunting hysteria" was hardly the result of four minutes on national television. It was rather the result of a growing realization, after four hundred or more years of animal mayhem, that a very small section of the public had for years hoodwinked the vast majority into believing that, if you were against hunting, you were also against apple pie, motherhood, America and, presumably a sissy to boot.

The body of Mr. East's scare article bore heavily on both

Say Goodbye and Stanley Kramer's movie about the buffalo hunt, *Bless the Beasts and Children*. It also decried the fact that "many of the anti-hunting people," as it said, "were TV personalities and movie actors." In an effort to score Brownie points for the little man against this august enemy, Mr. East managed to locate, for his readers, a Missouri housewife named Mrs. Marilyn Herberg. "The legal hunter," she said, "is a harvester of a wild menu." This extraordinary statement was followed by the usual management arguments, all of which were bolstered not by "facts"—which Mr. East and similar writers so decry the anti-hunters for not using—but by quotations from a large number of "authorities." Among these were our old friend Ray Arnett, Director of the California Department of Fish and Game; Les Voigt, head of the Wisconsin Department of Natural Resources; Glenn Bowers, Executive Director of the Pennsylvania Game Commission; O. E. Frye, Jr., Director of the Florida Game and Fresh Water Fish Commission; and Chester Phelps, President of the International Association of Game, Fish and Conservation Commissioners—all, of course, men in the hunter's jacket, if not in his ammo packs. Using such authorities to back up one's thesis is, obviously, tantamount to using your own family to back up your argument. And, if they weren't enough, other "authorities" cited were Bill Clede, president of the Outdoor Writers Association of America—an indoor writer apparently being ineligible— and Harold Glassen, a man whom Mr. East identified as "past president of the National Rifle Association and former chairman of the Michigan Conservation Commission, a man who has kept a finger on the pulse of the anti-hunting movement for more than 20 years."

His trigger finger, doubtless. The fact is, however, the hunters' persecution complex is not only evident from their reaction to television and films and motion pictures, it also carries over to virtually any unfavorable notice—no matter how mild. When, for example, in 1973 the publication *Science World* featured an article, "Hunting for Fun—Should We End It?" by Michael Cusack, once more the hunters went all-out. Again, this particular article was a balanced and even-handed argument which, if anything, quoted more authorities in favor of hunting than against it. Indeed, over and over the argument was made that wildlife "management" needed hunting. But the very fact that the article made mention of wounded animals, of deer strapped to automobiles and of the questionable "sheer delight" of killing was too much for the hunting fraternity. Henry Stowers, for example, a hunter-columnist of the Dallas *Morning News,* worked himself into a fine lather over the fact that *Science World* was a periodical circulated among the nation's secondary schools. "Read it slowly," he advised his readers about the article. "Then grab your pen and write your school superintendent."

Who, one wonders, censors the censors? Perhaps nothing, however, better illustrates the hunters' feeling of persecution than any indication that their numbers are not growing—in fact, perish the thought, that their numbers are actually declining. In 1971, for example, the Department of the Interior showed a major decrease of hunting popularity—the exact figure was 301,000 fewer licensed hunters. Immediately, the No. 2 patron saint of the hunters, the Wildlife Management Institute, was called into play, and its president, Daniel A. Poole, in an article in *Fur-Fish-Game,* promptly came to "the defense of the sportsmen." In short order, the same magazine reported, the Department of the Interior "corrected" its first release and, 23 days after the initial release, cited the fact that hunter licenses had actually *increased* in 1971—by 607,107.

This extraordinary occurrence was all due, declared *Fur-Fish-Game,* to the "now famous" letter "Dan" sent "Nat"—Nathaniel P. Reed, Assistant Secretary of the Interior:

> Dear Nat,
>   I am beginning to get through the pile of material that accumulated during my absence for the North American Wildlife and Natural Resources Conference. An interesting item is Interior Dept.'s news release of March 24, "Character of Hunting and Fishing in the United States Is Changing, Survey Indicates." Some of it is reasonable and makes sense. However, its overall thrust raises serious questions, in my view, because incorrect impressions may be left with the reader.
>   I am perplexed, as I was with the earlier 5-year reports, by Interior's willingness to use a projection from 9,000 samples or less to argue that the number of hunters is rising or declining. . . . Interior's best record is, and should be, the license sales certifications under the Federal Aid program. According to our records, which are based on previous annual Interior reports, the number of licensed hunters increased from 1960 to 1970 by 1.4 million, rather than decreased by 301,000 as the March 24 release indicates.
>   Those who have found some comfort and assurance in Interior's federal aid reports over the past five years will now undoubtedly wonder how hunters suddenly came out on the losing side of the ledger.

One thing was certain. "Dan" got the job done, and by the next release, as we have seen, the hunters were back in the victory column. In 1972, however, they faced the same problem when the Fish and Wildlife Service, in its annual review of hunting and fishing licenses, noted a drop of 674,084 in the sale of hunting licenses. Once more the hunters were quick to go to the blackboard. Wrote Walter Frank in his New Brunswick, New Jersey, "Outdoor Sportsman's" column:

> While this may seem like a large figure, it actually is not as bad as it looks. The statistics do not explain the cause of the decrease, which would include deaths of hunters through accidental and natural causes, oldtimers retiring from the field and similar reasons.

Those accidents again. Another problem that has plagued hunters in their attempt to overcome their complex has been their difficulty in obtaining their share of the "TV personalities and movie actors" they so deplore on the other side. There is, however, one man on whom they can count. That man is Robert Stack. A director of—what else?—the National Wildlife Federation, Stack entered the anti-hunting hunt with an article for the *Federation* Magazine entitled "Thanks, Hunter!" In this he claimed "sportsmen" have done more than any other group to preserve "our great wildlife heritage—one which, of course, he equates with "respect for gun":

> I was taught that respect by my father and grandfather when I was still a little boy. Later, I taught it to other young men in the Navy. To equate us with some nut who shoots up the neighborhood by saying that we "encourage" the use of firearms is patently ridiculous.
> Let's talk instead about all the good things hunting can lead to: the companionship of a father and son together . . . the close bond that builds between all hunters of whatever age . . . the oneness with nature that hunting instills. . . .

That ole-time oneness again between hunter and animal—particularly the oneness that comes after the hunter is the only one left. Stack stated, however, that "the brick-bats rankle"—as indeed they apparently rankle all hunters. In San Antonio, at the week-long Game Coin conference, 1,047 delegates pledged "a declaration of war" against anti-hunting groups. Declared President Harry L. Tennison, "We're tired of being shot at."

Amazingly enough, according to an observer, few of those 1,047 hunters even smiled at the line. But Mr. Tennison isn't by any means the only safari boy to feel put upon. So does James Rikhoff, president of something called the African Safari Club of New York. In *Track*, the magazine of the International Professional Hunters Association, Rikhoff sounded off on, what seemed to this writer at least, a personal note:

> The various individuals, ranging from Cleveland Amory to a whole covey of actresses of both sexes, have banded together in what they consider to be a now-popular children's crusade. We are being attacked on all sides and for a great many reasons, some of which even have a touch of logic to their presentation.

That surely was good to hear, at any rate. But Mr. Rikhoff continued:

> We can no longer laugh or shrug these people away because they have the money to buy the space and the names to attract attention of the previously vast uncommitted majority of non-hunters. They are winning battles and they intend to win the war. They have stopped the special deer hunt requested by game officials in New Jersey for the Wildlife Refuge in the Great Swamp and they are next going to court to try to stop all deer hunting in New Jersey.
>
> At the same time, there is an extremely active movement to obtain a federal law to ban all public and private hunting on any federal lands—which would mean national forests, wilderness areas, wildlife refuges—even those paid for by duck stamp funds and Pittman-Robinson money—as well as military reservations. I'm not sure if this would legally apply to Indian Reservations as well, but you can certainly bet they will attempt to do so.

If you will stop and think about this for one moment,
it should send shivers through your blood stream.

Blood, as a matter of fact, keeps cropping up in these arguments. It has, evidently, a special meaning for hunters. Perhaps
because of that age-old barbarity of "blooding the hounds" or
"blooding the hunter"—by dipping of a leaf in the blood of
the prey and then touching it to his forehead. When all other
arguments fail, the hunters turn on the anti-hunters by renam-
ing them. Hiram Southwick, Division of Natural Resources Regional Game Manager in Southwestern Minnesota—which is
quite a mouthful right there—recently penned what he called
an "Open Letter to Anti-Hunters":

> We refer to these people, militant or otherwise, as "do-
> gooders." But they are not doing good for wildlife. This
> is especially true of the militant groups. Instead of doing
> good, they are doing HARM. And so wildlife managers
> prefer to call them, "DO HARMERS!"

In Mr. Southwick's belief, the real culprit is neither the
hunter nor the anti-hunter but, of all things, the automobile:

> A game report from Thompson, New Mexico, showed
> a compilation of reports from other states, and the total
> estimated loss of deer from car accidents as 126,471
> during 1967. No estimate was made of the injured and
> maimed, but the experience indicates that the numbers
> may have been greater. The property damage per accident
> was reported to be an average of $272.79 and the total
> national property vehicle damage was $34,500,024—a
> staggering sum! And this does not include the additional
> damages to car grills, windshields, etc., caused by col-
> lisions with millions of other smaller animals and birds.
> Actually, *the automobile is the greatest killer and maimer
> of wildlife known to exist today.*

Perhaps the NRA could use a portion of what many people
consider its gun-gotten gains to build more and better fences

near highways, or even, as Sweden and several other enlightened countries have done, to build highway underpasses for the animals. An interesting associate for this venture with the NRA might be the Automobile Association of America. Up till now, the major contribution of the AAA to animals has been the dispensing to their members of hunting guidebooks. One thing, however, is certain—the hunters' persecution complex receives nothing but tender, loving care from a veritable army of outdoor writers, all of whom take severe umbrage at the slightest slur on the hunting fraternity. Almost daily in their newspaper columns they extoll the virtues of the gunmen. And if, in recent years, they have been called upon to fire virtually at will, they are also not averse to taking pot shots at random. One of the most remarkable statements came from a man named Richard Starnes, former editor of the New York *World Telegram & Sun*. A gunman from way back, he came up in *Field & Stream* with "A Lesson for Gun Bigots." Vietnam was beaten by the Communists, in Starnes's opinion, "because little Vietnamese boys didn't grow up with guns like U.S. boys." Less, well, bigoted, but only scarcely less extraordinary was the work of one Buck Russell in the Monterey Peninsula *Herald* in defending the hunting of, of all animals, the sea otter. "Some cringe at the thought of sea otters being hunted," he wrote. "Cropping excess population is a sound wildlife management tool, though, and a dedicated hunter like the sea otter might be just the one to explain such a program to his protectors."

We can see it now—Buck Otter explaining to his "protectors," at a lecture perhaps, the "valuable management tool." But make no mistake—the outdoor literati do not find humor in anti-hunting. "DISLIKE OF HUNTER IS BEWILDERING," wailed a headline of Gene Mueller's column in the Washington *Star-*

News. "Hunters are sick and tired of being blasted as murderers and bloodthirsty creatures," he wrote. "Wildlife must be harvested no different from agricultural crops." In some papers, perhaps in an effort to improve the grammar, even "outdoor" women are called upon to man the battlements. One of these was Harriot Geier who wrote a column entitled "Behind the Sportsman." Hunting, she pointed out, was exercise, and exercise meant "good circulation" to "stimulate" her husband's "brain." And, she added, "The more active his brain, the better job he can do for providing for his family." Also, she pointed out:

> The trips to the out-of-doors give him a chance to wear rugged clothes, let his beard grow, use indiscreet language and release his repressions. Therefore, he is usually a gentleman in civilized surroundings.

In another place in her column, she helpfully answers questions:

> Women often wonder how the outdoorsman can keep on doing the same thing year in and year out, pulling in the same fish or bagging the same game. The answer is he never tires of it, any more than a woman tires of shoping for clothes or redecorating the house. . . .
>
> A woman with a sportsman for a husband is actually lucky that her husband is able to release all those repressions which made him the upstanding, hard-working, well-trained family provider that he is. . . .
>
> He develops some idea of what it means to be a good sport and play fair. So, very often, he isn't too tired to lend a hand when you're worn out.

Surely a mere male outdoor writer could not have given gentler surcease to the hunters' complex. One case of this complex was, for this writer, particularly close to home. It began when a struggling young magazine, *Environmental Quality*, approached the giant Atlantic Richfield Oil Company—ARCO—and successfully persuaded them to send out a mailing to their 2.6 million credit-card customers to buy a subscription to the magazine, with the understanding that a portion of this subscription money would then be donated by the magazine to the environmental organization of its choice—this choice having already been determined to be The Fund for Animals. The public-relations department of ARCO dutifully had printed up, at an expense of some $25,000, 2.6 million copies of a four-color brochure announcing the project. This brochure was, in fact, already completed and ready to be mailed. At this point, however, word of the project reached the Outdoor Writers of America, which, by chance, was holding its convention in California, the site of ARCO headquarters. That very weekend, they began their pressure by telephoning to the home of one of the officers of the company. That same weekend, the Outdoor Writers also got in touch with the California Fish and Game Department, and we were told that the latter, in the person of our old friend Ray Arnett, also got in touch with the officer. Monday morning, when the officer walked into his office, he called off the project—at least as far as The Fund for Animals was concerned. A frantic search for another charitable organization began, and in short order, as the beneficiary of the extra subscription money, the Highway Action Coalition was substituted for The Fund for Animals. ARCO public-relations director Manny Jimenez dutifully issued the company denial. "There was a premature announcement that got out and caused some problems," he declared. "Unequivocally, we do not, nor do we intend, to back Fund for Animals nor any other anti-hunting organization."

A statement which, in number of negatives at least, was

certainly calculated to get the job, if not done, at least undone. There were, however, at least three remarkable ironies to the aftermath of the story. The first of these was the obvious one that the Highway Action Coalition—a militantly anti-road group—promised far more direct conflict with ARCO than The Fund for Animals ever would have. The second was that The Fund for Animals' own board of directors and officers had never been anything but extremely nervous about any association, no matter how profitable, with an organization which had as controversial an environmental record, not only in the matter of the Alaska Pipeline, but also elsewhere, as ARCO. The third and final irony was that the credit-card mailing, as it at last went through, was almost a total failure. It raised so little money for *Environmental Quality*, let alone the Highway Action Coalition, that the magazine shortly went bankrupt. ARCO might have 2.6 million credit-card customers, but they had, it seemed, where money for the environment was concerned, an extreme case of the shorts.

The outdoor writers, however, soon had bigger game and larger fish to fry than The Fund for Animals. In the space of one year—1972–73—the gunmen had also declared war on both the Salvation Army and the YWCA. Both, it seems, had had the temerity to suggest, albeit mildly, that one of the reasons for America's horrendous crime rate might be—just might be, mind you—that there was so little control of guns. The exact wording of the Salvation Army's editorial in its official publication, *The War Cry*, was as follows:

> Are we not encouraging crime by refusing to outlaw possession of guns, or even by displaying them on a policeman's uniform, thus providing an incitement to emulation in some and giving aggravation to those with a grievance against authority?

Ah, the horror of it. Yet this mild question immediately "touched off," according to *Gun Week*, "a storm of protests from firearms enthusiasts." To which Bob Cromie, Chicago *Tribune* columnist and a staunch supporter of animals, had a question of his own. "Would you rather," he asked, "be a gun lover or a 'firearms enthusiast'?"

The YWCA story was basically similar. This organization, at its national delegate assembly meeting, passed by an admittedly overwhelming majority a resolution to ban privately owned handguns, and to register and license firearms and ammunition. Again, not to take the guns of the "sportsmen" away, mind you, merely register them. But even this, of course, was too much for the arms-bearers. "GOODBYE TO THE Y," screamed a headline atop the column of Henry Stowers in the Dallas *Morning News*:

> It is difficult to understand how the organization, along with the Salvation Army and a few other groups, could adopt such an important stand without at least obtaining the views of those people they are taking such a hard poke at. Difficult, that is, until we consider that many large groups have been infiltrated by "hard workers" who rapidly rise to top positions and who are then able to put across their own often zany beliefs with the backing of a huge organization.

Mr. Stowers went on from there to make a prediction—that such "powerful" organizations as the Sportsmen's Alliance of Michigan, the National Rifle Association and such "power" groups as the "Sportsman's Club of Texas" would fight back with "the only weapon available in a free country":

> The target shooters and hunters have in turn a right to demand that none of their donations to United Fund drives and other fund-raising efforts go to the organizations that are taking such an unfair swipe at them. From

here, I predict that the YWCA's stand on guns will shoot
down at least a half, perhaps more, of their financial help
when this summer comes and the hat is passed.

This writer has many times been on the receiving end of
such bullying threats. Most of the time such threats are so
extreme they are just funny. I have been called not just a
"bleeding heart" or a "Bambi lover," or even a "do harmer."
I have even been dubbed—a not unflattering comparison—"an
Uncle Wiggly." Perhaps the most curious personal experience
along this line was the telephone conversation I had with an
editor of *Field & Stream*. As was explained in a Fund for
Animals bulletin, I had written in a *TV Guide* review about
an attempt, in a TV drama, to rescue a man on a mountain
ledge. Since the man was a hunter, I had written, I was cheer-
ing for the ledge. "That," the *Field & Stream* man told me,
"is the most despicable thing that has ever appeared in a national magazine." I told him I did not agree—that I felt certain
that somewhere, sometime, possibly in the dim past, something
equally "despicable" might have been allowed to slip by. I
told him further that what it was was a joke, and that if *Field
& Stream* was all out of jokes possibly I could persuade The
Fund for Animals to lend them a couple. At this the editor
declared that he didn't have to sit there and listen to this sort
of thing, and that anyway it was not the first time I had written
something despicable. "You once said," he continued, "that a
hunter was caught in an avalanche. And you were hoping for
the avalanche!" I admitted that he had me there—that I had
indeed so written. But, I urged, what he must remember is
that avalanches and ledges are very different things. There
are very few avalanches left these days. They are virtually an
endangered species.

*

In no field of hunting does the outdoor writer have a more difficult time than in the matter of hunting accidents—accidents, that is, to the hunter. But make no mistake, if outdoor writers cannot defend the accidents as unavoidable, they manfully attempt to explain them as overemphasized—and unfair criticism. Possibly the most remarkable effort in this latter direction was made by the Chabot Gun Club of San Francisco, when one member was quoted in the *Wall Street Journal* as saying that nonhunters were always complaining about hunting accidents, but he lived next door to a golf course and his car had been hit by golf balls as many as "five times in a single day." He could not understand why the authorities were, as he put it, "unwilling" to criticize golfers the way they did hunters.

Another man, Gordon Charles, in the Ann Arbor (Michigan) *News* took a more historical approach. "Hunting accidents," he wrote, "are nothing new. History is full of hunting accidents. He then proceeded to recount the story of King William II of England, who was shot "by one of his favorite hunting companions." The date was 1100. Mr. Charles also advised that Greek mythology was "full of hunting accidents," and here he recounted the story of Peleus, son of Aeacus—neither of whom were favored in my dictionary—who accidentally killed the son of his host on a hunting trip. Even Marco Polo, Mr. Charles continued, told of hunting accidents, and as proof of this he related Polo's account of the death of the Apostle St. Thomas, who was kneeling in prayer in a monastery in the midst of a flock of peacocks. "A native on a hunting expedition," Charles wrote, "came by and let fly with an arrow. It missed the flock of birds, but bagged St. Thomas."

"No matter that this is the 20th Century," Charles cheerfully concluded. "Hunting accidents are still with us."

Jack O'Connor of *Outdoor Life* also attempted a stirring, if less scholarly, analysis, if not defense, of hunting accidents in an article remarkably enough entitled "Why You Shoot Your Uncle for an Elk." Mr. O'Connor pointed out that a hunter is something more than his own worst enemy—he is also apparently his mortal one. "If what I have written so far," he wrote, "has made many readers feel that half the gunners in the world are out to get them, let me say that the one person most apt to shoot you is YOU. In a recent year, 37 percent of persons who died in hunting accidents in California were their own victims." Mr. O'Connor also advises you, however, what to do when the trouble is not apparently, you:

> Across the canyon, at a distance of 300 yards or so, I had from time to time seen another hunter. I had looked at him once with a funny little French binocular I had at the time. He was wearing a pair of blue bib overalls, a green sweater and a blue stocking cap.
>
> Suddenly I heard the *crack-boom* of a bullet fired in my direction—the crack of the bullet breaking the sound barrier, followed by the boom that is the report of the rifle. That bullet passed within probably 15 or 20 feet of me. I shouted. Across the canyon I could see the other hunter kneeling and aiming at me. I let out another yell and threw myself behind a log on the ground. Again I heard the *crack-boom* as the bullet came my way.
>
> I crawled around to one end of the log and peeked. The hunter was still on one knee with his rifle turned toward my log. My life was in jeopardy, and yelling had done no good. I had to take radical action.

What did the intrepid Mr. O'Connor do? Tune in tomorrow. No, what he did was the only thing he evidently felt he could do—he fired back. It turned out later that the fellow in blue bib overalls and green sweater and blue stocking cap thought

Mr. O'Connor was a turkey. Mr. O'Connor was understandably furious. How, he wanted to know, could "a tall guy in a 10-gallon hat, a red plaid shirt resemble a turkey?" We have no idea. However, the idea of hunters shooting back and forth at each other—as, of course, a "safety measure"—is not without its appeal. In any case, at least one song writer, Tom Lehrer has, in "The Hunting Song," put it to music:

> People ask me how I do it
> And I say there's nothing to it.
> You just stand there looking cute,
> And when something moves, you shoot.
> And there's ten stuffed heads in my trophy room right now:
> Two game wardens, seven hunters and a cow.

Exact hunting-accident figures are difficult to come by, except via the National Rifle Association, which is obviously an organization with a vast vested interest in minimizing them. The National Safety Coucil, however, not long ago estimated as an annual figure seven hundred killed and nine thousand wounded. In that particular year, there were three times as many hunting deaths as passenger deaths in commercial airlines, train wrecks and bus accidents combined. Yet somehow the California Fish and Game Department can even make pro-hunting propaganda out of such strange statistics. According to Hilton Bergstrom, "Hunter Safety" training officer of California Fish and Game, it is "23 times as safe to go out hunting as it is to go out in an automobile." How Mr. Bergstrom arrived at such a conclusion, let alone a comparison, I hesitate to imagine, but I do know that there was a recent case in Michigan where a man thought he saw a deer by the side of the road and blasted away. When he arrived at the scene, he found he had hit what he had shot at all right—he had shot off the top of his own convertible.

There is, of course, nothing funny about most hunting accidents. In Florida, in 1973, four game wardens were shot—two fatally. In one incident, veteran wildlife officer Harry Chapin and his associates were crossing a field one night near Quincy, Florida, and approaching a tree where three hunters were sitting. The hunters shone a light on the officers and, when the light hit the officers, all of them dove to the ground except Chapin, who bravely shone his own light back at the men. "As soon as the light hit them," the sheriff recorded, "there was a shot and Chapin went down." He was dead.

In California a National Park Service ranger was killed by members of a hunters' ring—operating with silent and deadly crossbows. And in Michigan a game warden was run down and killed by a bear hunter in an automobile. The penalty? The Michigan killer got two years for "negligent homicide." A few years ago, Donald Foltz, director of the Indiana Department of Conservation, bluntly stated the truth about hunting accidents in the *Saturday Evening Post* in an article entitled "Boobs in the Woods":

> I am forced by law to issue hunting licenses to anyone who has the fee—even the feebleminded or half-blind. . . . In Minnesota "mistaken for game" killing is a criminal offense, punishable by imprisonment from five to twenty years. But there hasn't been a conviction under this statute in fifty-seven years. In New Jersey it is illegal to hunt while under the influence of liquor or a drug, but no one has been prosecuted for this offense in fifteen years.
>
> The classic case occurred in Colorado several years ago, when seventeen hunters were slain in a two-week preseason hunt. Not a single hunter who caused a death was prosecuted. . . . In many states the hunting codes have not been substantially reviewed in twenty years.

> Indiana is one of the states that do not forbid people to hunt while intoxicated. When I asked one of our conservation officers what he would do if he came across a drunken hunter, he replied, "I'd run like hell!"

It is small wonder, in view of this, that a recent survey conducted by the New York Cooperative Wildlife Research Unit at Cornell University indicated that 56 percent of landowners listed, as the chief reason for posting their property, a "bad experience" with hunters. The next major reason was a "bad experience" on the part of friends and neighbors. To counteract such bad experiences, the hunters have turned, as always, to the authorities. Not long ago, they prevailed upon the U.S. Government to pay farmers to allow hunting on land it already pays them not to farm. The program, a $1-million "pilot one," was announced by Secretary of Agriculture Earl L. Butz to be operated in fifty counties of Colorado, Indiana, Iowa, Louisiana, Michigan, North Dakota, Oklahoma, Oregon, Pennsylvania and South Carolina. The fifty thousand farmers, Butz said, would be paid an average of $200 each, in an effort "to increase recreational use of the countryside." One can only wonder how many farmers will have, from such "recreation," a "bad experience." Such an experience, for example, as that of the Miller-Stringer families of Kinross, in the upper peninsula of Michigan. In December, 1972, Clyde Stringer went out hunting and took with him his fourteen-year-old son, Michael, although Michael's mother never liked the idea of hunting. Arriving on the land of another hunter, Harry Miller, they were told to get off the land. Apparently they did not get far enough off. Miller shot Michael. The shot severed Michael's spinal cord and paralyzed him from the waist down—he will never walk again. Whereupon Stringer shot Harry Miller—dead.

That is not, obviously, the average hunting story. But any country landowner who has gone through any hunting season can tell you horrifying stories. Author Jerrold Mundis of West Shokan, New York, has best summarized a typical "scene":

> Forget the moral questions about hunting. . . . Walk with me through the woods immediately around my house. Within an hour of setting out, I'll show you the carcasses of eleven does. Livestock and pets of all kinds are shot each season in large numbers. I know a farmer who in desperation painted the sides of his cows with large, white COW. One animal was drilled neatly in the center of the O.
>
> Someone sent four slugs through the radiator of a car parked next to a house; the owner had tossed on old bear-skin rug over the hood to protect the engine against wind. Most pets and livestock are killed on private property with "No Hunting" signs. A neighbor's dog was killed while it was tied in the yard twenty-five feet from the house. There is need, when you have a gun in your hand, sometimes, to kill something.
>
> Midway through this season I was working in my den and watching two does in my back field. It was well past sunset, a murky grey. A car with three hunters slowed to a stop on the road. One jumped out, fired a shot, which missed and sent the deer bolting away, then got back in and the car sped off. Illegally, the man had (1) attempted to kill a doe, (2) fired from a public road, (3) fired after hunting hours, (4) violated private, posted land, (5) discharged a firearm within 500 feet of an inhabited building without the owner's consent. Five major violations in as many seconds.
>
> So tell me about conscientious, responsible sportsmen.

If one thinks that Mr. Mundis is exaggerating, take, from another part of the country, the view of another author—Dan Satran of Eagle River, Wisconsin:

> First it was the early bear season and the bow hunting season, then the ruffed grouse and the duck seasons and now the deer season.

When hunters indicate they're perplexed that they're bad-mouthed by so many people, perhaps a review of what has been happening will help them understand why some folks are upset.

Most of the news relative to hunting season comes from the game experts at the various DNR offices and the doctors who tend the injured and killed hunters. But the animal doctors, the veterinarians, are never consulted. And their business really perks up during hunting season.

Dr. Roger VanProoen, Hazelhurst, performed surgery on a Guernsey cow recently, removing a hunting arrow from its front shoulder. . . . Dr. Tom Dunn was dismayed that an archer had shot a black Labrador dog, the arrow with a broad-point blade imbedded in its hindquarters. . . . He said another hunter victim, a Chihuahua, was brought in, wounded by a shotgun blast into its hindquarters.

Dr. Dunn said this hunting season two horses were shot—one in the Crandon area, the other in Lake Tomahawk. The horse at Crandon was hit at close range with a shotgun. The horse at Tomahawk was shot at night, killed instantly by rifle fire. The owner said it was apparently the victim of deer shiners, who mistook it for a whitetail.

Dr. Francine Gough said opening weekend of bow season, she had several dogs brought in shot with arrows. She said she managed to perform surgery on the animals and save them, noting that "all had been hit in the pelvis or hindquarters." Talking with the owners of these pets, she said "they were all in the immediate vicinity of their homes when they were shot." . . .

Gary Howe, employed at the St. Germain shopping center, said this bow season he heard what sounded like a small child crying from the back of the store. Hurrying to locate the source of the trouble, he found a small raccoon, an arrow completely through its stomach. . . .

Hunters can't resist gunning down ducks, even if they're

paddling around in the front-yard of a residence. Five
pet Ruan ducks were shot by two young men combing the
shoreline illegally carrying uncased guns in open water.
The ducks, so tame and hand-fed that they responded to a
human calling "quack" were all gunned down by the
hunters.

*

All the arguments of all the Federal and state governments,
their fish and game departments, their commissioners and
even their "biostitutes"—i..e., biologists who have prostituted
themselves to the hunters' ethic—boiled down, in the final
analysis, to one basic argument—that, if they didn't shoot the
deer, the deer would die of starvation. Even if this argument
were true—which most of the time it is not—it is basically no
argument at all. In the first place, the reason that there are too
many deer is that the hunters either (a) shot off their natural
predators or (b) "managed" them in such a way, that hoping to
have more to kill, they actually produced starvation. In the
second place, while it is certainly true that there are examples,
be they elephants in the Tsavo or deer in the Catskills, where
there is actually overpopulation and therefore some animals
will have to be either relocated or, as a too final resort, "culled"
or "cropped" or whatever, this still does not make it a "sport"
any more than it is "sport" to "put down" or "put to sleep" or
whatever an excess of dogs or cats in an animal shelter. In the
third and final place, the use of the starvation argument for
the hunting of virtually all animals, as it is so used, is simply
absurd—if for no other reason than that, in state after state
and, for that matter, in country after country, the hunters'
own published "limits" and "seasons" show that they shoot
literally scores of animal species all year long with no limit,
no season, no "bags," no nothing.

Take the sovereign state of Connecticut—surely a highly

"urbanized" state and one supposedly far from totally hunter dominated. Here you can kill all year long, with no limits, black bear, fisher, fox, opossum, porcupine, red squirrel, skunk, weasel and woodchuck. Isn't that nice? Think of all the "starvation" you stop. And if you think I am singling out Connecticut, take my own home state of Massachusetts. There you can kill red squirrel, flying squirrel, chipmunk, porcupine, skunk, weasel, woodchuck, English sparrow and starling all year too, except—Massachusetts being Massachusetts—*Sundays.* And hunting licenses are, in Massachusetts, for all people over seventy years of age, *free.* Our senior starvation stoppers —failing eyesight and all.

Turning to the Midwest, in Michigan you can kill all year red squirrel, opossum, fox and coyote—and, for your added starvation-saving pleasure, you have the extra special inducement of receiving a bounty for every coyote killed. In Ohio, you can kill all year fox, skunk, weasel, woodchuck, raccoon and opossum—all year, that is, except during "gun" season. Meaning, presumably, when everybody is out shooting deer and so, during that period, it doesn't matter whether the others starve or not.* In Mississippi, you can even kill all year, of all animals, the beaver; in Kentucky you can kill groundhogs all year—except from November 1 to "midnight" November 14. Moving farther west, in Kansas you can kill all year red and gray fox, raccoon, coyote, bobcat and badger; in Idaho ground squirrel, coyote, jackrabbit, snowshoe rabbit, bobcat, badger and rockachuck. In Utah, you can even have the satisfaction of saving an endangered species from starva-

---

* Ohio permits hunters down to the age of ten. Yes, ten! It is nice to know, however, they must be accompanied by a "licensed non-hunting adult"—eighteen or over—and there must be no more than two of them per adult.

tion—you can kill mountain lion all year. In Montana you can have the fun of killing *two* rare and endangered species all year—lynx and wolf. In Arizona you can have a ball too— and save from starvation all year not only the mountan lion but also bobcat, coyote, fox, cottontail, muskrat, opossum, ringtail cat and even beaver and coati-mundi.

In Hawaii, you can kill wild goat, wild pig and even wild sheep virtually all year, except that on Hawaii Island you can shoot wild sheep on "Unit A" only on the third weekend of each month except February and October. In Alaska, you can kill wolf all year, all the arctic fox you want, both blue and white, and at least up until the passage of the Marine Mammals Act, you could even shoot sea lion all year and, in at least four "units" of the state, walrus. In Texas, well, Texas being what it is I decided on a personal interview with one "Cap" Talbert, staff assistant to the Director of Law Enforcement of the Texas Parks and Wildlife Department. I asked Cap to tell me the animals I could kill all year round with no limit. "Waal," he drawled, "I may be kinda bad at snarin' all of 'em, and I may jus' miss quite a few, but I'll take a crack at it." He paused. "Lessee," he said. "Mebbe the easiest way to do this would be to tell you that you've got *all* the furbearers open to you for year-roun' huntin', less'n you're huntin' 'em for the pelts, and then mainly you gotta take 'em in December an' January." Honestly, *mainly*—that's what the man said. In any case how, I asked him, about rabbits. "Rabbits!" he expressed surprise. "Down here rabbits aren't considered furbearers—they got no protection 'tall." Which, judging from the "protection" he gave the furbearers, was obviously not a great privation. In any event, as a final question, I asked Cap Talbert if he had the experience of having game wardens shot in Texas. "Oh," he said, "that. Down here, you're shot at on a regular basis." He paused again. "We don't think a whole lot of it, but there it is. We just lost an officer last July." What, I wanted to know, was the officer trying to do when he was shot? "Nothin' particular," Cap told me. "He was jus' tryin' to enforce a fishin' law."

So much for the "starvation" arguments. Before passing on to other aspects of "management," however, one state and one animal deserve special mention. The state is Arizona. The following quotation appeared in a brochure entitled *Wildlife Guard* written by Paul Anthony of Phoenix in 1971:

> Twenty years ago wildlife was fairly abundant in Arizona. The last Merriam Elk had been shot years ago, but Rocky Mountain Elk had been imported and deer were still much in evidence. You often saw hawks and occasionally eagles. You could hear coyotes at night, not far from town, and your headlights often picked out raccoons and skunks and ringtails. The State was far from swarming with wildlife, but wild animals and birds were still in evidence to the population at large. There were still more javelina than men hunting them. . . . Today there are almost 2,000,000 people in Arizona, and you have to make a very determined effort before you have a chance of seeing a deer, elk, antelope, hawk, eagle or javelina.

One reason surely is the "Game Management Data Survey" of 1969 of the Arizona Game and Fish Department. Under the headline "Number of Javelinas Seen in Survey," it gave the figure 948, yet the survey gave the number of "Javelina Hunters Afield" at 30,226 and the number of "Javelina Killed" at 5,903.

"Sure enough," Mr. Anthony pointed out, "30,000 guns finished shooting 5,000 more javelinas than were known to exist."

The javelina is a small, harmless, root-eating, piglike crea-ture with very poor eyesight. In the literature of the Arizona hunt, however, he is, of course, blown up into being a terrify-ing wild boar. As if this were not enough, in 1973 the Chamber of Commerce of Globe, Arizona, announced, in connection with the annual javelina slaughter, a brand-new hunting horror. This was a free-for-all, in which a prize was offered each day for the biggest "point kill" of bobcat, coyote or fox killed by any means. The points were "tallied"—five for bobcat, three for coyote, two for fox. After it was over, the Chamber of Commerce had done its work—but in reverse. "This year's hunt," said Tom Anderson, president of the Chamber, "will be the last. It just isn't worth it. We received so many letters criticizing Globe."

The "rules" for bear hunting are perhaps the most extraor-dinary of all. They were recently detailed in *Sports Afield*. In Maine, for example, dogs and "baits" are allowed. In New York, however, the wording is "Dogs not allowed." But under "Baits" in New York, one reads, "Hunting over bait discour-aged, but allowed." With two years for "negligent homicide" for the murder of a game warden, one wonders what kind of "discouragement" one receives for killing a bear with bait. In Vermont, on the other hand, bait hunting is illegal. But under "Use of Dogs" the wording is "Maximum of six dogs for hunting and treeing bear." Which, one presumes, is either Vermont sense of justice—or economy.

For bear hunting in New Mexico, one reads, "Best chances by hunting on horseback with dogs." Nothing, though, about using the horse as bait. Michigan, too, evidently has remarkable bear hunting—witness the fact that, at the opening of the bear-hunting season of 1973, bear hunters from Detroit, Port Huron, Grand Rapids and Kalamazoo crowded around the town dump of Copper Harbor, Michigan. Each year thousands of tourists regularly came to the dump—which has been the town's No. 1 tourist attraction—just to see the bears. The bears, of course, searching the dump for food, are used to the humans and not the slightest bit afraid of them. Then, on the day the 1973 "season" began, the bold hunters arrived at the dump and, on the dot of the beginning of the season, began potting away. "It was like shooting fish in a barrel," declared Mrs. James, a local tourist-camp operator. "The poor things just stood there and looked at the hunters." Mrs. James and other residents were, according to the United Press, "especially angered that the hunters probably go back home and boast about their hunting ability." But the United Press also noted, "there was not a single thing the residents could do about it —the hunters were not violating any state or local laws."*

For "varmint hunters"—the quotation marks being usually confined to the "varmint"—there are no rules at all. The "varmints," including, of course, raccoon, are hunted 365 days a year, 24 hours a day, night and day, by any method whatever. And no matter that such varmints as the coyote, as well as

---

* In the spring of 1974, despite the heroic efforts of Lucile and Harry Hunt, of the Society for Humane Legislation, and Ruth McCloud, of Defenders of Animals, Governor Patrick Lucey of Wisconsin vetoed a bill banning the use of bait or dogs by Wisconsin bear hunters. The dogs were added in an amendment which may well have been a ploy to get the bill killed—in any case even the baiting ban was not a real ban. All it did was restrict the types of bait for bears to "soft" materials such as honey, scents, grease, vegetable matter, and bakery products. Virtually the only mess in the woods actually prohibited were "meat bones." Each licensed bear hunter would also have been limited to only two bait stations. Now, since the bill was defeated, he can have all the garbage and dogs he wants. "I have vetoed the bill," Governor Lucey said, "not because I like the practice of bear baiting, but because I do not like the sweeping and un-qualified manner in which regulation is being sought. Bear hunting has a place in Wisconsin, but it must be conducted in such a way as to reflect favor and not disfavor on our humanity." And without, apparently, any regulations at all.

the raccoon, are the brightest, friendliest, most curious animals of all. Take the case of Charles Richard Feezer of San Diego, who teaches history to gifted students at Helix High. He has a son, Shawn, who, he says, is "one of his hunting buddies." Mr. Feezer, who weighs 270 pounds, has been at the "varmint calling game," as he puts it, for about five years. And, he admits, he and another buddy, Charley Kahan, a fellow Helix teacher, make "quite a sight" in the toy department of the stores while shopping for "squeakers." "You can imagine how we must look, a couple of thirty-year-old men, big as we are, testing children's toys for the right sounds. But those twenty-nine-cent squeakers do the job." Mr. Feezer also declares that he has hunted Mexico, but didn't like it. "The laws," he says "are such that you can easily make a mistake and be in violation. You can't use calls or lights, and that makes it almost impossible to hunt with any great success."

But the killers of everything, including their own starvation arguments, are not confined to any one section of the country. In 1970, for example, in New York State alone 64,581 deer were slaughtered. Of these, it was proudly announced by the New York State Department of Environmental Conservation, 11,690 were fawns. And at least one kind of "challenging sport," as the outdoor writers put it, would seem to have absolutely nothing to do with starvation. This is the killing of a bird which in many states is classified as a songbird but which in twenty-eight states—pretty generally in those states where "game management" can be classed as primitive, even by primitive standards—is classified as a "game bird." The bird is the mourning dove. Each year they are shot not by the thousands but by the millions. The annual kill, in fact, is over 40 million. Their tiny carcasses, laid end to end, would make a bloody chain from Los Angeles to New York and back to

Chicago—and yet even this would not be accurate, because it has been estimated by the great mourning-dove authority, Dr. Henry Weber, that at least one mourning dove is unretrieved for every one killed. So the actual chain, bodies end to end, would go from Los Angeles to New York, back to Los Angeles and almost back to New York.

*

One of the most telling whistles ever blown on the billion-dollar butchery business which is hunting was blown by, of all people, an ex-hunter. His name is Bil Gilbert, and he is a Pennsylvania naturalist who has, among other things, taught survival techniques to members of the Peace Corps. His article, "Hunting Is a Dirty Business," was a landmark one in the last days of the late *Saturday Evening Post*:

> At the lowest critical level, in my experience, the average hunter is a hypocritical nuisance. . . . Each one seems to believe that because he is trying to shoot an inoffensive animal, he is a tough, crafty, courageous woodsman whose chest is covered with hair, a figure out of James Fenimore Cooper by Ernest Hemingway. Frankly I suffer these clowns more as a composite of Studs Lonigan and Walter Mitty.
>
> Physically they run to paunch and red faces. They are slow of foot, expensively dressed from the tips of their down bootees to the knobs of their silver hip flasks. They have little desire to search for game, but a great desire to kill something that can be tied to a fender or held up in a barroom. They shoot from the road ("Don't slam the door, Jack, you'll scare him"). They rarely pursue wounded game, and after a hunting season, the woods are filled with cripples. Hunters are noisy, belligerent, and the dirtiest of all outdoors users, littering the landscape with bottles, corn plasters and aspirin tins. They are also dangerous. . . .

Beyond the fact that sport hunters are, as a rule, disreputable, the most obvious complaint against them is that they are destructive of wildlife. Several species—the passenger pigeon, heath hen, Eskimo curlew—were simply hunted into extinction. Many more—buffalo, antelope, grizzly bear, wolf, mountain lion, eagle, certain waterfowl—now barely survive.

Hunters say that these were merely atrocities of the past, committed by gunmen who had not been saved by the National Wildlife Federation or the National Rifle Association. Today's hunters are said to be enlightened conservationists whose fees and political support make possible all sorts of wildlife research, protection and preservation. In fact, about half of the funds of state game agencies is spent to hire, equip and arm wardens to protect wildlife from gunners. Hunters are therefore in the position of would-be bank robbers who, upon encountering armed guards in front of a vault, decline to blow it open and then demand a good conduct medal.

The most shattering part of Mr. Gilbert's thesis was that he not only took issue with the hunters' sacred belief that they are the only ones who put their money where their muzzles are, where "conservation" is concerned, but that actually the reverse was true—that the hunters were in his opinion closer to something they would least like to be—welfare chiselers:

The most irksome aspect of all of this is that, unlike bridge players, Boy Scouts, pool hustlers or any other sporting group, hunters are more or less public wards. I, you, we are required to subsidize hunters with our taxes and set aside large chunks of our increasingly scarce wild lands and wildlife for their use. Somewhere in the neighborhood of 25,000 public wildlife "conservation" workers, state and Federal, consume upwards of a half-billion dollars a year mostly to make it easier and quicker for gunners to gun things. No other sport comes anywhere near to being so pampered and coddled.

Take, for example, the National Wildlife Refuge system operated by the Department of the Interior. Some 29 million acres of public land (2 million more than are in the National Park System) are set aside for wildlife refuges. Much of this land is managed and maintained for the primary benefit of waterfowl gunners. Hunters point out that they buy duck stamps and assert that this money pays for the refuge system. The truth is that the annual refuge budget is about $30 million and the annual income from duck stamps is $5 million. In other words, about 85 percent of the refuge money comes from general tax revenues. . . .

Hunters attempt to justify this obvious inequity by explaining that the work of state and Federal wildlife agencies benefits all wildlife. It is claimed that state and Federal hunting lands also serve as sanctuary for many non-game birds and mammals. They do sometimes, but it is largely accidental. . . . You seldom find public wildlife employees out ministering to a bluebird, chipmunk or owl, since they are occupied almost exclusively with about 30 shootable species out of approximately 1,000 of North American birds and mammals. "You may be hired as a wildlife manager, biologist or whatever, but you soon find that you are paid to put out so much meat on the hoof," explains a man who, until last year, was an official in a "conservation" department. He is now employed by a private *conservation* foundation. "I just got tired of being a butcher's assistant, and quit."

Mr. Gilbert concluded that the results of our hunter-dominated national wildlife policy have been "disastrous." He also reminded his readers that hunters, despite their many privileges, were not only minority users of wildlife, but that their numbers were declining. And probably nothing in his article, strong as it was, would have irritated the hunters more than this. Their efforts to show that their numbers are increasing have at times, as we have seen, reached ferocious proportions. Nonetheless, Mr. Gilbert was accurate. And his reference to the declining number of hunters—as well as to their small number in relation to the total population—was, shortly after his article, amply demonstrated by the curious history of a Sunday afternoon television program with the extraordinary name of *The American Sportsman*. From the outset this program was, among other things, the pet of Thomas Moore, at that time vice-president of programming for the American Broadcasting Company. Mr. Moore, a hunter himself, as well as one of many hunters on the board of directors of the World Wildlife Fund, saw to it that the project received the full treatment available to him—including all manner of promotion and even a whole houseful of hunting books to be sold in conjunction with it. In addition, the so-called American Sportsman's Club produced a brochure with a slogan: MAKE THE WORLD YOUR GAME. Among the big shots— in all senses of the word—who were constantly publicizing the program was none other than Bing Crosby. Whatever program he was on, he always seemed to be talking or wisecracking about *The American Sportsman*, and when he was on the program itself he was still wisecracking, at the same time blasting away with his gun at whatever particular "game" was being shot that Sunday. A full roster of celebrities was hired to take treks to just about everywhere, from Alaska to Africa, and in short order they were assassinating everything within their sights—not only all manner of birds and small game but also big game and even endangered species. *TV Guide* accorded the program unusual privilege—it permitted me to review it twice. My first review in March, 1965, ran in part as follows:

> The narration is inept, the fishing is boring, the bird-shooting pathetic, and the "he-man" exchanges embarrassing ("Look at those ever-lovin' birds! Hey man! Cock-a-baby!"). As for the African safaris, they are almost incredible in their ingenuousness. The hunters, miles away, whisper—then, right next to their prey, they smoke and talk in loud voices. And everything they kill, of course, they're killing for the good of the poor, fear-maddened natives, all of whom are apparently refugees from the latest Joe Levine picture. In one sequence actor Robert Stack "bravely" shoots, at a distance of approximately one light mile, a feeble old lion who is billed as a "killer." ("The tribe will remember a man named Robert Stack—a friendly, capable man, an American Sportsman.") In another, Joe Foss brings down, again a country mile away, an elderly, bewildered, one-tusk elephant who is gently trotting along—and Joe, in turn, is billed as "standing in the way of the thundering, massive charge of a rogue elephant." In one show, we heard the "sportsman" defined as "the certain sense of good in each of us." Honestly, sport, that's what the man said.

My second review was in February, 1967—by which time bona-fide celebrities were beginning to show marked reluctance to appear on the program. This read, again in part, as follows:

> Out of regard for their families, we will not mention the names of anyone connected with this show. Suffice it to say, however, that we have as host a man whose idea of communicating excitement seems to be to express even the most obvious explanatory remarks in a tone previously reserved for the deaths of heads of state. Along with him each week we have a curious assortment of white hunters in living color, about all of whose fearless exploits we hear *ad nauseam*—particularly as, armed with

full arsenal of weapons, they boldly advance to test wits and match virilities with, say, a mourning dove. We also have guest "stars," a preponderance of them nonentities, each of whom apparently has to be identified as a "television personality," because otherwise you wouldn't know he had one, let alone is one. To top it off, as they approach their victims, they invariably speak in such school-girlish stage whispers that the only thing missing is for a house mother to shout "lights out!"

Animal people had, of course, from the beginning turned on the program—in all senses of the phrase—in fury. By this time they were not only writing letters to the network and the sponsors and the host, but also to the "guests" who shot the animals. One of these guests, the actor Cliff Robertson, received so many letters after shooting another supposedly "rogue elephant" that, in expiation, he produced, partly at his own expense, and also appeared in, a pro-elephant special entitled *Elephant Country*. Bing Crosby, in a telephone interview, practically disowned the show altogether—for all his previous promotion. "I never hunt anything except birds," he protested. "I just don't believe in it." Faced with such defections, the hunters redoubled their efforts and desperately attempted to bolster the show with cables and letters. It was no use. First Eastman Kodak dropped its sponsorship of the show, after an advertising executive admitted that his company never should have been part of it in the first place. And, perhaps more important, after admitting that never was a slogan better designed for a company than the nonhunters' slogan for Kodak —"Hunt with a camera, instead of a gun." Then the program's other sponsor, Chevrolet, also received an extraordinary number of complaints. In the final analysis, there were just too many people out there who were too angry—and at long last, in 1971, *The American Sportsman* announced a change in policy. No longer would the hunting of big game be featured —instead, rescue and relocation would be the keynote of all "game" segments. The hunters had lost. Again, in the final analysis, the fact was that their numbers had been exaggerated by everybody—by the network, by the sponsors, even by the "guests." They could not keep on the air even one program— and that one only ten weeks a year on Sunday afternoon in so-called "ghetto" time.

Before the horrors of the "old" *Sportsman* have been laid to rest, however, one story from Sid Brooks, a writer who did two *Sportsman* shows, deserves to be told. One of these, for one Sunday's show, involved the death of no fewer than three tigers in India—at a time when the tiger population was rapidly approaching extinction. "We went 'hunting' for five weeks," Brooks recalls, "to get the proper 'action' picture. We had to kill two scrawny tigers before we got a 'photogenic' one. That 'good-looking kill,' as they called it, demanded a 'good-looking'—i.e., fierce—animal."

The particular segment of this particular episode was, supposedly, a "true" tiger hunt with the Maharajah of Bundi. The "television personality" was Craig Stevens. One of the Maharajah's men located the tiger to be used in the final kill. The tiger was asleep in a cave. The Indians put a flag on the cave. A few hundred yards away there was a concrete structure which Brooks promptly named "The Bunker Hill Monument." It had been constructed near the turn of the century by the Maharajah's grandfather when tigers were considered vermin. In any case, it was complete with thick concrete walls and slits or small windows from which, safely inside, hunters could shoot. The Maharajah had hired half a hundred "beaters" who were paid the equivalent of thirty cents a day. Equipped with old muskets and tin cans to make noise, they had as their job to wake the tiger. Finally, bewildered, he came out of the cave. At first he started to move slowly up the hill, then faster and faster as he was spurred on by the shots, shouts and tin-can banging of the beaters. He headed in the general direction of the bunker, but one of the Maharajah's trained marksmen actually "steered" him—by firing bullets all around him, one of which actually grazed him—directly to the bunker. In this bunker, peering out of the slits, were the Maharajah and Mr. Stevens. There were cameras in there too, behind them, looking over their shoulders. So while it seemed as if the tiger was actually coming at them with no bunker at all, the fact was they were, inside, completely safe. When the tiger, frantic to escape, leaped up, Mr. Stevens shot him.

That was what really happened. But, of course, for the program it was just the beginning. They had to go back and "re-create"—to make the whole thing look dangerous. First they returned to the Maharajah's palace. Here the Indians had constructed right on the palace grounds, especially for the show, a *machan*—a leafy tree platform from which, in the jungle, animals are shot. The Maharajah and Mr. Stevens climbed up on it and were told to have a conversation as if they were hunting together for the first time. Mr. Stevens was directed to whisper to the Maharajah as if there were a tiger in the vicinity. His script called for him so say something about being nervous. "Quiet, Mr. Stevens," the Maharajah whispered. "The tiger has ears." After this, the crew took film of Mr. Stevens's shooting, his rifle pointed up at nothing at all. This "shooting" was then, of course, spliced in with the actual shots of the tiger leaping in front of the bunker. The impression the television viewer had was that the Maharajah and Mr. Stevens were sitting in a flimsy, open observation post with a fierce tiger attacking them—whereas in reality, the Maharajah and Mr.

Stevens were on the *machan* and there was no tiger anywhere around. When they had actually faced the tiger, they had done so from behind thick concrete. In fact, the wildest animals around the Maharajah's estate were peacocks.

No less remarkable was the aftermath to this "true hunt." It occurred when Mr. Brooks and Mr. Stevens were present at the final screening of the show in New York. After seeing it, Stevens turned to Brooks. "That," he said, "was the scariest moment of my life." To this day, Mr. Brooks does not think Mr. Stevens was joking—he thinks rather that Stevens, by that time, believed he really had been in danger.

Even the tiger "hunt," however, was not the end of the experience for Mr. Brooks. For, besides Mr. Stevens, another "star," Joe Foss, had also been taken to India—to do another segment for the same show. It got off to a difficult start. Upon meeting the Maharajah for the first time, Mr. Foss's first words were "Hello, Your Royalty." From then on his dialogue in front of the cameras had to be watched carefully. Before Foss's segment was even programmed, the Maharajah's trackers had found a female sloth bear with her cub beside her. The idea had been to find a male sloth bear in the jungle, face up to it and shoot it. Here was a female with her cub, ambling down the path, returning from a fruit hunt. Nonetheless, Mr. Foss, high on a cliff above the bear, decided to shoot it anyway. "He shot right down on it," Brooks recalls. "That bear never even saw him. And I still remember that cub's crying. Even one of the associate producers, who loved hunting, was so disgusted he walked away. I said to Foss, 'Why don't we find you one in a cage and you can also shoot that?' Foss replied, 'Well, you've got to remember ABC's spending a lot of money for this show.'" The final irony was that the footage was, of course, totally unusable and was never shown.

In fairness to the hunting "establishment," there have been numerous instances of late of its card-carrying members being seriously worried about the future of hunting. An example of this was the fine book by *Field & Stream* columnist Michael Frome, *Battle for the Wilderness*. Not only did the book contain much justly deserved praise of the work of the dedicated Wilderness Society—it was also sharply critical of hunting:

> Although hunting plays a valid role as an outdoors experience, the rightness of one being to kill another for sport is now extremely moot. The need to hunt for food is gone. Much of sport hunting has scent relevancy to primitive instincts or old traditions. It does little to instill a conservation conscience. Blasting polar bears from airplanes, hunting the Arabian oryx—or deer—from automobiles, trail bikes, or snowmobiles, tracking a quarry with walkie-talkie radios, killing for the sake of killing annihilate the hunt's essential character. There can't be much thrill to "the chase" when there is little chase. At one end of the spectrum, "slob hunters" shoot farmers' livestock, road signs, and each other. At the opposite end are the superpredators: jet-set gunners whose greatest goal is to mount on their walls one of everything that walked Noah's plank.

Even in the heart of the hunting establishment there are deep worries. One example of this was the speech delivered to the San Antonio Game Coin Hunters Convention in 1973 by A. Starker Leopold, Professor of Zoology and Forestry at Berkeley—a man who fought the first California mountain-lion-hunting ban because he said it would be "dangerous to the sport of hunting." In this San Antonio speech, however, Mr. Leopold offered the hunters sobering thoughts:

> We cannot afford to overlook the wave of anti-hunting sentiment or to charge it to the rantings of an impotent,

lunatic minority. It has, in fact, become a real political force, not only in the State and the Nation, but in international wildlife affairs. Ray Gasmann, senior ecologist of the International Union for the Conservation of Nature in Morges, Switzerland, was in my office recently. He told me that one of the biggest impediments he must deal with today in trying to develop rational programs of wildlife utilization and management in underdeveloped countries of the world, is the rash of anti-killing propaganda from America. Not from any other country, mind you—just from America.

Mr. Leopold's speech was written that way, but, when he delivered the speech, he added phrases to the last line which made it read, "not particularly from any other country, mind you—primarily from America." Which, was, of course, even more encouraging news. And Mr. Leopold is not alone in his concern. In a two-part article in *Field & Stream* in 1972, entitled "Can Public Hunting Survive?," Stuart Williams, the magazine's "shooting editor" evidently felt doubtful: "No Trespassing and No Hunting signs," he says, "are multiplying across the country to bar hunters from more and more private land." Mr. Williams declared that "the second great threat to hunting is hunters themselves . . . that boorish fringe who are conspicuous way out of proportion to their numbers, and who call damnation down upon the rest of us, i.e. Joe Slobswine and his Yahoo buddies."

We know them all too well. They are the slobs who stay up all night long at the deer hunting camp, roaring and drinking over a poker game, and then go out in the morning, hung over and irresponsible, to blast away wildly at anything that remotely resembles a deer. They are the ones who kill does when the law specifies bucks only. They are the ones who use underpowered calibres and who do not sight in their rifles precisely and who therefore often wound game. They are the ones who will make only a half-hearted attempt to track down a wounded animal, then blithely go on and find another. They are the ones who will tie a deer across the hood of the car—thereby surely spoiling the meat—to make a public display. They are the gamehogs and jacklighters, the out-of-season hunters and trespassers. They are the goons who hunt in mobs, who leave open gates, who shoot up NO TRESPASSING signs to articulate their sentiments toward the landowner, and who are never around in the off-season to help him out when he needs a hand. They are the "sky busters" who ruin the shooting for everybody around them. I could go on *ad infinitum*—or should I say *ad nauseam*. Our ranks contain the seeds of our own destruction and we must cut them out or perish. We must police our own ranks; the number of game wardens is insufficient to do the job.

The difficulties of such a "job" were perhaps best described by Glen Sherwood, a wildlife ecologist and former employee of the U.S. Bureau of Sport Fisheries and Wildlife. In the fall of 1969, Mr. Sherwood's work took him to a goose hunt on Sand Lake in northeastern South Dakota. Herewith his observations, as excerpted from the National Audubon Society magazine—a society, you will recall, not against sport hunting:

> The concentration of geese at Sand Lake simply had attracted far too many eager hunters. Manager Schoonover told me that as many as 1,500 hunters surrounded the Lake on some days. In the frenzy and excitement to see and hunt geese, accidents occurred—including head on collisions and a number of vehicles run into ditches. One carload of hunters plowed into a ditch, narrowly missing three other hunters. The most outrageous accident took place when one hunter was wounded in the head when he peered out of the pit to look for geese. The hunter who shot him mistook his head for a badger. . . . Firing-line shooting along the boundaries would be comi-

cal were it not contributing so tragically to the slaughter of geese. Hunters claim fenceposts to "hide" behind, usually stationing themselves behind alternate posts. In the hottest areas, however, hunters can be found hunkered behind every fencepost. Sometimes two or three behind a single post. . . . Most of the hunters I saw or talked with around Sand Lake had no respect or compassion for the birds or concern for what they were doing to them. The geese were simply targets to be shot at. There was no remorse over the cripples, the broken families of geese or the wasted resource. Hunters repeatedly shot at geese over the line and at in-coming flights when there was no possible chance for retrieving. After watching one hunter shoot and cripple several geese, which fell inside, I asked him if he had any idea how many geese he had lost in that manner. He was surly about the interruption and replied, "I don't have time to watch my cripples. I'm too busy shooting." In another instance I saw a hunter drop a beautiful adult blue goose. Thinking he would want the bird, I told him I had the authority to enter and would retrieve the bird for him. His reply: "I don't care what you do with the damn bird."

Time and again I was shocked at the behavior of the hunters. I heard them laugh at the plight of dazed cripples, which stumbled about. I saw them striking the heads of retrieved cripples against fenceposts.

The attitude of most of the hunters towards the geese, I fear, was most clearly demonstrated when I examined six geese bagged by several young men. Every goose had a cigarette jammed into the corner of its mouth. The incident in itself was relatively harmless, but the attitude it connoted was disgusting. It is the same type of irreverence for life that has put our entire environment in peril.

Four things should be borne in mind here. First, these were migrating geese—blue geese and snow geese—perhaps the most beautiful birds in the world. Second, the total number of geese which were killed at Sand Lake in that one hunt, in a hail of lead, was fifty thousand—and of these nearly half were left to rot. Third, the massacre was entirely within the law and without the possibility of legal prosecution. And fourth, finally and almost unbelievably, it all occurred at the Sand Lake *National Wildlife Refuge.*

Indeed, in about half of the nation's wildlife "refuges," this kind of slaughter is not only permitted—it has, of recent years, increased. However, the Interior Department has touchingly provided refuge "managers" with a thirteen-page "policy statement." This statement warns these managers "to buffer the non-hunting public from the sights and sounds of the hunt." To *buffer*, mind you. "The roar of the guns," the official report goes on, "with geese falling out of the sky, may be offensive and confusing to persons who visit refuges while hunts are in progress." *Confusing*? "Likewise," the report concludes, "large numbers of deer carcasses hanging at a check-station may create an unpleasant atmosphere if viewed by visitors not kindly disposed to hunting."

Such solicitude, curious at it is, on the part of the Federal Government is the kind of thing that has proved too much for the State hunting establishment to stomach. In the summer of 1974 an obscure bill (H.R. 11537) was introduced to take the management of wildlife—on, of all places, *Federal* lands— virtually out of Federal hands entirely. This bill, which was described as "a goal which has been unsuccessfully sought by the National Rifle Association since time immemorial," required that "No conservation or rehabilitation program, nor any recommendation in any preliminary study or survey undertaken with respect to any program, may be implemented unless included within a 'cooperative agreement' with a State." And the bill also demanded, or course, that hunting be permitted

on Federal public land except by such "cooperative agreement." In sum, the object of the bill was to deliver all wildlife
on public lands into the blood-stained hands of the State Fish
and Game Departments, the NRA, and the hunting lobbies.
Literally, in other words, lock, stock, and barrel.

*

For impartial answers to some basic questions posed by the
increasing polarization of hunter and nonhunter, I journeyed
to Windsor, Ontario, to local Bill Grosscup. Mr. Grosscup is
one of North America's most remarkable outdoorsmen. His
program, *Woods and Wheels,* is as admired in Canada as it is
in the United States; he himself won the 1973 Outdoor
Writers' combined overall award, for television and radio
writing.

Q. Mr. Grosscup, may I ask what made you different
from the average outdoor writer who feels himself sorely
beset and put upon by the namby-pamby Bambi lovers?

A. First of all, my father and mother had quite a bit
to do with it—and my upbringing in the state of Florida,
near the Everglades. That, and a very remarkable woman
we knew named Rachel Carson. When ecology first came
on the scene in the early 60's, I already knew what it was
—and what it wasn't. Right off the bat, I had a gut feeling
about it. I could understand the interaction among animals—among predators and prey. I never had the inclina-
tion to take advantage of Mother Nature, because I had
too much love for her. I was just part of it, and when
you're part of something—and a very small part of it—
you have no business fooling around with it.

Q. And how have you been able to stay that way
against all the pressures of your fellow hunters?

A. I don't have to go out and stalk the wily quail for
$150 an article. A lot of those articles are written simply

because there's money involved, and of course this pro-
liferates the "sport" and the "adventure." It's very good
writing, but I just wonder how many of those writers
have actually gone out and done it.

Q. How do you really feel about the situation today?

A. Mostly, I'm scared. I'm scared of what's going to
happen. I've seen the forces against nature—of game
depletion, of faulty legislation. I'm afraid for my children
and my children's children. If we don't stop the pillaging
and the carnaging. The hunter says he's got to go out with
a gun to get the feel of nature. Well, the best way to get
the feel of nature is to take a camera and let nature take
its course—not to go out killing. If you want something to
eat, go to a supermarket. I'm frightened for mankind.
If we don't stop taking away the habitat of animals and
all the pillaging and the carnaging, *we're* in trouble.

Q. What is your answer to the hunter who says the
non-hunter just bleats and bleats but he doesn't put up a
damn dime for the habitat—that the hunters are the ones
who put up the money for conservation?

A. The hunters don't put up the money for conservation. The hunters are out there for their own special purpose and they put up the money for the proliferation of
their own special sport—hunting. A great portion of the
money comes from the arms companies, and the gasoline
industries. The hunting license per se doesn't do anything.
If you're going to have a hunting license that really does
something for conservation—I've told this to hunters and
I've said it repeatedly over the years—I say let's boost
the hunting license fee to about $100 per person per ani-
mal. Then at least there can afford to be a reasonable
hard-hitting program of conservation. I can't see any
hunter telling me that his lousy eight dollars for a hunting
license is going to do one diddly damn thing for the
conservation of wildlife.

Q. But isn't the way the hunter sees it that it's eight
times millions?

A. That just won't wash. Even if the hunters turn around and say there's thousands and thousands of us in each state. Sure, there's plenty of hunters—in fact there are too damn many hunters—but what is even $800,000 going to do when we've had hundreds of years of encroachment on our land? It won't do anything. It's illogical to begin with. If you're going to have hunting and be honest about it and say with a straight face that your hunting fees are improving the outdoors, then let's boost it up to maybe a thousand dollars a license to go hunting. The states and even the Federal government can do an awful lot with that kind of money—if that's the way man's going to go. But the way it is, every time an animal dies, we're losing—man's losing. The hunter doesn't see this, because his father hunted there and his grandfather hunted there. There are thousands of stories about "How I Stalked the Whitetail Buck Through My Grandfather's Hunting Land." If a hunter stops for a moment and thinks—I bring this up many times when I talk with hunters—"you go out," I say, "where your grandfather hunted and you just find how many whitetail buck are there now. And you're telling me your license fee is doing so much?" Let them answer the question.

Q. I'm told there are more deer out there than there were in the days of the Indians—that through Ducks Unlimited and all those marvelous programs, there are more animals to be shot than there ever were.

A. Where are they? They're all in tight little areas. Redhead ducks used to be all over North America, and now the greatest flock of redhead ducks is now in Laguna Anascosa in south Texas, 5,000 of them. Hunters would just love to go out there and shoot redhead ducks. Fortunately, it's a National Game Refuge, and you can't do it. Yes, there are more animals, but they're all in those segmented, close-knit little places that are so fragile now that the animals are overbred through man's messing around with nature. Man has this thing about fooling around with nature, and the more he fools around with it, the more responsible he becomes for it, and then he has this perfect excuse that he's got to go out and "harvest." What's happened to the wolf in the state of Michigan? What's happened to the deer herd in the state of Michigan? They're all gone to naught. Right now we have an antlerless deer season. Man's fooled around with it to a point where the Department of Natural Resources says the does are starving to death, so we've got to go up and harvest them. If we had predators—natural predators—we wouldn't have to harvest them like that. We wouldn't have the starving does, we wouldn't have the problem. There are more animals but they are only there for man's taking. They're overbred and five years from now the land is going to deplete. Everything is based on land. You've got to have land. When the Indians were here, there was plenty of land. And plenty of animals. They were all over the place. There was enough for every species, there was enough for every predator, there was even enough for every man. Now everything has been shoved back—by the building companies, by the developers, by the DNR, by the Federal and State and County Governments. It's been shoved back and back. Where we used to have 100,000 deer roaming the entire state of Michigan, we now have 150,000 in four counties. Sure, there's more—but where are they? Besides, we don't have enough money. Nobody can tell me that there's a single state government in this whole country that has enough money even to take a reasonable census. I don't even believe that we have as many as they say. There's no way you can count them.

Q. What kind of person is today's hunter?

A. Today's hunter is not the hunter we have read about—the Zane Grey hunter of the old days—when a gun was passed from father to son and down through the generations. Today's hunter can go to any one of the discount stores and buy a shotgun for $26 or $27, a box of shells and a couple of jugs of whatever it is the hunters take out with them. For $150 you're a hunter—all of a sudden—and then you try to live up to the stories that appear in *Field & Stream* and *Outdoor Life.* Those great white hunter stories. They get up in the morning and they get out of the car and they expect to have parties and learn something about the wilderness, and relive some of those old Zane Grey and Ernest Hemingway stories. Well, those days are gone. They get up in the morning, and they drive along the road and they get out of their car, and they find there's a housing development going up. They go back maybe 150 yards off the highway and they don't see any game and they get frustrated and they get mad. And they want to come back and show their wives or their girlfriends what great hunters they are. And they have no business being up there in the first place—except that it's become very big business for the arms people to get them up there.

Q. Are there *any* good hunters left?

A. Yes—but they're not trophy hunters. I haven't met an honest, down-to-earth hunter who's a trophy hunter yet. But the vast majority are. They're trying to relive this dream of 150 years ago—of the pioneers. That's gone. Sure, there are the stories and the cards and the camaraderie. But you don't need a gun over your shoulder to do that. I have yet to go to a hunting club or a gun club or a so-called conservation club and not see trophies. All you see draped on the walls are heads and horns and hides—skins and furs and stuffed animals—everything from fish to wolves. All this does is create the aura of the great white hunter. I have nothing but disgust for a man like Fred Bear shooting a polar bear. I have nothing but utter disgust for hunters shooting what they call "varmint"—the coyotes, those valuable, wonderful animals. But we need every animal we have left. We need every single bit of animal life we have left. If there is any person who is thinking of getting into hunting, if he would sit down and have all this logically put before him and take the time to read something about it, and listen to a few people—pros and cons—well, I don't think there'd be a single, sane, logical, intelligent or even halfway intelligent human being who would even think about going out and investing in a shotgun or a rifle.

*

Mr. Grosscup's strong feeling against trophy hunting— "Scratch any hunter," he says, "and underneath you will find a trophy hunter"—brings up a subject which not only deals the final, mortal blow to the hunters' favorite argument, starvation, it also permanently hoists them on the petard of their second major argument—that, since there are now not enough predators, they must be the predators. Obviously they must be the predators, since they have succeeded in shooting off all the real predators. And the question may well be asked what kind of predators are they? In New York's Bronx Zoo there is a sign: "You Are Looking," it says, "at the Worst Predator on the Face of the Earth." The sign is over a mirror. Nonetheless, the paradox is inescapable. The trophy hunter, of course, does not kill like a good predator—the old, the sick, the weak, the ones who really won't make it through the winter; he kills instead the very best, the herd leader.

Russell Barnett Aitken, whom we met earlier, is perhaps today's outstanding trophy hunter. He was voted one of the "Six Greatest Living Hunters" by "an international jury" in 1963. And, although it is not quite clear why the jury has not since sat, the fact remains he makes no bones about why men hunt. "The compulsion to hunt," he writes in *Great Game Animals,* "is as basic a part of man's nature as the mating urge. When the frost is on the ground and antlered bucks are pawing the timbered ridges, it might well take the combined wiles of a Cleopatra, a Helen of Troy and a Fanny Hill to keep Nimrod home by his hearthside." Mr. Aitken also writes of the fieldside. "The big game hunter," he continues, "is a bear for punishment"—a phrase one might have wished he could have foreborne. "Without complaint he will endure back-breaking toil, hikes of marathon distance, and discomfort normally encountered only in jungle warfare. Intense heat and humidity, foul weather, poor food, and assault by mosquitoes, by tsetse flies, fire ants, scorpions and poisonous snakes are all taken in stride. Although at home, he may avoid his own child when it has the mumps, on the trail of a top trophy, he will cheerfully risk exposure to malaria, sleeping sickness, hook-worm, dysentery and even leprosy. . . . Galahad in his quest for the Holy Grail never suffered half the tribulations which beset the sportsman who elects to spoor up a bongo in the stinking swamps of the Moyen Congo." And then, at last, Mr. Aitken comes to what might be loosely described as the gist:

> What makes a hunter willing and eager to endure such ordeals?
> Primarily it is the unconscious desire to fulfill a boy-hood ambition—to slay the savage lion or tiger which had leaped at him from the picture books of his impressionable youth. There is, however, a more compelling reason.
> He is a collector.
> Just as other people choose to amass stamps, modern art, autographs, vintage automobiles or antique Colt revolvers, *he* collects trophy heads. These values matter inordinately because they represent tangible evidence of a successful stalk. They also prove his prowess with a rifle—a prowess which in pioneer days made heroes of Daniel Boone, Kit Carson and Davy Crockett.

The Boones of thar's-bars-in-them-thar-woods fame and the Crocketts in their ridiculous coonskin caps have been, as we

have seen, commemorated in the Boone and Crockett Club
—one which from the beginning nominated itself to be the
arbiter of trophy records. "The interest of men in trophies of
the chase," says James Trefethen, historian of the Boone and
Crockett, "antedates civilization." With that, surely, one can
agree. In any case, no one can fault the club on not taking
its burden with extraordinary seriousness. And let no one
underestimate the problems faced:

> For years sportsmen had rated their deer trophies on
> the basis of the number of points and elk on the basis of
> spread; but a super abundance of points in itself is an
> abnormality which often is attended by lack of beauty
> and symmetry. Spread was a criterion preferred by many
> serious collectors, although there was a difference of
> opinion as to whether the inside spread or the outside
> spread should be the governing measurement. Then there
> remained the problem of freakish outspreading tines or
> beams, warped or twisted through injury, glandular mal-
> adjustments or disease, factors which could put an other-
> wise inferior head well up in the record class if based on
> spread alone.

A hunter, surely, did not live on spread alone. But, as
Trefethen sternly continues, "When it came to evaluating the
bears and cats . . . even more basic problems arose":

> Weight of the animals was a worthless criterion since
> few hunters or guides are equipped to weigh a specimen
> that may scale from 500 to nearly 1,000 pounds in the
> case of the larger bears; and verifying each claim would
> be a near impossibility. Then, too, two animals with the
> same general measurements might vary as much as sev-
> eral hundred pounds in weight, depending upon their
> physical condition and the food supply. The weight of the
> same animal might vary as much as 500 pounds between
> spring and fall. . . . Field measurement of freshly killed
> animals presented similar difficulties, and the measure-

ments of the hides of two animals of comparable weight and measurements in the flesh might vary as much as several feet because of difficulty in stretching and processing.

Into this terrifying situation leaped a man steeped in Boone and Crockett probity. His name was Prentiss N. Gray, and together with his trusty committee of Kermit Roosevelt, Madison Grant, W. Redmond Cross, George Harrison and E. Hubert Litchfield, after three solid years' work, he produced the famed Gray Committee Report:

> Deer were rated solely on the length of the outside curve of the longer antler, although circumference of main beam, greatest spread, and number of points on each antler also were listed. Moose were ranked on the basis of extreme spread and caribou on the basis of the length of the antler to the tip of the uppermost point. . . . On the troublesome cats and bears length of the skull, although not itself as a trophy, was considered to be the fairest and most practical standard of excellence.

There was just one trouble. When Gray finished his masterpiece, only five hundred copies were printed, and in no time at all the inevitable happened—they were all gone. But once more the club was saved through the graciousness of the ever-at-the-ready Remington Arms Company. Without asking so much as a dime for their services, they reprinted it. But, even at this, there were still bugs—as Trefethen solemnly recalls:

> One particularly ingenious taxidermist specialized in constructing "World's Record" trophies, adding points, steaming and spreading antlers, and splitting and broadening skulls to squeeze an inch or two of spread from the average specimen. The masterpiece of this artist was a stupendous bighorn sheep head, which, upon closer examination, was found to have been built up from the

horns of three sheep painstakingly and skillfully spliced together!

Following the death of Gray, the Gray Committee was supplanted by a Committee on Records consisting of Dr. H. E. Anthony and R. R. M. Carpenter under the chairmanship of Alfred Ely. But this committee too was dogged by the same problem that had plagued the efforts of Gray. Into the breach this time leaped Dr. James L. Clark. According to Trefethen, he was the man who "devised and copyrighted a system of scoring based upon a single numerical rating, arrived at by adding up certain fundamental measurements and subtracting various 'penalty' measurements to rule out unsymmetrical heads." But once more there was dissent—this time in the person of Grancel Fitz, noted big-game hunter:

> Clark, for example, had included the tip-to-tip of the main beam measurement as a credit in deer heads; Fitz contended, proving his point with examples, that in many of the better white-tailed deer antlers, the tips of the main beam may almost meet in the normal dichotomously branch antler of the mule deer. The Clark method differed from Fitz's conception as to which points should be regarded as the extention of the main beam. Fitz also found fault with Clark's definition of what constituted the length and definition of a point. On Clark's method of scoring sheep, Fitz took exception to Clark's inclusion of both tip-to-tip and extreme spread measurements as penalizing truly massive heads with tight curls, a highly desirable characteristic in some races of the bighorn.

There was now all hell to pay—not one but two world's records; one based on the Clark method, the other on the gospel according to Fitz. For a while it even looked as if there would be a Boone Club *and* a Crockett Club. But once more wiser heads prevailed, albeit this time the great march forward was primarily due to a man named Samuel B. Webb—who, as Trefethen manfully notes, was "a non-member of The Club." But he was at least to the manner born. "He stemmed," Trefethen tells us, "from a long line of prominent big game hunters and killed his first whitetail deer in the Adirondacks at the age of eight." To this man was entrusted by Archibald Roosevelt, then president of the club, on behalf of the executive committee, the responsibility "to see what he could do to untangle the prevailing chaos." Webb rose to the challenge. He determined on an Independent Revisions Committee and, it is recalled, hand-picked his task force for their experience and interest in the field—Dr. Anthony, Dr. Clark, Grancel Fitz, Milford Baker and Frederick K. Barbour. Webb and Fitz personally measured more than three hundred trophies to evaluate the proposed formulae, which were adopted officially at the next annual meeting of the club in 1950. "Webb," Trefethen notes, "became a regular member of the Club at this time."

However much credit belongs to now Member Webb, in the final analysis there were extraordinary ironies in the Official Scoring System of the Independent Revisions Committee of the Records Committee. One was that the record of the president of the club himself, Archibald Roosevelt's famed wapiti head—one with, in Trefethen's words, "a 63.7/8ths inch beam length but with little else to recommend it, which had dominated the old records"—sank in the new list, to forty-second place. The other was the fact that out of Arizona in 1959 came the "world record" for the largest desert bighorn ram ever taken. It was shot by a sixteen-year-old schoolgirl.

It is not fair, of course, to single out the Boone and Crockett Club alone for its trophy hangup. Natural history museums from one end of the country to the other have been equally so.

So too have gentlemen's clubs. At the Harvard Club of New York, however, the heads around the Great Hall and dining room have been viewed with some suspicion ever since a younger member complained that they made him nervous. They bore, he felt, too close a resemblance to some of the elderly members. Atop New York's famed "21" Club, the penthouse office of Francis T. Hunter, president of "21" Brands, was for years, according to *True* Magazine, a sight. "Visitors to his office," the magazine said, "can sit on fur-covered chairs with their feet on bearskins while they admire the North American small and big game trophies." As time went on, however, there were too few admirers—in 1970 Mr. Hunter attempted to sell, lock, stock and barrel, the entire collection. At present they are still at a warehouse. At the New York Explorers Club, when a member attempted to donate a mammoth stuffed polar bear, the club, already crammed to the rafters with the results of such explorations, thought long and hard about the deal. If they refused, the man might refuse further largesse—even a future will might be jeopardized. Finally, the house committee of the Explorers Club hit on a solution: they would accept the polar bear, but that would be the last. The Explorers Club would thenceforth refuse all trophies. Following this decision, the house committee, in company with other members of the club, held their annual meeting and ate their way through—according to the published menu—"Hors d'oeuvres of loin of lion tidbits, pickled sirloin niblets of hippo, bites of beaver in beer, snacks of smoked mountain sheep and braised hump of buffalo." For snacks, apparently, they could climb the walls.

There are hundreds, if not thousands, of private trophy rooms around the country. The photographs taken of these chambers of horrors are notable for two reasons. One is that the gunman himself is often pictured in them—sometimes even with gun at the ready. The other is that in that latter case the gunman is not only, in comparison to the animals around him, a rather sad-looking figure, he is also frequently not a distinguished specimen. Indeed, if it were not for the animals, you would not look at him twice. And when you do look at him, after looking at the animals, it is perhaps lucky that the same insensitivity which led to his slaughtering also prevents him from knowing *how* you are looking at him.

"Trophy hunting," says Russell Barnett Aitken, "has increased enormously in popularity since the end of the last war." One wonders which war—a guess would be the Boer. Nonetheless, of more than 32,000 killed deer in Missouri in 1972 only 51 qualified for what the Kansas City *Times* called "the most exclusive sportsmen's group in the state," the Show-Me Big Buck Club. The real trophy club of trophy clubs today is probably Shikar Safari International, its "worldwide membership," as its brochure states, being limited to 200. Among the Americans who belong are John Connally, Maurice Stans, and Hollywood's James Stewart. One of Mr. Stans's recent safaris was given the honor of being recorded, not just among the shikaris, but also in a Jack Anderson column of February, 1972.

> WASHINGTON—While President Nixon was signing a bill to protect rare animals around the world, his Commerce Secretary, Maurice Stans, was oiling up his guns to kill two rare African animals that may well come under the act.
>
> Over the objections of furriers and animal collectors, the White House helped push through the "Endangered Species Act" this month. But Stans, a big game hunter for years before he took over his Cabinet post, was not deterred from an African safari where he and Ethiopian

King Haile Selassie hope to gun down an Abyssinian wild ass, and a Nyala Mountain antelope, both very rare.

In March, Stans' son, Steve, and his son-in-law, Walter Helmeck, plan to carry on the family traditions. They will track down an African rhinoceros, also listed as rare by the esteemed International Union for the Conservation of Nature and Natural Resources.

The Union's list of rare and endangered animals is a basic guide used by the Interior Department in getting up its own list under the new law. It bars import of such animals without special permission of the Interior Secretary.

The elder Stans is combining his pleasure trip to Ethiopia with a visit to Yugoslavia for trade talks and similar meetings in Addis Ababa with the old king and Ethiopian commerce officials.

Then, thick-skinned as a rhino against the criticism of conservationists, Stans and his beaters, bearers and gunholders will be off to shoot the two graceful and helpless animals.

To Stans' credit, he has no wish to bathe Ethiopia in the blood of antelopes and asses. His plan is to shoot only a single one of each species and to present the mounted skins to the Stans African Hall in Rock Hill, S.C.

There, some 88 animals killed by Stans in his previous 10 safaris and by other collectors are on display. The museum's executive director, J. Lee Settlemyer, said the family-controlled Stans Foundation pays for many of the exhibits' costs.

Stans is president and his son Steve is vice president and a director of the tax-exempt foundation. Young Steve's safari will be financed by the foundation, said Settlemyer.

Southern California, according to Lupi Saldana of the Los Angeles *Times,* has more trophy hunters than any other area. The Los Angeles chapter of Safari Club International alone has

189 members, while the Southern California club has 80. "I love animals," says Arthur Carlsberg, one of these. "And I love to hunt them on their own grounds, because it presents a real challenge." The same idea was expounded by J. C. McElroy of Englewood: "I hunt mainly to escape from the concrete jungle and to see and enjoy the wilderness. I like to pit my knowledge, skill and endurance against wildlife in their own environment." An eastern trophy hunter, Dr. Edward S. Bundy, a general practitioner of Meriden, Connecticut, concurred. Declared Dr. Bundy of a forthcoming safari: "This one will be for my son's indoctrination. I don't expect to fire a shot, but I'm sure it will be my greatest hunting thrill. To watch my son meet the challenge of the world's greatest animals on their home territory has long been my dream."

Just why all three of these trophy hunters feel they're doing something admirable by assassinating the animals at "home" —just as if, instead of doing it on Astroturf, say, they were giving the animals the advantage of a "home crowd"—is difficult to fathom, but then so is just about everything else about these headhunters. Since they all say approximately the same thing, however, it is probable that they are programmed either consciously or perhaps—which in their cases should be easier—subconsciously. This is usually done at hunters' "conservation" conventions. J. C. McElroy, for example, even repeats, almost word for word, what was actually programmed at such a convention. "The United States," he said, "is the only country where the hunters are maligned and mistreated. In other countries, hunters are respected and admired. The difference is that Americans live in a world of fantasy where all animals are supposed to be Bambi, the story book deer. These just aren't the facts."

One would like to ask Mr. McElroy to reply to such a fact

as that when a hunting safari leaves the New Stanley Hotel in Nairobi, the natives jeer—or indeed to the fact that countries varying from Taiwan to Tanzania have ordered a ban on all hunting, and not just the Great White Hunter, either, but all hunting, period. On the other hand there are, it is true, still some countries which feel differently. The tabs for Dr. Bundy's safaris, for example, have been picked up by Zambia Safaris, Ltd., in deference to the fact that Dr. Bundy is their "Eastern U.S. representative." Incidentally, Dr. Bundy has admitted that more than half the inquiries he gets about such safaris are from doctors; at last report he had more than twenty waiting to go on one. Dr. Bundy himself told the story of "The Most Challenging Big Game You Can Hunt" in *Medical Economics*. He chose the elephant:

> An eternity of seconds seemed to pass as I waited in this David and Goliath situation for the towering tusker to turn. All at once he wheeled, and my shot—the one I was waiting for—was suddenly over. I fired, plowing more than 3 tons of missile energy into his brain. Instantly decerebrated, he remained frozen in death, still on his feet. Then, under the impact of an insurance shot into his heart, he plunged to the ground.
>
> The exhilaration, triumph and emotional fever of an elephant confrontation cannot be adequately described except, perhaps, to another hunter.

With that we agree—particularly with the "perhaps."

In the privacy of their private trophy rooms, of course, what trophy hunters love best is publicity—apparently on the theory that they and their rooms are much admired. J. C. McElroy, for example, or Mac, as he prefers to be called, happily gives interviews in a trophy room with 187 "mounts" in it. In this room, Mac declares, he keeps fit by jogging three miles daily round it. At which times, apparently, he is unarmed. Mac's room, however, is different from most in that it is actually open to the public—"for educational purposes" and, presumably, attendant tax benefits. "It is," he told the Los Angeles *Times,* "widely used by Boy Scouts, Cub Scouts, Campfire Girls, school groups and church organizations." And in Chicago, Dr. T. R. N. Howard, a black physician, also has a "Safari Room" which, according to *Ebony* Magazine, "occasionally fulfills an educational purpose as troops of awestruck schoolchildren roam the red-carpeted plain lit by hundreds of tiny, twinkling 'stars' set in a cloudy, grey, pseudo-sky." Dr. Howard is particularly proud of his son, Barrett, who has already, in Dr. Howard's words, "bagged" three of Africa's "Big Five"— leopard, lion, Cape buffalo, rhino and elephant. Dr. Howard's son is thirteen.

Finally, in New York City, William I. Spencer, president of the First National City Bank, has gone so far as to have his private office made into a private trophy room. He too is apparently not loath to boast about it. He might have felt differently, however, after an article on banks, in which his room was featured, appeared in *Cosmopolitan* Magazine. In any case, afterward, one reader wrote, "I am sure many depositors would react upon learning that the President of their bank uses earnings derived from their money to murder wildlife and then brag about it."

If no one else appreciates such trophies, one group which assuredly does is the taxidermists. "LET JONAS RECREATE THE THRILL OF YOUR HUNT," reads one advertisement. Underneath, it states, "Your safari cost you a lot of time and effort"— tactfully, as at a funeral home, no mention is made at the beginning of money—"when it is over, you return with a wealth of memories . . . memories of tried and true companions, the joy of the hunt when noble game fell to your skill." Then the same advertisement shows you a "noble" polar bear—standing up with its front legs toward you in a boxer's pose. It was just little you, after all, against that great, huge, fierce bear. "LIFE SIZE MOUNTS," reads the headline of the Knopp Bros., and then, "Head mounts are nice and rugs beautiful, but the ultimate is life size mounts!" To prove it they show a tiger not only ready to box with you but with a kind of combination snarl and roar. Jonas offers a life-size "Buffalo or Bison" for $1,650. However, they can also supply, obviously whether you yourself did the shooting or not, a "Bear Paw Ashtray" for just $95. "Two Feet," the advertisement states, it not being clear whether it is two feet in size, or two of the bear's four feet. One thing is certain, they are big on feet—there is also a "Mountain Goat Feet Cigarette Lighter," advertised for just $31.50. On the head mountings, Jonas warns, "We do not use the natural teeth, since artificial teeth are far superior and will last indefinitely." The Knopp Bros., meanwhile , warn of many things. "THRIFTY PRODUCTION MODELS" and "CUT-RATE TYPE," they emphasize, "have no place in both the hunting and the taxidermy." And they put it in terms the businessman-hunter can surely understand. Yes, they say, you can get your taxidermy done for less, but they ask him to realize he may be jeopardizing "his costs thus far." And here they list five of them—carefully, of course, prepared for the "important" businessman:

1. Cost of the hunt
2. Cost of transportation to and from the hunt area
3. His valuable time which he has to take off from his important work
4. Cost of his licenses and miscellaneous fees
5. Most important of all, something that cannot be put

into cost figure—his "Good Fortune" in getting an irreplaceable valued trophy, which is the most important factor of all.

Many taxidermists double as "hunting consultants" and will literally do everything for you except pull the trigger—and some of them, through their guides, will even do that. Jack Atcheson and Son, of Butte, Montana, for example, bills itself as "international hunting consultant and taxidermist." "The purpose of this letter," it recently informed potential customers, "is to give you as much information as possible on arranging hunts in Mongolia." The letter then continued:

> Most everyone is looking for gigantic sheep, but like sheep hunting everywhere, the sheep are not always that big. I am told that in the past, some people brought back horns of rams that were not really taken from the ram they actually shot themselves, but rather picked them up or they were those poached by Mongolian hunters. Also, a lot of the big rams have huge bases, but their horns are busted back anywhere from a few inches to a foot. Some of these have huge bases but not too many inches in curl. They still make an excellent trophy and if taken to a good taxidermist, the horns can be extended out to their normal length if so desired.

The company is not recommending any particular taxidermist, of course. But the letter goes on:

> How does one get to Mongolia? That's not really much of a problem. Primarily you fly from New York to Moscow . . . then, by Mongolian Airlines, you fly down to the capital of Mongolia, Ulan Bator, where you will be met and taken through customs by members of the Mongolian Travel Agency, Zhuulchin. I might add that the Russian Tourist Bureau in Moscow is right near the Customs Office at the Airport, should you have problems.

Mr. Atcheson lists the "high altitude" price for one sheep and one ibex at $7,300. He is, apparently big on sheep everywhere. But for North America he has a warning: "I'm convinced that sheep have the power to create bad weather, as well as being able to notify all other game to be scarce the day after a hunter arrives. Jack O'Connor told me he thinks sheep even see through thin rock and around corners." Mr. Atcheson also rewarns of that old taxidermist bugaboo, price cutting:

> There is no such thing as a *good, cheap* hunt—it's either one or the other.
>
> 1. Few guides make much profit. Why should he work for less unless he gives you less. Would you work for less in your business?
>
> 2. Accommodations seldom have much to do with the cost of the hunts we arrange. You are paying for a man's time, ability, knowledge and his area.
>
> 3. People who cannot feel the true meaning of sport hunting should not hunt. Even if you pay the price—everything can go wrong. It's that kind of sport—kind of like marriage!
>
> 4. If you take enough time, most anything can work out. When you limit your time and cut costs, you also cut down your chances at game.

And, after this, Mr. Atcheson gave the hunters some affirmative thoughts:

> *The longer you hunt, the more likely you are to get all the species available, especially the Grizzly.* Expect about one animal for each 5 full days of actual hunting. Expect less if weather is bad, if you can't walk, if you miss shots, or if you are among the 10 percent who are doomed to bad luck no matter what they do in life.

The most incredible story of combining taxidermy with "hunting consultancy" in recent years was the 1971 desert-bighorn-sheep case of one Gary Swanson, of Yucaipa, California. Operator of World Safari Taxidermy, he was accused of being the leader of a ring that, according to the Los Angeles *Times*, "for 4½ years had guided trophy-seeking big game hunters to the shy creatures that, since 1872, have been protected by state law." Swanson was jailed and pleaded guilty to poaching charges—a state felony—and to violation of the federal Lacey Act which bars transporting illegal game across state lines. He drew $1,500 in fines. Three others were convicted with him and, while awaiting sentence, he was severely beaten by eight jail inmates who called him a "snitcher."

Once he turned pro, Swanson told Lupi Saldana, he became a "magnet" for trophy hunters. They telephoned him, and made it plain they wanted a ram regardless of legality. Only a handful of legal permits are issued in Arizona, Nevada and New Mexico. But a hunter yearning for a grand slam needs a chance at a desert bighorn. "Trophy big game hunting is for me," he said, "like alcohol to the alcoholic and drugs to the addict. . . . The only real threat to the bighorns is man."

The Swanson case stirred even the National Audubon Society magazine—although the editor, Les Line, in writing of it, included the usual Audubon disclaimer: "Let me emphasize right now that I've done my share of killing in the past . . . and neither I, nor the National Audubon Society, advocate the end of sport hunting." Having incorporated this obeisance to Audubon officialdom, however, Mr. Line, to his credit, cut loose:

> These words are written in anger. Anger at the perfidy of men who call themselves sportsmen. . . . Anger at the cult of trophy hunting, a rich man's cult for the most part and a cult that holds that the rack of horns or the bear's hide is the whole object, and to hell with the way it was

obtained. Which is why Alaska probably has as many dishonest guides as honest ones, men who will break every law to get their customer a ram or a moose or a brown bear or a polar bear in a hurry, the easiest way possible. . . .

Pause, now, and listen to all the cries of "Foul" from the sportsmen. . . . The fact is, however, that the sportsman's code of ethics just doesn't exist anymore. . . . If you don't believe it . . . watch the bang bang books to see if they report this odious episode, complete with names and addresses of every hunter involved, which are readily available. If they do, perhaps there is some hope for the future of hunting.

The headline, "35 Named in Raid on Bighorn Sheep": for fees as high as $3500 apiece, wealthy sportsmen from across the country—from Washington, California, Vermont, Oregon, Colorado, Idaho, Pennsylvania, New York, Texas, Oklahoma, Missouri, Hawaii and Canada —were led into these sere hills to shoot an animal that has been totally protected in California since 1872. Three races of the bighorn were slain and two are on the U.S. Fish and Wildlife Service list of America's rare and endangered species.

Their guide . . . was a man who until recently had been a director and a charter member of the National Society for the Conservation of Bighorn Sheep, . . . who for years had aided the California Department of Fish and Game on its annual bighorn census—and thus knew all of the rams' haunts. . . .

And he not only led the expedition, but he mounted the trophies at his own taxidermist shop. . . .

So this is why I'm angry. And why it's time hunters stopped flaunting their reputations as conservationists. Their hands are dirty and bloody and had better be washed.

*

If trophy hunting is not the bottom of the barrel, then that honor must surely go to hunting or shooting "preserves." The first three American Heritage Dictionary definitions for the word "preserve" are (1) "To protect from injury, peril, or other adversity; maintain in safety," (2) "To keep in perfect or unaltered condition . . . ," and (3) "To keep or maintain intact."

The animals in hunting "preserves" are not so preserved. They are, however, reasonably close to dictionary definition number 4: "To prepare for future use as by canning. . . ." Indeed, preserves are of course the final answer to all hunter arguments about starvation, predation, or whatever. If the hunter were seriously interested even in the word "hunt," he would not go near a preserve. It is, literally, shooting fish— i.e., substitute *game* for *fish*—in a barrel. And the success of these preserves is proof positive that what the hunter has is not the love of animals, not the love of "conservation," not the love of "Nature," not indeed any kind of love except the love of death. There are more than two thousand "private" preserves, or clubs, around this country—and as many as seven hundred more commercial preserves. You pays your money and you shoots your animal—or bird. And occasionally, of course, on crowded days, you shoots each other. In fact, as I write these lines, this very evening the New York *Post* carried a story of a member of the Sportsman's Club of Farmingdale, Long Island, a father of four, who was out hunting for rabbits with one of his sons and another boy when he was approached by still another boy, Ronald Eng, and three companions on property that is used by the Club. A "scuffle" ensued, whereupon, police said, the "alleged assailant" fired his shotgun and the blast hit Eng in the face. Eng, eighteen, was killed.

"LET'S GO HUNTING!" is the headline on the brochure of the North American Shooting Preserve directory. "It's fall again," the brochure continues. "There's hunting in the air, and it's time to be out and at 'em—out in the golden fields with dog and gun. And one of the best ways to get there is to head for a good shooting preserve that offers action-packed no-limit gunning at reasonable cost. This directory of public, daily fee shooting preserves tells you where the action is." In New York State alone, in this one brochure, there are twenty-seven preserves listed; in Wisconsin, forty-two; in California, forty-four. Their names: The Duck and Buck Club, Fox Valley, Pheasant City, Quail Haven, Goose Hill, Rabbit Creek, Restless Feathers, Bird Island, It's for the Birds, Inc., The Lazy S, The Lazy Z, and finally, of course, The Conservation Club.

And who "compiled" this wondrous directory? Why, none other, we are told, than the Conservation Department of Winchester-Western. And on the back is a reproduction of a rather idealized painting of Mr. John Olin, gun in hand, patting his hunting dog. "When John Olin began Nilo Farms," we read, "he sure started something. The modern game preserve industry . . . a great way to solve the modern hunting question. We're glad Mr. Olin started hunting for answers."

Mr. Olin's company, the Olin Corporation, owners of Winchester-Western, must be glad too. Think of all the additional guns they can sell, not to mention the additional ammo thudding into the bodies of fenced-in, semi-tame "wild" animals. Another brochure comes from the American Sportsman's Club. "ATTENTION," this one reads. "Fellow hunter. Do you have adequate uncrowded places to hunt? Are you satisfied with your hunting conditions? Do you usually fill your game bag? If you answers are 'No!' we have the answers you are looking for." Underneath, the brochure declares: "The American Sportsman's Club owns, leases or controls the following acreage":

	Deer	Elk	Antelope
Calif.	98,530		2,375
Colo.	92,864	24,546	60,400
Nevada	19,500		
Texas	48,718		
Utah	57,100	12,000	
Total	316,712	36,546	62,775

	Pheasant	Quail	Dove
Calif.	11,532	41,500	16,200
Colo.	67,066	6,004	67,555
Nevada		10,500	5,600
Texas		8,094	
Utah	11,732		600
Total	90,330	66,098	98,049

Following this table, there is a large headline. "You," it says, "ARE AN ENDANGERED SPECIES." With this is reproduced the apparent emblem of the American Sportsman's Club. This is an eagle—a bird which, considering what the hunters have done to it, is a curious choice indeed. But the hunters can be tough on other birds, too.

Here's the way one "duck preserve" was described on the CBS *Evening News*:

CRONKITE: The perils of duck hunting are great, especially for the duck. But some four million Americans are

Pig	Bear	Varmint	Duck	Geese
12,500	16,000	32,000	13,767	12,987
	77,665	75,400	29,795	24,304
		7,000	20,300	13,100
41,758		2,780	980	640
		20	12,494	5,962
54,258	93,665	117,200	77,306	63,993

Grouse	Chukar	Turkey
14,885		
	10,500	
		38,327
14,885	10,500	38,327

presently going to a good deal of trouble to shoot a bird: hunting frequently involves expensive equipment, long hours in a chilly blind after a long trip to get there, bourbon and bird dogs. Well tomorrow, however, may be a better day for Nimrod, but certainly not for his prey. Warren Olney of KNXT has the story.

OLNEY: American hunters have been working out the easy way to do things since the Indians learned to drive buffaloes off cliffs. But the Meadowview Wild Life Preserve, a private establishment not to be confused with a real wildlife preserve, has carried the principle to extreme. Here, near Marysville, 13-week-old ducklings are being trained to live out their lives between an artificial pond and a chicken wire pen. In the morning, the ducks are released from the pen. They can't fly yet, so they walk, down a fenced path to the pond. At five PM, a horn is sounded, the fence around the pen is opened, and the ducks waddle eagerly back to the pen for supper. For the Meadowview Wild Life Preserve this easily manipulated, instinctive behavior is a potential gold mine.

The idea is to sell gun club membership at $1,000 apiece. When the ducks learn to fly the 900 feet from the pen to the pond, hunters will be waiting along the way. Each club member is guaranteed 100 ducks for his thousand dollars over a three-month period. If he doesn't shoot that many, the club will kill the balance, and send them along anyway, all cleaned and dressed. Ten dollars a duck isn't bad on an original investment of 75 cents, and Manager Clyde McRunnels says he thinks it will work.

What kind of people do you expect to interest in it?

McRunnels: Well, more or less, the man behind the desk. In other words, I mean, he don't like to invest $100 or $200 to—for gear for—to wade through the mud and water and everything like that. In other words, I mean, he can come out in his suit if he wishes.

Olney: This is sort of duck hunting for the sedentary man, huh?

McRunnels: That's right.

Olney: Is there any sport in that, do you think?

McRunnels: Oh, I think so, very much so.

Olney: Well, where's the sport, if you release the duck and the chances of his surviving are zero?

McRUNNELS: Well, I, in—I would say maybe there's a little betting going on, who gets what.

OLNEY: So the— sport comes from that rather than from the shooting itself?

McRUNNELS: Could be.

OLNEY: McRunnels and his partner have bet $25,000 on their scheme. If it works, they'll build bigger and better clubs for pheasants, partridge and quail. In the meantime, the ducks will be marching up the ramp to the tower and winging off one by one toward the pond, with the Meadowview Wild Life Preserve guaranteeing that they'll never make it.

On another kind of bird shooting, a book of advice to "operators" is entitled *Releasing Game Birds.* "In general," it says, "the longer and harder you rock the bird, the dizzier he becomes and the longer he'll stay put." Another dizzying method suggested elsewhere is "to grasp the bird firmly and compress its chest with the heels of your hand. The correct amount of pressure causes the bird to faint, and then you can just set it down and leave it." After the birds are so "treated," Horace Sutton describes the rest of a typical "hunt":

> Hunters are fetched to the field of valor in jeep-pulled caravans, special wagons with built-in dog kennels and high upholstered seats for the sports. Some trucks are equipped with soft chairs welded onto the front fender. Hunting is getting more homelike every day. Next year or so, they'll have it all worked out so you can stay home and they'll just ship you the bird, all plucked, dressed, frozen and lardered with enough buckshot to make enormously chic conversation.

And, when bird and deer fail, you can go on to other targets. One preserve in New Jersey offers aoudad and mouflon. In

Virginia you are offered ibex and Russian bear. In Michigan, Louis's Big Game Preserve offers Corsican ram and even buffalo. Texas, as might be expected, not only has the most and the biggest shooting preserves, it also offers the widest range of targets. A Texas Parks and Wildlife Department survey taken a few years ago turned up 13,160 exotic animals representing 13 different species, all residing within deer-proof fences—in other words, all not only available for killing but easily accessible for so doing. Today the number is estimated to be over double that. Just why these "protected" animals are permitted to be shot is one more irony in the billion-dollar butcher business—particularly since the U.S. Department of Agriculture has ruled that exotics imported into the United States must spend all their "natural lives" in an "approved zoo." The catch is that though *they* must spend their lives in zoos, their *offspring* do not. And, since the vast majority of zoos in this country have nothing whatever against hunting, these offspring are then sold by zoos to preserves by the truckload—there to spend all their "unnatural" lives. Furthermore, since these exotics are fenced in and on private land, there is not even any "control" of them by the Texas Parks and Wildlife Department. However, since we have already seen what the Texas Parks and Wildlife Department does with "control" when it does have it, the difference to the animals must somehow be bearable.

Perhaps the most Texan of the Texas preserves is the Guajolote Ranch northwest of San Antonio—one which is run by a man named, aptly enough, Frank Huntress. Although Mr. Huntress is not averse to celebrities like Wally Schirra, who chased down—in a jeep—a blackbuck, he caters primarily to "the big boys," as he calls them, businessmen from Dallas and Houston. "These men," he said, "like their comfort and I give it to them, deluxe. Every bed in our lodge has a box spring and every room has its own bath with pink, lime or baby-blue tiles." "The hunting at Guajolote," wrote Duncan Barnes, in *Sports Illustrated,* "is equally deluxe."

> Hunters' blinds are made of sheet tin and are fitted with wooden benches, sliding glass, shooting ports and telephones connected to the main lodge. Too spartan? Well, there is the Brigitte Bardot Blind, which features a television set ("You keep the sound down low, so you don't spook the game"), an icebox stocked with beer and soft drinks, electric outlets for heater, hot plate and coffee percolator and pink-and-blue curtains. And there is a life-size photograph of BB—yea!—to which Huntress has pinned a red cloth bikini—boo!—Some hunters have been known to unpin the bikini. Huntress can tell by the number of pinholes.

The largest and most relentlessly publicized of Texas preserves is the Y.O. Ranch in Mountain Home. Here, over your breakfast menu, you pick out, from an "exotic" list your choice of trophies. Then you ride out in a car with a guide, and when the animal comes over, thinking it's *his* breakfast, you kill him. And you do so, if you wish, without even getting out of your car—unless, possibly, you want to pat him first. The rates are high but there are times, as the rates below illustrate, when you can get some super (market) bargains:

"DEER FOLKS," headlines one Y.O. brochure, and farther on there is another headline, "NO LICENSE REQUIRED TO HUNT EXOTICS." Sitting over their kills, guns in hands, are the smiling faces of "X-15 pilot and astronaut, Major Joe Engel," as well as "Continental Airlines executive, Charles Bucks." Another picture shows fifty deer hung upside down, standing in front of which are fifty young boys. "ANOTHER BUNCH OF

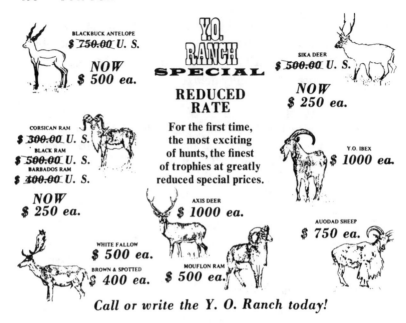

BLACKBUCK ANTELOPE
$ 750.00 U. S.
NOW
$ 500 ea.

Y.O. RANCH
SPECIAL
REDUCED RATE

SIKA DEER
$ 500.00 U. S.
NOW
$ 250 ea.

CORSICAN RAM
$ 300.00 U. S.
BLACK RAM
$ 500.00 U. S.
BARBADOS RAM
$ 400.00 U. S.
NOW
$ 250 ea.

For the first time, the most exciting of hunts, the finest of trophies at greatly reduced special prices.

Y.O. IBEX
$ 1000 ea.

AXIS DEER
$ 1000 ea.

AUODAD SHEEP
$ 750 ea.

WHITE FALLOW
$ 500 ea.
BROWN & SPOTTED
$ 400 ea.

MOUFLON RAM
$ 500 ea.

Call or write the Y. O. Ranch today!

HAPPY HUNTERS," reads the capitalized caption, "were these Kerr County youngsters who participated in the annual Free Hunt at the Y.O. Ranch, the world's largest and quickest deer hunt in the world." The Y.O. is big on that word "world." Another article on the ranch tells us:

> At the ranch's "Chuck Wagon," where you eat family style, you might find yourself seated next to astronaut Captain James Lovell [the Y.O. is also big on astronauts] or Weatherby Award winners like Prince Abdorreza Pahlavi, Iran; Julio Estrada, Mexico, or C. J. McElroy, Los Angeles. . . . Charles Bucks, senior vice president of marketing for Continental Airlines, can tell you of the thrills and excitement of bagging the trophy black-buck that adorns the wall of his office.

"Two thirds of the Y.O.'s 'sportsmen,'" reported Roy Bongartz in the *New York Times*, "don't even want to bother with the meat of the animals, which is then sometimes used in various exotic dishes served at the ranchhouse. . . . The main purpose of a kill, everyone agrees, is to get that trophy to hang on the wall at home."

Another writer, Craig Karpel, preparing a special report on the Y.O. for The Fund for Animals, went on a typical hunt:

> In the kill we witnessed, that of a fallow deer, the guide worked on the guest, convincing him that this specimen was indeed a "nice, well-developed fallow buck," until finally the hunter, an oil trucker from Pennsylvania, who obviously had his doubts as to whether the buck was indeed worth the $300 and, in any case, about where he was going to find space on his office wall to hang up the trophy, got ready to shoot. "I've extended my office 12 feet just to hang up all my trophies—I've been on 27 hunts—but damned if I have room for this one." The trucker shot the deer from about 15 yards. . . . After the dead deer had ceased to squirm and the trucker was able to approach the carcass, he seemed disappointed. "Why don't we shoot us one of them armadilloes on the way home, and eat him for supper," said the guide. "No," said the hunter, "what the hell, they like to live like everything else." At that moment a doe came into the clearing to sniff the remains of her lord and master. "Look at that," said the trucker, "isn't that a shame? She knows what has happened and she's lonely now. Isn't it a shame?"

Mr. Karpel found that, although the Y.O. has a strict no-kill, no-pay policy—in other words, if the gunman doesn't get his game, he doesn't have to pay for anything except his board and lodging—at the same time the guides are reluctant to do the shooting for him. "We're not in business for that," manager Vernon Jones told him. "Now we'll do anything humanly possible to get a hunter a deer. But when it gets right down to it, he'd better be able to kill it." Why? Mr. Karpel wanted to know. "Because," replied Mr. Jones, "well, hell, just because."

Mr. Jones is no longer manager of the Y.O. He has been replaced by a man named Robert J. Snow, Jr. And it was under the new manager that the ranch racked up a new "world record." And it was an animal killed by one clean shot, too. The killer was a six-year-old boy. The animal was a goat.

Here and there, however, there are signs that the day of the preserve may be over—that the preserves of the future may have some difficulty preserving themselves. Take the case of Pete Gee, founder of the Tioga Boar Hunting Preserve in Tioga, New York. Mr. Gee guides hunters out, but he himself refuses to hunt any more. "It's like bartending," he says. "You lose your taste for it when you're with it every day." Mr. Gee also took pride, on the day he was interviewed, in the fact that one of his boars had chased a hunter up a tree. "And that's nothing," he added. "I've seen as many as five hunters up the same tree."

And, as if that were not a hopeful enough sign, take the case of the Royal Hunting Preserve of Pine Mountain, Georgia. Here, twenty-one exotic animals were not just shot—they were poisoned. And Mrs. J. C. Yarbrough and a stalwart group of humane workers went to work with such effect that, in short order, the preserve was closed. "The killing of the animals was a big factor, but not the only factor," said John B. Amos, owner. "I can put up with the do-gooders, but not the do-badders. I didn't realize when I started this thing," Amos continued, "that there was such a strong feeling against hunting. I might not have ever started this if I had known that. I don't think the feeling is just against preserves like this, but against all hunting."

*

So far our tour of the Nimrod nobility has been confined to gun hunting. No discussion would be complete, however, without some attention to the ancient but relatively lately revived sport of bow hunting. To the credit of the bowmen, they took it up originally to even the odds a little bit—to make out of their game, in a sense, a better game. It did not, unfortunately, turn out that way, but this has not stopped the bowmen from truly extraordinary efforts at promotion. In December, 1973, for example, a "senior" writer for *Sports Illustrated,* bow hunter Robert Jones, extolled the sport in glowing terms:

> The man who would kill a deer with a weapon as "primitive" as a bow and arrow must acquire certain talents that seem as distant from today's world as the skills of the Paleolithic: patience, quiet, immobility, stoicism, the suppression of movement and whim and imagination to so deep a level of control that the game literally comes to him to be killed. In a way, it almost seems un-American.

Surely after what we have seen elsewhere in the field, Mr. Jones's concern for bow hunting's being considered un-American is touching solicitude. But Mr. Jones is even more sensitive when he compares the bow hunter to the gun hunter: "The bow-hunter," he writes, "is not so readily categorized as a man with a penis problem." Mercy. And to think it was a hunter himself who brought up something which I had not only successfully avoided for all these many pages but also had been resolved to leave out entirely on the theory that it was—well, hitting below the belt. No matter. Mr. Jones cannot be stopped. He does however declare his preference for bow-killing a buck rather than a doe. "To kill a buck," he writes, "is to give another, perhaps wilier, buck a chance at inseminating many does with his superior genes."

Let us hope one day another, perhaps wilier, *Sports Illustrated* writer—maybe even a junior one instead of a senior—will have the chance at inseminating readers with a rather different view of bow hunting. In any case, Mr. Jones writes of a hunt on which his "partner" is Judge Vincent Gurahian. "To hell with the buck," Mr. Jones quotes Judge Gurahian as saying. "What I want is a nice, fat, young doe, about eighty pounds of tender meat." Mr. Jones has already identified Judge Gurahian as "a New York State judge who sits in the Family Court of Westchester County . . . a humanist of the first order, whether on the bench or deep in the woods."

Having not heard the judge on the bench, I'll have to go with the woods. Meanwhile, in the interests of equal time, it is surely high time for the appearance of another witness. And the man I choose to call as chief witness for the prosecution in the case against bow hunting is a man named Clare Conley, a champion archer. There is justice here, too. For, just as it was a well-known ex-gun hunter, Bil Gilbert, who blew the whistle on modern hunting, so it was a well-known ex-bow hunter who blew the whistle on bow hunting. Furthermore, Mr. Conley blew his whistle in, of all places, *True, the Man's Magazine.* His article was entitled, simply, "Butchers with Bows and Arrows." "The sport," he said, "should not be allowed. *There is no sure way to kill a deer instantly with a bow!*" (The italics are Mr. Conley's.) His article ran, in parts, as follows:

> Consider this: It is against the law in Wyoming to kill a deer with a rifle having a bore diameter smaller than .23 inch. This includes, among others, the .220 Swift. Yet in that same state you can, with perfect legality, shoot any big-game animal, from antelope to moose, with a weapon made obsolete for military purposes by the first crude, muzzle-loading firearms: the bow and arrow.

Wyoming, like many other states, prohibits the use of small-caliber rifles, including those of extremely high velocity such as the Swift, in an attempt to prevent the crippling and loss of big-game animals. Yet, also like many others, it encourages the use of bows and arrows by giving archers special privileges, including an early open season before riflemen are allowed to take the field.

This is ridiculous. It is absurd. It is as illogical as cutting off a dog's tail an inch at a time in the belief that it won't hurt so much.

An arrow—any arrow from any bow—compared to the bullet from a .220 Swift is as a falling feather to a bolt of lightning. The first rabbit—rabbit, mind you—that I killed with a bow was fairly hit. The arrow went through its chest. Yet it screamed in agony, running, falling and stumbling, struggling when the arrow caught in weeds, leaping blindly and always screaming, until I ran after it and ended its agony by crushing out its life with my heel.

Mr. Jones and many other historians of the modern bow hunt date its birth from the day when an Indian named Ishi wandered into the California town of Oroville, and pronounced himself, "the last of the Yanas"—the Yanas having been, according to Ishi, terrific bow hunters. Declares Jones:

> Ishi's closest friend was a physician, Dr. Saxton Pope, who learned bow-hunting techniques from him and fired the romantic imagination of hunters everywhere with tales of deer hunts and salmon slaughters in the outdoor magazines of the day. Pope himself was an incurable Robin Hood romantic, but he and his hunting partner, Art Young, drummed up such enthusiasm for the bow and arrow that they virtually created a whole new sport. Just as gun hunters have their trophies accredited by the Boone and Crockett Club, bow hunters measure their kills against the records of the Pope and Young Club.

With all due respect to Ishi, it is certainly remarkable how his "closest" friend and fellow bow-hunting tub thumper, Dr. Pope, turned out to have a brother, Gustavus Pope, who together with *his* friend William Chanler were both pillars of the Boone and Crockett. Also they both were soon in bow-hunting promotion up to their elbows—even to the seeing to it that a fine new hunting industry, that of making bows and arrows, could march ahead side by side with the guns and ammo industry toward the making of a better America. "Through their accomplishments on the hunting fields of North America and Africa and their writings," says James Trefethen, "they maintained a small nucleus of devoted followers during a generation in which the archer was often regarded as a fop, a fool, or a crank. The bow-hunter today is regarded . . . as the paragon of sportsmanship."

As long, of course, as one confines such regard to the membership of the club. Or rather, two clubs—the Boone and Crockett and the Pope and Young. Elsewhere it seems, the record is less of a paragon—it is, however, easy to follow because it is a trail of blood. Take, for example, the opinion of the late Dr. J. M. Kolisch, founder-president of The Pines to Palms Wildlife Committee of California, and for decades the West's leading authority on hunter cruelty. His opinion on bow hunting was given as far back as 1959 to the California Fish and Game Department—then and now not only pro-gun but also pro-bow:

> Does nursing their fawns are made the target of archers who sit in ambush for them at one of the scarce water-holes, waiting for the buck to approach. The archers use a chemical luring device imitating the scent of a doe in heat. The use of this luring device is permitted during this hunt which lasts throughout the entire sex season of

the deer. This chemical device is sprinkled on the clothes of the hunter to lure the animal through the scent to the place of ambush. Phonetic luring devices imitating the call of a doe are also used. These devices are being advertised as a "must for the archer" in a so-called sports magazine.

If the doe approaches, it is wounded and escapes into the dense brush. The wound made by the arrow becomes infected by blowflies and maggots, which soon commence to eat the animal alive. The little fawn at its mother's side either dies of thirst or, like its mother, is torn to pieces by predators who soon become trained to attack deer.

Some sport! Some outdoor recreation! Some state conservation method! . . .

Hunting with bow and arrow is not only a retrogression to the use of weapons which have been given up hundreds of years ago because of their lesser efficiency, but also a retrogression to utter barbarism.

In the entire state of Florida, in the 1930's, in the first three *years* of bow hunting, not one single deer was actually killed —although hundreds and perhaps thousands were wounded. The next year one deer was killed, and then the fifth year was a big year—two deer were killed. Of late years, in the North, the outstanding authority on the cruelty of the bow hunt is Carl Marty, propietor of Northernaire, the famed hotel resort at Three Lakes, Wisconsin, which he now runs as an oasis-reserve in the midst of the surrounding bloodbath which, each season, is the bow hunt. Although his thousands of acres are posted with NO HUNTING signs, the week I was there I saw a score of animals, all of which had been wounded within the no-hunting area, and many of which bore the telltale marks of the arrowheads with the dread razor blades attached. One animal, a three-month-old fawn, was one Mr. Marty himself had raised as a pet. He had been terribly wounded by a bow hunter, and not even finished off—just left to die. Mr. Marty himself had to shoot him. Afterward, Mr. Marty ran an announcement in the local paper of his intention to form an admittedly anti-bow-hunting society. It was a small announcement in a relatively small paper—yet within days Mr. Marty had the incredible number of sixteen hundred letters, asking to join, and almost every single one of them had an individual story of some bow hunter's mindless mayhem. Out of that mailing was born the Vilas-Oneida Wilderness Society, its membership now many thousands. "The Wisconsin Conservation Department," Mr. Marty told me, "with their budget reaching toward half a hundred million dollars, does not need the blood-soaked dollars from the bow-hunting season. For every deer they kill quickly, at least five or six die lingering, agonizing, gruesome deaths." Mr. Marty also gave me a letter from a former hunter, the late J. R. Marnich:

> Did you ever see a man and woman bow-hunter fire at several deer being fed in a yard, their arrows hitting the house and woodpile, barely missing humans? I did.
>
> Did you ever see a hunter cutting off the hindquarters of a wounded doe while she watched him? I did.
>
> Why did the Indian discard the bow and arrow 100 years ago for the rifle, only to have the white man take up the bow and arrow? Would you say that the eighty bears killed by archers this year were all legal kills? A treed bear looking like a pincushion, suffering excruciating pain with every arrow that entered his body—can you call this sport? Can the hunter be proud of such a cruel kill?
>
> Why a dollar license fee for teenage bow-hunters, when many of them are not strong enough to pull a bow to make a clean kill? Why encourage our youth to participate in bow-hunting butchery? What is more nauseating than to see a full-grown man in a camouflage suit sneak-

ing up to get a shot at a five-month-old fawn? The cruelty of bow-hunting is completely indefensible, and when the book of life is closed on those who sanction it, they may pray for more merciful judgment than they are giving our wildlife, who have no voice of their own to plead their cause.

The State of Pennsylvania, in keeping with its position as the No. 1 gun-hunting state in the nation, is also No. 1 in its promotion of bow hunting. Like other states, Pennsylvania has a Game Commission, which publishes a beautiful monthly four-color magazine—at the expense of the taxpayers, of course—which, in its case, is called *Pennsylvania Game News.* Each issue seems to concern itself with almost any kind of possible live target it might have overlooked in the previous issue. The September, 1970, issue, for example, had an article entitled "Wanted! Snipe Hunters." To drum up enthusiasm for sniping snipe, the writer, Byron W. Dalrymple, even went so far as to tell you what delicious eating they were—the "ultimate delicacy," he called them:

> There is the tale, oft told using different settings, about the waiter in a plush hotel who served to a gourmet a half dozen broiled snipe. The customer stared in horror, noting that each had been wrapped in bacon. Then he flew into a towering rage, arose and shot the waiter dead.

The Pennsylvania Game Commission does not, I gather, actually promote the sport of gun-shooting waiters, but of bow-shooting same I would not be certain. For, along with their sniping, went an article entitled "ARCHERY FOR EVERYONE —ARCHERY." Their readers are apparently extremely forgetful. The article extolled in particular something called "The Forksville Festival"—which, it said, "Probably draws more participants than any other sporting event held in the United

States." In the very next paragraph, one reads, "In recent years participation in the Festival has averaged in excess of 2,000." Suffice it to say that I have attended more popular chess tournaments.

The keynote of the Forksville Fun, according to the *Game News,* is informality. "People wander back and forth in all different directions at once throughout the three days. Each has a specific goal in mind, but there is no one to tell him or her what to do." The first "organized activity," we are told, occurs on Friday night—a raccoon hunt:

> Only a person who has gone out at night with a few good dogs to rout out some shooting up the beam of a flashlight can appreciate the excitement that goes with this one. . . . Just standing in a patch of woodland or along a hedgerow, waiting for the dogs to tree a 'coon, is worth the price of admission. . . . And when a raccoon is finally treed, the activity which follows is a fair example of pandemonium. While hound dogs try to climb the trees, lights are thrown on the raccoon and hopeful archers attempt to bring it down for a score. . . . Those who don't care for night hunting, or already have sore fingers from shooting, are treated to outdoor films in the new show building built with profits from previous Festivals. . . . On Saturday morning, the first wild boar hunt usually starts at nine o'clock. About eight or ten feral pigs from the Georgia swamps are turned loose in a predetermined area. Upwards of 300 bow-hunters will be lined up to take their chances against heavy human odds and the sharp instincts of the Southland porkers. Each of the pigs is previously checked for hog cholera. . . . The second hunt on Sunday usually brings out even more participants. Over the years, such prizes as chipmunks and rattlesnakes have gained the attention of those archers who fail to get a glimpse of wild boar. Return of successful hunters is always a big event, loudly an-

nounced so that photographers and spectators can view the trophies.

Always that trophy.

I have never had the honor of attending the Forksville Festival, but I did have the memorable experience of attending, in Oil City, Pennsylvania, what was called a "Bow Hunters Jamboree." "FIVE WILD BOARS," said the advertisement. "FIVE SPANISH GOATS." In the company of Harriet Bleakley and Fran Frye, editor of the Franklin, Pennsylvania, *News Herald,* I arrived early, while the bow hunters were having breakfast. "SIGN HERE," said one sign. "AGITATORS," said another, "KEEP OUT!" I signed away. Three hundred archers, I saw, had also signed. First I looked at the animals. The "wild boars" were not even full-sized pigs. They were, in reality, piglets. The "Spanish goats" looked like tame nannies. All the animals were huddled, shivering with fear, guarded by a teenager, in two crates— one for the boars, one for the goats. "Nine out of ten of them," one archer explained to me, peering at the crates, "will be killed with one arrow." "No," said another, also peering in, "we haven't got ten, now. We've only got nine. We had to throw one out. He was blind."

For me the most incredible thing about the whole "hunt" was the presence throughout it of no fewer than six members of the Pennsylvania Game Commission. On the badges of these gentlemen was written "Game Protector." I questioned the word "Protector." "You see," the leader explained, "the boars and goats aren't 'game.'" Oh, I said. "They're wild animals," he said. Oh, I said again. "After they're *released*," he continued helpfully, "they'll be *predators*." I looked back on the truck and saw—still in their crates—the shivering, quivering nannies and piglets. Beside the truck now there was also another truck—a Red Cross vehicle. I questioned the attendant. "Hunting is very dangerous," he told me. "So many of them go out when they are too old. They get heart attacks."

When the crate was placed on the truck and the truck was driven out to the place where the animals were going to be released—completely surrounded by archers—even that didn't suffice. The archers crowded right in around the back of the truck. "I'm not going to let them out," the boy driving the truck said, "until you back away." But the archers wouldn't back away, and so finally the driver got in and drove on down the road. Suddenly he stopped, jumped out and quickly let the animals out. The goats, tired from being in their crate for over twenty-four hours, hardly moved at all. One was shot right on the road. He died, however, hard. Another, barely off the road, looked like a dartboard before he finally expired. The boars tried harder to get away. But there was no real hope. One boar was shot first in the foot, then in the rump and finally in the eye. Another boar was thrashing around in a bush while an archer was literally pumping arrows into him. I learned firsthand that the bow, as a *coup de grace* weapon ranks somewhat above a hacksaw or a chisel but well below a hatchet or a blowgun.

Afterward I talked with one of the leaders of the hunt. "We went into the whole thing morally," he told me. "We had a meeting of the entire membership and we discussed it from every angle." How long, I asked him, did the meeting last? "Fifteen minutes," he replied. I also talked once more with the leader of the Pennsylvania Game Commission—and I did so with all five of his men standing there and listening. I asked him to give me his definition of cruelty to animals. He did not do so but told me that, in his opinion, he did not have the power to stop the hunt. I told him that in my opinion he was a coward. He turned red but moved away—which did not surprise me. I did, however, a little later, hear one of his men, a younger one, talking to another. "You know," he said quietly, "I agree with that guy. I think we should have stopped it."

Second only to Pennsylvania as bow-hunt promotion paradise is the State of Michigan, whose animal laws are so archaic it still has a bounty on coyotes. Michigan's Grand Dragon of the bow hunt is a man named, aptly enough, Fred Bear, of Grayling. He started bow hunting in 1936 and shortly afterward entered business—that of making bows. For many years president of the Bear Archery Company, he has, for a trophy room, a whole museum of his own. Among other honors, he claims to have shot, with a single arrow, a four-ton elephant—a rogue dinosaur preying, apparently, on primitive, fear-maddened natives. Irene Portnoy tells of his bravery in the Ann Arbor *News*:

> It takes a friend or one of Bear's adventure films to tell you about the close brush with death, at the claws of a polar bear. Or about the time in 1963 when Bear was invited by the Maharajah of Bundi to be a guest in his palace in Rajasthan, India, and hunt tigers in the royal way.
>
> This involved flushing the tiger out with native beaters. The bowmen were stationed in tree platforms, and when Bear saw the tiger about 100 yards away, he planned to shoot beyond him in an effort to get elbow range.
>
> The arrow hit the big cat in a vital spot, however, which brought him roaring toward the platforms before he collapsed in a nearby thicket.
>
> Bear was on ABC "American Sportsman" show and spent 25 days on an icepack before spotting a polar bear. With the cameras grinding, Bear made an almost perfect hit, close to the left shoulder, felling the 1,000 pound giant. It was his third attempt at the polar bear.

Twice before, polar bears charged after being pierced by arrows and backup riflemen had to step in to save Bear.

Bear admits to several close calls, but brushes them off. "At a point, all game is dangerous," he says.

Even, apparently, on *The American Sportsman.* But Mr. Bear isn't the only one of Michigan's intrepid bow hunters to be highly publicized. Another is Ruth Ryan, a sixty-eight-year-old great-grandmother, who didn't even take up the "sport" until she was forty-nine. "What else," she asked writer Kathleen Hampton, "could women our age do?" Miss Hampton described Mrs. Ryan's technique:

> Mrs. Ryan explains that there are two kinds of shooters—the instinctive, or bare-bow, shot and the free-stylers, who use sights.
>
> "There used to be a terrific amount of conflict between free-stylers and bare-bows," she continues. "Fifteen years ago if you shot with a sight, the bare-bows wouldn't even look at you."
>
> An instinctive shot aims his bow according to the distance of the target, whereas a free-styler will center the target in the crosshairs of his sight.
>
> "You have to learn how to elevate to get your distance, and this is easier said than done. The further the target, the more you have to elevate. And with a light bow you aim for the clouds," Mrs. Ryan explains. . . .
>
> Mrs. Ryan doesn't think she is a hunter by nature. "But if I get a shot, I'll take it—even though when that arrow hits, your stomach kind of goes blooock. But after a while it settles down."

"Deer hunting," says a typical article by one of Michigan's outdoor writers extolling the sport of bow hunting, "is only a small part of the fun." The article points out that you can add to your fun "the kinds of wildlife that can be hunted anytime of the year." And, to encourage this amusement, the

Michigan Bow-Hunters Association set up, on such year-round targets, a year-round "point system": for bobcat, coyotes, wild turkey or wild goose—thirty points; for fox, woodchuck, quail, grouse, jacksnipe or duck—fifteen points; for badger, weasel, mink, cock pheasant, woodcock or rattle-snake—ten points; for porcupine, opossum, skunk, squirrel, hare, rabbit or crow—five points. Following this announce-ment—which included the injunction that "points may not be saved from one year to the next"—a bow hunter promptly went out and shot a Black Angus cow. He was not, however, awarded any points.

To Michigan's credit, it has occasionally balked at some aspects of the bow hunt. In 1972, for example, a bill was proposed to allow bow hunters to shoot from trees. During the discussion at the State House in Lansing, Representative Thomas Anderson, one of the proponents, said the bill would, in his words, "stop the very thing opponents of the bill are complaining about—the wounding of animals." Just how the bow hunters' pursuit of wounded game would be facilitated by their being up a tree, Representative Anderson did not make clear, possibly he saw Michigan's bow hunters swinging, like Tarzan, from tree to tree. Representative Richard Friske, on the other hand, felt that for the state bow hunters to be up a tree was "dangerous and unrealistic." And, although he did not say whether he saw the danger to them, the animals or the tree, the bill was finally defeated 47–44. Similarly, in the state of Connecticut, a bill to allow deer hunting on Sunday was defeated—but not without a remarkable appeal made by a man named Michael Fedora of West Haven. Mr. Fedora, like Mr. Bear, is not only a bow hunter—he also makes and sells bows; he wrote the New Haven *Register* as follows:

> The attendant pain of an arrow head is slight, about the same as a clap on the shoulder; the arrow does not kill

by shock, nor is it intended to, it kills by hemorrhage. If the wound is slight, not striking a vital area or cutting an artery, the deer will often clear the arrow and heal quickly. If the animal is mortally wounded, it will normally lie down, go to sleep and not awake. The "clap on the shoulder" may startle the animal, cause it to run and quicken the end result. In any case, death is relatively painless. There is not one recorded instance of a deer being found dead with an arrow stuck in it; bow-hunters do not abandon their game.

It is doubtful that any writer has ever managed in similar space what in this writer's opinion is self-serving nonsense. But another bow-hunting writer, Dave Harbour, in the May, 1973, *Sports Afield,* would at least have none of such twaddle:

> Not one bow-hunter out of ten that I know can hit a deer in the spine or put his arrow through the heart or lung of even a standing deer every time, even at reasonable bow ranges—and these are the only conventional arrow shots which are likely to drop a deer quickly. When a deer crouches or jumps, and when the hunters' hands are shaking and his heart is pounding, a quick-killing hit with a conventional arrow is even more unlikely. What bow-hunter can really call himself a sportsman and enjoy trailing stumbling, suffering deer for long periods? This is exactly what too many of us bow-hunters are doing today.

Mr. Harbour makes a case for drug-tipped arrows—something permitted, curiously, only in the state of Mississippi. The reason for this is that the drug or pod-tipped arrow—succinylcholine chloride—was developed by a Mississippi doctor, Dr. R. P. Herrington of Jackson. A bow hunter himself, one season Dr. Herrington hit five deer in a row with conventional arrows and was unable to retrieve a single one of them. "At that point," he told Harbour, "I was ready to give up bow-hunting completely. The thought of those five wounded deer dragging themselves around the woods until a painful death overtook them was more than I could stand." Dr. Herrington went to work. The drug he came up with is not a poison and not a tranquilizer; it is, however, a powerful muscle relaxant. It is also inexpensive and works remarkably quickly. The animal is down in about six seconds, and dead—in a sense, relaxed to death—in about thirty seconds, all with a minimum of pain. The meat, even at the site of the wound is, within a half hour, fit for human consumption. Since developing the arrow, Dr. Herrington, his wife, three sons, a daughter and a daughter-in-law have hit sixty-four deer—and retrieved every one of them.

Although the arrow could obviously kill people too, for ten years some 8,000 bowhunters in Mississippi have been using it with no accidents. This, Dr. Herrington believes, is because they know the danger involved and are extremely careful. Since 1961 the Mississippi Game & Fish Department have not only not opposed the idea of the drug-tipped arrow, they have encouraged it. The reason for this was the fact that in Mississippi as in other states the bow season precedes the gun season. However, in gun season, Mississippi hunts with dogs as well as guns—and the extremely large number of wounded deer flushed by the dogs early in the gun season, deer with obvious bow-hunt wounds, convinced the Game & Fish to try something else. Now the wounded at the beginning of the gun season are practically nonexistent.

Other states, however, have been reluctant to follow suit. For one thing, the Food & Drug Administration has been slow to countenence the use of the drug. For another, the American

Bowhunters Society has objected strongly. Being a typical hunting society, going by the big brave hunter syndrome, they are, in the first place presumably reluctant to enjoy the fact that anyone—as can happen with the drug-tipped arrow—who can bend a thirty-pound bow can kill a deer quickly. In the second place, if the Bowhunters Society did go for the arrow, they would also obviously have to admit the staggering statistics about wounded animals that Mississippi proved—and which necessitated the arrow to begin with.

There are two areas in which bow hunting is widely used and yet for which it is perhaps most widely criticized. One is its use in wildlife "refuges." The other, curiously, is its use on Government installations—particularly military ones. When Ohio's Ravenna Arsenal opened its gates to public bow hunting, for example, on an area of some twenty-five hundred acres surrounded by chain-link fencing, the deer were driven in a pack against one corner of the property. "The panic of the animals, huddled together," an eyewitness reported, "with their rolling eyes and slavering tongues made for me an unforgettable sight. They made no sound. The only noise was the howling of the jerks pumping arrows into them." When, for another example, Kentucky's Lexington-Bluegrass Army Depot was also opened to bow hunters, at least forty deer were "arrowed" but uncollected by hunters. "I saw one doe," an eyewitness there reported, "her right shoulder arrowed and swollen, still leading her half-grown fawn." The result, in the words of one reporter, was that something which had been promoted as a possible public-relations success turned out to be, for the Army, more of a public albatross. One retired Army colonel, William L. Stoughton, was moved to write an article about such bow-hunting slaughter. "I implore every Field Archer," he wrote, "to make his own contribution to universal peace by bringing his portion of the world's violence and destruction of life to an end."

As for the wildlife refuges, these too have paid dearly in the public prints when they have seen fit to allow their animals to be bow trimmed. In a recent deer hunt in Virginia's Chincoteague National Wildlife Refuge, the refuge discovered that it could get almost as bad publicity from bow hunting as it could from rounding up wild ponies. Only thirty-four deer were killed —the bowmen admitted having left arrows in thirty-three. The Mark Twain National Wildlife Refuge near Quincy, Illinois, has had five bow hunts so far on its four Mississippi River islands. The limit of dead deer is supposed to be one to a customer—there is, however, no limit to a customer's wounded. Strangest of all these refuge hunts is the bow hunt at the Aransas National Wildlife Refuge in south Texas. Aransas' claim to fame is that it is the principal wintering ground for the last remaining whooping cranes—which, as of 1974, numbered just forty-three world-wide. Gun hunting of excess deer —like the later problem of the test bombing by the Department of Defense of nearby Matagorda Island—would, it was felt, disturb the whooping crane, so a bow hunt was decided upon. It was a strange decision, in view of the fact that when Possum Kingdom Lake, a state park operated by the Brazos River Authority, had been previously open to bow hunting, the Texas Parks and Wildlife Commission—not known for statistics unfavorable to any kind of hunting—itself estimated that over two hundred deer were wounded, abandoned and subsequently died. This time Ed Ragsdale, of the Irving Bowhunters, suggested that a nine-inch paper pie plate be put up and that anyone who hunted must first be able to put five out of six arrows in the pie plate from seventeen yards. The U.S. Fish and Wildlife Service, however, told Ragsdale that this could not be done—that any restrictions would be "discrimi-natory" and that "public hunts" should be open to everyone. Texas' Committee for Wildlife Protection also tried to block the hunt. But when this committee wrote a San Antonio paper requesting a copy of a photograph it had printed showing a deer in full flight with an arrow still stuck in its body, the paper did not even answer the letter. In any case, the hunt proceeded. Writer Craig Karpel kept a diary. Here are some excerpts:

"Did you get a shot?" was the question of the mo-ment. The answer of the moment was "No." One hunter complained that he *almost* had a shot—a still buck at 15 yards, bow drawn back, then "some idiot comes thrashing the underbrush, yelling, 'Seen anything this morning?' " "I'm out a half hour," says a benign young face in-congruously surrounded with camouflage material and daubed with black grease, "when some old boy comes up behind me, shouting 'Louie . . . Louie . . . Louie.' Six o'clock in the dad-gum morning and this son of a gun is looking for his Louie. Some people."

Along the side of the road to the refuge, hung from a low limb on one of those big shade trees, was the swing-ing carcass of a ten point whitetail buck. Two hunters, one in camouflage suit, one in camouflage pants and a blood-smeared white undershirt, were preparing to butcher their kill. "You can see where the arrow was," said the white undershirt, "this was a rib shot—it entered here on the left, pierced that lung, and went on through diagonally. The arrow stayed in him, but the first thing we do is remove it. Hell, those broadheads cost $14 a dozen. This buck took about fourteen minutes to die and stiffen up.

"These arrows kill by hemorrhaging—you can see the extra set of edges on this broadhead, at right angles to the main head. The whole thing is razor-edged—in fact, on this one here, you can see where we actually set in pieces of razor blade to make the edges even sharper. . . . Sometimes you'll get a situation where you see the deer is not bleeding all that profusely and you may have to wait an hour or more for him to stiffen up. That's why we try and beef up the arrow.

"We've been at this five years now. I remember the first time I went after a deer with a bow—I took eleven shots. *Eleven shots!* Didn't kill him, either."

At this point a hunter came up wearing a plaid shirt and cowboy hat. He kibbitzed with the other two as they continued dressing their kill. "I had me a beautiful shot this morning, but damned if I missed him," he said. The other two were not particularly listening. "Got him right here." He pointed to the hanging carcass, the point at which the hind leg joins the body. "You should have seen the bastard take off. Lost an arrow."

A landmark event, not only in bow hunting but all hunting, occurred in Los Angeles in 1971. For years anti-hunting sentiment had been building all over the country. It was particularly strong in California, where a very large number of people feel close to nature, and it was strongest of all about the matter of bow hunting. This feeling came to a head when the California Fish and Game Department announced a special bow hunt—one which had nothing to do with the regular pre-gun season in the fall, but which was to be a spring season, and was to occur, of all places, within the City of Los Angeles. The reason for the hunt, the Fish and Game explained, was that they had had "hundreds of citizen complaints about deer depredation." Deer, presumably, at the Bank of America and Grauman's Chinese.

Actually, in fairness, the "City" of Los Angeles does include many semi-open and even wooded areas, but from the beginning, to many people at least, the hunt was extremely suspect. The few deer occasionally visible were, generally speaking, far from a subject for complaint. On the contrary, they were a source of so much enjoyment to people that they were only too happy to pay for this enjoyment with the price of an occasional bush. Usually such matters as the forthcoming bow hunt were decided at hearings before the very same committee, the Fish and Game, which wanted the hunt in the first place. If you were a nonhunter, in other words, you were in somewhat the position of a banker asked to attend hearings held by the James brothers on the subject of robbing banks. This time, however, the nonhunters resolved that they would have a different kind of hearing—a real hearing. Before the hunters knew what was happening, Los Angeles City Councilman Robert Stevenson introduced a bill to prohibit bow hunting. It was still, mind you, just a bill to prohibit bow hunting within the city limits. But, from the reaction of the hunters, one would have thought that nothing less was at stake than their right to bear bows.

In short order, it became a national issue. Hunters are accustomed, at certain periods, to appear in large and intimidating numbers; they invariably include in their "testimony" by no means veiled threats about their vast political power. This time they prepared with a vengeance. Bow hunters were shanghaied from far and wide—if they had been able to produce a direct descendant of William Tell, make no mistake, he would have been there. The difference was that this time, for once, the nonhunters were also prepared. When the hunters arrived at Los Angeles' City Hall—and they came by the hundreds—they were faced for the first time with at least equality in numbers and at times it seemed far better than that. They were also faced for the first time with a basically unintimidatable council—one which brought with it, among other

Zimmerman's in Nairobi. The spoils of the war on wildlife.
Everything anyone could ask—from elephant-foot wastebaskets to
giraffe-tail flyswatters.

White wolf—Baffin Island

Giraffe—Kenya

Fun with a gun—via helicopter

Trophy time—a grizzly death

Joe Kordick, Chicago Sun Times

Girl meets wolf—the late "Jethro"

A sing-in—the late "Clem"

Walt Scheider

A "shooting preserve." The Y. O. Ranch in Texas. You pick your target as you would your breakfast. You don't even have to get out of your vehicle. The animals think you've come with *their* breakfast.

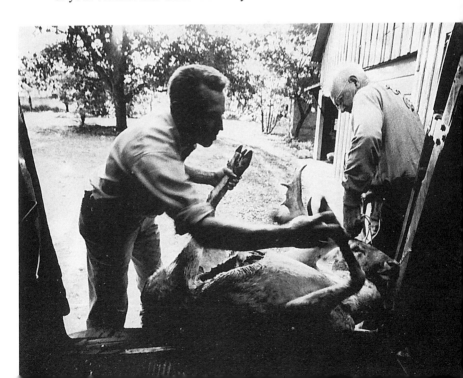

Jack Paar and "Amani."
"He was the very *best* lion
I ever knew."

Jim Fowler and
"Arthur."
"Cheetahs are so
very special."

Dick Cavett and "Mariah."
"I never met an
animal I didn't like."

Bow and arrow hunt in Oil City, Pa. Despite the sign, I attended.
There were 300 archers after five "wild boar" and five "Spanish
goats"—to be released from a truck.
(Below) Final release

Here I hold one of my
very favorites—the otter.

A wolf and her person—"Cadillac," a black timberwolf at
Mountain Place Sanctuary, California.

C. W. Telford

"Coon on a log." Raccoons are sometimes chained on logs, sometimes, as here, in boxes on water, or, as below, in barrel or tied to it. The "contest"—to see how many dogs the raccoon can fight off before they finally kill him.

The famous Fund for Animals advertisement—by the E. F. Timme
Co.—in favor of synthetic fur. Members of The Fund's National
Board, clockwise, Doris Day, Amanda Blake, Jayne Meadows,
Angie Dickinson. In front, at six o'clock, Mary Tyler Moore,
National Chairman of The Fund.

One of the so-called "fun" furs. This coyote, approached by a dog, will make a great addition to someone's amusing wardrobe.

Here's what that darling fox jacket came from—only it takes about six foxes like this and it takes them so long to die.

Summer of '74. Fund for Animals volunteers picket Casa de Pets in Studio City, California, offensive "exotic" dealer.

Below, the late "Skandy" in New York's awful Central Park Zoo. When a man stuck his arm in Skandy's cage, Skandy grabbed it. The headline read: "COP SHOOTS VICIOUS BEAR."

Coyotes strung up—to teach other coyotes a lesson.

(Below) Another lesson. First the trucks, then fresh dogs loosed from the trucks, then, finally, after fighting as bravely as he can, the coyote will, in his traditional sign of submission, present his throat—only to be torn to pieces anyway.

Thomas Felix Bolack of New Mexico. The caption, in a 1967 *Saturday Evening Post,* read: "He is a busy civic booster, an ex-Governor of New Mexico and a noted conservationist."

things, some memorable statistics. Indeed, early in the hearings it was pointed out that exactly 3.4 percent of the citizens in the entire state of California hunt with anything—a gun, a bow or a peashooter. Also, it was soon apparent that the nonhunters had done their homework. They produced, along with a variety of incredibly razored arrows, firsthand, eyewitness accounts of bow-hunting accidents—accidents not to animals or to other hunters, but to all kinds of ordinary people, people in automobiles, people out walking, bystanders, housewives, even people in their own homes. Even a child actually struck by an arrow. One housewife, on the way to her garage, had a double-razored arrow whistle past her head and imbed itself in the frame of her screen door. An inch one way and it would have killed her. An inch the other way, and it would have killed her child inside in the doorway. One councilman, Arthur Snyder, related the fact that his brother had been hit in the head with an arrow, and the arrow had penetrated his brain. He had been killed.

The bow hunters, who had prepared for arguments about cruelty to animals, were soon entirely on the defensive. The Southern California Archery Association turned to "statistics" about how many of their number came from out of Los Angeles and hence brought money to the city; one of them even pointed out how much food they ate and "in driving around" how much gas they used. He was interrupted. "We are not," said one councilman, "discussing pollution." At this point another archer came forward to try to counter the accident statistics. "We all take out insurance policies," he said. At this, a black councilman, Gilbert Lindsey, asked him the amount of such policy. "Ten thousand dollars," the archer replied firmly. "You mean," Councilman Lindsey went on, "that if I'm out walking with my grandson and you shoot him

with one of your arrows you're going to give me $10,000 and
that's going to make up for it?" To this the archer made no
reply. Councilman Lindsey stared at him. "I am not going to
vote for you," he said quietly.

When it came the turn of the "conservation" societies, the
National Wildlife Federation entered the lists, as usual, on
the side of the hunters. But it was no use. In vain did California
Fish and Game protest that they had "evidence" of their citizens' complaints about depredation. Asked to produce such
evidence, the best they could come up with was a telephone
call that a deer somewhere was in someone's garden eating a
rosebush. When it came my turn to testify, I pointed to the
hunters on one side and the nonhunters on the other, and asked
where the depredators were—the people who were the reason
for us all being there. No army of rosebush fanciers had appeared—in fact, not one single person complaining of depredation had appeared. The bow hunters had lost.

The most moving single piece of testimony was filed with
the council but never read. It was written by a bow hunter, too,
the same Clare Conley whose article in *True* Magazine,
"Butchers with Bows and Arrows," was cited earlier. Mr. Conley had no human accident stories in his article, but nonetheless
he said it all:

> Well, four of us were hunting together last fall, spread
> out in a line about 20 yards apart. We jumped a doe
> that ran across in front of the line. One of the men in the
> center whipped up his bow, drew and shot. He made a
> perfect—and lucky—hit. The arrow went through the
> doe's neck. We all saw it strike, and we all saw it sticking
> out both sides as she bounded away.
>
> The blood was easy to find, but we waited the cus-
> tomary hour for her to lie down and stiffen up so that we
> could approach her a second time. We followed the scar-

let trail for most of another hour, expecting to find her dead momentarily, but going doggedly on when we did not.

We came to several pools of blood with prints of her knees beside them, where she had gone down to hang her head and bleed in the bright sun. We saw spots where she had stumbled. But still her life blood ran, and still she went on.

At last we found her. She was dying. She was on her knees and hocks. Her ears, no longer the wonderful, alert warning system to detect any danger, were sagging. Her head was down. Her nose was in her blood. We could hear her breath bubbling in the warm blood.

We paused, then silently separated so as to come at her from four directions. The archer who had hit her first approached her head. At a range of 15 feet he drew his bow and released another arrow . . . and missed! He had tried to hit her in the brain at 15 feet, and though he held an Expert A rating in the National Field Archery Association, his arrow slipped between her ears and thudded into the ground beyond.

Somehow the doe lurched up. Stumbling, bounding, crashing blindly into the brush, she managed to reach the rim of a plateau we were on and disappear. None of us was able to hit her again. We ran to the edge of the steep, brushy slope below. She was nowhere in sight!

Her trail was plain enough where she had slid and stumbled down the first steep pitch, however. We took it, but now there was no more blood. The original arrow had broken off somewhere along the way and the two wounds had closed. We followed her halting tracks carefully in the dust and rock, but soon they were lost among a maze of deer tracks. We fanned out and combed the hillside. We failed.

Altogether, we lost four wounded deer on that one hunting trip, but the doe that I saw dying stayed with me.

Her heartbroken, dulling eyes haunted me. At odd moments I'd see her, wild and free, then dying in the sun, her breath choking in a pool of blood. I resolved never again to shoot any living creature with a bow.

*

Even when you come to the end of bow hunting, you are, in a sense, just beginning. The blood-soaked hunting trail is, literally, endless. In Wyoming hundreds of eagles are shot from helicopters for—what else?—the hell of it. In the Great Lakes region, snowmobilers have a new sport—trapping wild animals, releasing them and then running them to death. In Maine, the Governor signs a law against shooting of bears— in cages. In Grand Junction, Colorado, a former Wildlife Services man, Paul Maxwell, can stand it no longer—he tells the story of a hunting "guide" who takes a mountain lion out of a cage, and when, seeking protection, it runs under an automobile the hunters shoot it there. In New York, Dick Cavett on his television program tells another story—this of two men who, having caught their mountain lion, beat it to death. In Chicago, Bob Cromie writes in his Chicago *Tribune* column about fox hunting and beagling. "It's a damn healthy thing to do," Morgan Wing, president of the National Beagle Club of America is quoted as saying. And Wing goes on, "Beagling is great family fun." Writes Cromie, "If any member of *my* family considered it 'great fun' to watch an animal be torn to pieces, I'd send him to the nearest shrink."

In the South, they still fancy "coon-on-a-log." In this, raccoons are chained or roped on logs or on kegs and set upon, in relays, by dogs. But just plain "cooning" is enough. Of all hunting cruelty, this may well be the worst—the one which probably comes closest to what Dr. Karl Menninger has called "an erotic, sadistic motivation." Witness this account by Herb Phipps in the October, 1972, *Together Magazine*:

> Since raccoon hunting with hounds was popular among the boys of the region—and because I didn't want to appear different—I accepted a hunting invitation from two acquaintances.
>
> We hadn't been in the woods long when the two hounds had treed a large coon. One of the boys dislodged it with a noncrippling shot. Instantly the dogs charged and knocked the coon on his back. But the ripping power of its sharp claws and teeth caused the hounds—each twice the coon's 20-pound weight—to bound back.
>
> As the dogs continued a dash-in, dash-out attack, all three animals became bloody from numerous wounds. I was amazed by the courage and fighting skill of the coon and wished I could help it. I suppressed an urge to protest, aware that it would only cause me to be laughed at for being sissy and softhearted.
>
> Blood blinded one of the dogs and he was withdrawn. The other was near exhaustion and defeat. Then one of my companions hurled a hatchet at the coon, intending to split its head. Missing its mark, the weapon chopped off two hind toes.
>
> As the coon tried to escape up a nearby tree, it was shot down again. After a few wobbly steps its hind legs collapsed, and the dog was at its throat. With the remaining strength in its battered body, the dying coon placed its front paws on the dog's head and tried to push it away.
>
> I turned home feeling sick. I resented it when my father asked about the hunt. "We got one coon," I said.

If one cannot save, from the worst kind of hunting torture, such a bright, interesting, friendly, charming creature as the raccoon, what chance is there to save the warthog? Mr. Phipps' article was entitled, "The Day I Stopped Hunting." It is good advice, and it has been repeated countless times by countless other ex-hunters—Edmund Gilligan in *The Saturday Evening Post*, A. Kulik in *The Reader's Digest*, Robb Sagendorf in *The Old Farmer's Almanac*. But even hundreds, even thousands, of hunters quitting will not get the job done quickly. It will take millions and it will take time.*

Meanwhile, there are hopeful signs. At the 1974 convention of the National Wildlife Federation, Thomas Kimball himself, executive vice president, admitted not only that the number of hunters in his membership had dropped, but also that 72 percent of his membership did not hunt. In 1966, he reminded the hunters, the percentage that did not hunt had been only 59 percent. "These statistics prove," he said, "that there is a definite trend toward the non-consumptive use of wildlife. The time is at hand," he went on, "for the formulation and implementation of programs that attract *all* conservationists." And, although the convention's program, under the ten minutes allotted to the subject "Social—Ethics and Morality," was left blank, and there was no speaker listed, at the last moment there was indeed a speaker. He turned out to be Robert E. Le Resche, who was, of all things, a "game biologist," who

---

* In 1974, at a meeting of California's newly formed Wildlife Advisory Committee, which includes both hunters and non-hunters and which is one of the very few efforts anywhere to see that wildlife be represented by something besides hunters, this writer asked the regional head of the California Fish & Game Department about his statement that out of the department's $28,000,000 total budget, three-quarters of it went for non-game animals. I told him that by my figures that came to $21,000,000, and I asked him what non-game animals he was protecting with it. After a very long pause he managed to come up with just two—the Big Horn Sheep and the Tule Elk. We have already seen what kind of protection the Big Horn Sheep were receiving. As for the 500 Tule Elk remaining, their half of the budget came by my figuring to $21,000 per elk—enough to set each one of them up on Park Avenue. And yet I had just left Washington, D.C., where Beula Edmiston, of the Tule Elk Committee, the real protectors of that great little animal, had been fighting for a Tule Elk refuge. Ray Arnett, head of the California Fish & Game, had been there too. He had testified *against* the refuge.

worked for, of all offices, the Department of Fish and Game, and who came from, of all places, Alaska. Mr. Le Resche gave a speech which indicated from the very outset that it was going to be something very different. "I have been assured," he said, "by the organizers of this meeting that there is no relevance to the fact that they had to go all the way to Alaska to find someone to speak on ethics for ten minutes." Then Mr. Le Resche proceeded to the part of this talk which he called "To the Hunter":

> First—sit down with yourself sometime soon and decide, "What *are* my own personal ethics regarding hunting and conservation?" That question is more difficult to answer than you might think, but the answer will come. Then—*consciously* stick to these ethics, whether in a crowd or in the wilderness 100 miles from the nearest human. How many of you have—just once—chased an animal with a snowmachine? Hazed one with an aircraft? Failed to kill cleanly and humanely? Left just a bit of edible meat in the field? Hunted a species we knew little about? Forgotten for a moment that hunting is much more than killing something and getting home fast? Ethics have a way of eroding very quickly at the tiniest breech.
>
> Once you know your principles and follow them yourself, talk about them. Don't ignore acts by other "hunters" that are wrong in your eyes. You can't make that fellow who just shot from the road share your ethics, but you *can* let him know you find his behavior offensive. Have an opinion; anti-hunters certainly do.
>
> Second—don't be defensive about hunting. Don't say "it isn't any worse than letting animals starve," or "the game can take it." . . . As a corollary, never get into a position where you defend *all* hunting. Admit that there *are* some slobs who hunt (there are also slobs who belong to anti-hunting groups), and make it plain you disapprove of them as much as anyone does. Many practices lumped

in the public's mind under "sport hunting" *are* despicable.

Third—accept the fact that anti-hunters are sincere, that many people are actually made ill by the sight or even the thought of a dead wild animal. They don't deserve to be written off as "kooks" any more than do hunters. So have some concern for the sensibilities of others. Take them seriously and try to understand them. Practically translated this means asking what do I gain by leaving a gut-pile in view of the road, by tying a bloody deer carcass on the hood of my car, by carrying an easy rider gun rack full of loaded firearms in plain view on my pickup? These acts are nothing less than gross disrespect for the sincere feelings of others.

Fourth—acknowledge, personally and as a group, that there are other legitimate uses of wildlife than hunting, and support them where appropriate. Never forget that wildlife belongs to all the people and not just to hunters.

At the same meeting, the same A. Starker Leopold who at an earlier meeting had sounded a first warning now added a second. "The hunting establishment," he said, "has got to learn to bend or it's going to break. The public at large has recently discovered wildlife. There is no room in the Fish and Game Departments for this."

Even more jarring to the hunters was the report of Dale L. Shaw, of the Colorado State Forestry Service. "Sport hunting of wild animals," he said, "has almost overnight become unacceptable to increasing numbers of people in our society." Mr. Shaw reported he had sent a questionnaire to 937 students in ten colleges and universities. He found by far the majority were against sport hunting, even those from the rural areas. Their five major reasons were (1) sport hunting endangers some species, (2) they didn't believe in trophy hunting, (3) they didn't believe in killing for pleasure or sport, (4) too much game went to waste and (5) too many hunters were game hogs.

The two major influences, Mr. Shaw stated, were (1) general philosophy and (2) personal experience with hunters. Their "reasons for being against" were, in a tie for first place, "TV" and "personal experience." After that came "parents" and then "movies and magazines." The TV shows which, he said, most influenced them to be against hunting were (1) *Wild Kingdom,* (2) *The American Sportsman,* (3) clubbing-of-seals newsreel, (4) *National Geographic* specials, (5) *The Wonderful World of Disney* and (6) Jacques Cousteau specials. The movies which most influenced them against were (1) *Bless the Beasts and Children,* (2) Disney wildlife movies, (3) *Born Free,* (4) *Deliverance* and (5) *Alaskan Safari.*

The fact that *Alaskan Safari* was a pro-hunting film but influenced these students against hunting was an interesting note —so was, in the same way, on the TV list, *The American Sportsman.* But what was perhaps most interesting in this reverse regard was the three magazines that they listed as having been most responsible for turning them off hunting. These were, in order, *Sports Afield, Field & Stream* and *Outdoor Life.*

II: For Money

Real People Wear
Fake Furs

A few years ago something called The Fur Information and Fashion Council put out a promotion brochure. It was entitled *The Softest Touch*. Its text began as follows:

> A fur garment is like a beauty salon. The lady who goes in comes out different. She not only looks different, but *feels* it.
>
> She enters restaurants, living rooms, department stores and PTA meetings with the quiet, knowing confidence that radiates from her luxurious fur garment. . . .
>
> She presides over a station-wagon full of howling Brownies with the calm that comes only to one who knows that every eye at the traffic light is on the little fur cardigan topping her tweeds.

Howling Brownies aside, today that lady might have something besides the "quiet, knowing confidence" and the "calm." The eyes might be on her fur, all right, but for every eye of approval there would be at least one and probably more of something very different. In Boston, not long ago, a woman I know started out for a luncheon date wearing a fur. At the door, she had the misfortune to be stopped, and sternly, by her outward-bound teenage son. He gave his mother and her coat short shrift. "Mom," he said, "it just *had* to look better on the original owner." Mercifully on her way, the woman thought she had clear sailing. Not a chance. Right on the sidewalk, she was stopped by an animal-minded friend. "Tell me," the latter asked, actually fingering her coat, "what kind of an animal was that? I mean, of course," she added, "before it was killed." By the time the woman reached her destination, she was a nervous wreck. Her lunch, however, turned out to be with another woman who was also wearing a fur. For a moment she could relax. But the relaxation—for both women —was short-lived. A man, a total stranger, walked by their table on the way out. "Why," he asked quietly, "don't you wear each other?"

Such an experience is not unusual anywhere in the country today—or indeed around the world. Near Boston, in Cambridge, in Harvard Square, a group of Harvard students fall in behind a woman in a fur coat. "Tramp," they say. Then, in unison and in step, they sound off. "Tramp, tramp, tramp." In Rome, Gina Lollobrigida sports a full-length tiger coat made out of the skins of ten tigers. Considering the matching process involved, she has on her back, it is estimated, one-tenth of all that species of tiger left in the world. Miss Lollobrigida is amazed at the protests. "They were dead," she says, "when I got them." So, replies a nonfan, is she—from the neck up.

In Chicago, the Kroehler Manufacturing Company, largest manufacturer of household effects in the world, announces that it will no longer make *furniture* out of fur. In Los Angeles, on the other hand, in Bel Air, California, basketball star Wilt Chamberlain decorates two rooms of his new mansion with just wolf muzzles. "I bought seventeen thousand of them," he explains proudly, "from some Alaskan bounty hunters." He claimed he bought all the wolves killed in Alaska in 1964, which were then kept in cold storage. And Mr. Chamberlain is not the only athlete. Joe Namath appears in an elegant mink. "See," he says, grinning, "double-breasted." His apartment, too, is liberally befurred. Boxer Joe Frazier sports— what else?—a white mink. Pitcher Tom Seaver, a mountain lion. "It has," he says, "an air of masculinity." In the same vein *Playboy* publisher Hugh Hefner shows reporters the covering on the elliptical bed in his private DC-9 airplane. The spread, six by nine feet, is Tasmanian opossum. "They didn't," he says smiling, "die in vain." The reporter, wondering if Hefner didn't protest too much, didn't smile. And, in San Francisco, animal worker Virginia Handley has a formidable run-in with an interior decorator whose office is covered with fur. "You animal nuts," he says sarcastically, "have a problem." "So," she replies, "do you—which is probably why you got into the business in the first place."

In London, Richard Burton, who with his then wife, Elizabeth Taylor, already owns two of the most expensive matching furs in the world, also buys her a $125,000 Russian sable but, in short order, he is sorry. "Elizabeth has taken the pledge," he says, "and I wouldn't mind if she sold them all." Celebrities as diverse as Princess Grace of Monaco and Mae West condemn wild fur. "I cannot stand," says Princess Grace, "the idea that wild animals can be killed to satisfy fashion." Says Mae West, "I love all animals. I haven't bought a fur since 1956." Yet in New York Mayor Lindsay declares Fur Festival Week. In the fur district, buttons appear. "Animals Have Rights, Too," reads one. "Boycott Fur-Wearing People," reads another. "You eat meat, don't you?" shouts a fur worker. "You wear shoes." "Yes," replies an animal woman, "and I work for humane slaughter. Furs aren't even slaughtered— they're tortured."

Mr. and Mrs. Samuel Newhouse, he the owner of *Vogue*
and a large number of newspapers, she the owner of a brand-
new lynx coat, arrive at a New York cocktail party. Both are
so criticized that they shortly leave. On the other hand, etiquet-
teer Amy Vanderbilt would say they have done nothing wrong.
"I have absolutely no compunction," she says, "about wearing
home grown furs." But Violet Porte, a Glenoit Mills executive,
has such compunction. "If I were the richest woman in the
world," she says, "I wouldn't want to kill an animal to put
fur on my back." To this position, Mrs. Francine Farkas,
wife of the owner and fashion director of Alexander's Department Stores, has perhaps the most extraordinary answer. "We
aren't killing," she says, "any animals that aren't *supposed* to
be killed."

"Question," asks an animal-society brochure. "If you see
a woman in a seal coat, what should you do?" "Answer: Throw
her a fish."

Say the furriers, "Furs are warm, furs are smart, furs are
fun." Say the animal people, "Furs are wrong, furs are ugly,
furs are cruel."

*

The furor over fur is a comparatively new story. But the
use of fur itself goes back to caveman days. Indeed, the
brochure *The Softest Touch* entitles its "history" of furs "From
Caveman to Cape-Stole":

> Of the few customs we retain from our primitive fore-
> bears, covering ourselves with soft, warm, lustrous animal
> pelts is one.
> The caveman probably started the fashion because he
> had all those skins lying around from past meals. Besides,
> he must have been chilly.

The point at which furs shifted from necessity to luxury isn't certain, but we do know that fur was a valuable ornament in just about every civilization in recorded history.

To the Chinese of 3,500 years ago, fur was a definite badge of esteem. Greek warriors were decorated from the furs they hauled home from the wars. Roman nobles picked up the fur habit along with other trappings of gracious living from the Greeks.

Furs really got their boost as the prime status symbol in medieval Europe. Italian Cardinals wore ermine as a symbol of purity.

It was some jump from Italian Cardinals to American chorus girls, and somehow the "purity" seems to have fallen by the wayside. In any case, in America, once upon a time, the dream of every girl was to own a fur coat. To the little girl dressing up, Mother's mink was second only to Mother's milk. The society woman's bank account, or rather that of her husband, was effectively broadcast by the length and quality of—well, her broadtail. The virtue of the Ziegfeld girl, and later the Hollywood starlet—or, rather, the lack of same—was measured in mink. Farther back, in Indian and early trapper days, fur literally was money. The very first company on the North American continent, chartered in 1670 by King Charles II to his uncle, Prince Rupert, was a fur company—its name, "The Company of Gentlemen and Adventurers Trading into Hudson's Bay." America's first millionaire was a furrier— John Jacob Astor—the man for whom, on his death, the word "millionaire" was first coined.

The death of the thousands, if not millions, of animals on which Mr. Astor's fortune was built was not so commemorative. I have read book after book about the early days of the fur industry and hardly one of them mentions anything about the death of the animals, let alone what kind of death. The vast majority of them met their deaths in the steel leghold trap or gin trap, as it is called in England—by far the most widely used trap there is. It is also the trap on which there have been no improvements—at least from the animals' point of view— since it was "perfected" by a seventeen-year-old trapper named Sewell Newhouse in upstate New York in 1823.

The leghold trap is deceptively simple in appearance and the principle on which it works is also simple. The "jaws" are opened by pressing on the spring, and the trap is set either on the trail of the animal, in its burrow or den, or close to a "bait" or strong-smelling lure. The triggering device is the "pan," which, when the animal steps on it, releases the spring so that the jaws snap closed on his leg. From that moment on, the best the animal can hope for is to chew off his leg—the trappers call this "wring-off"—so he can get away leaving just part of his leg behind. If he cannot do this—and indeed when he makes any movement of his paw between the jaws, the result is an immediate cutting, tearing and soring of flesh and even bone—the animal may remain in the trap for days on end, sometimes weeks, enduring every possible variety of fear, pain and suffering, until it finally dies either by exhaustion, starvation, cold, heat or the attacks of other animals, or is killed by the trapper.

There are various modifications of the leghold trap. These include the jump trap, a trap structurally modified so that it springs up as the animal is trapped and catches it higher up the leg (to prevent wring-off); the so-called stop-loss trap, also to prevent wring-off, in which an auxiliary guard on a trap moves high up on the body of an animal, holding him in such a position that he cannot gnaw himself free; the pole trap, a leghold set on a tree or pole, so that the animal caught falls with the trap and dangles from it and hence, by a paw, hangs to death; and finally, the spring pole trap, which is designed to prevent killing of the trapped animal by another animal, and hence the harming of the pelt. In this, the trap is attached to a bent sapling or pole in such a way that the animal is caught and the trap and the animal are hoisted up in the air and again the animal hangs by its trapped leg until it dies. A leghold trap is also used in a "drowning set," which is not a special trap but an ordinary leghold set beside deep water and weighted in order to pull the trapped animal, when it dives for its natural cover, down to final drowning. Used primarily for beaver, otter and muskrat, and claimed by the trappers to be relatively humane, the drowning set is far from always so. It can take a beaver, for example, twenty minutes to drown.

Canadian trapper Frank Conibear, of Victoria, British Columbia, the world's most famous trapper, has best told the story of the leghold trap. A tall, lean man, now in his seventies, he went to the Canadian West as a young man. He started trapping in an area so wild that for many years his was the only white family within five hundred miles. He learned both the ways of animals from Indians and the ways of Indians with animals. And, although it is popular today to believe that the Indians were basically kind to animals, this view is, in Conibear's opinion, as far from the truth as the opposite belief that Indians were nothing but bloodthirsty savages. Indian trappers, in Conibear's experience, were as indifferent to the sufferings of the animals as white trappers. As, in fact, Mr. Conibear himself then was. His traplines were from 150 to 200 miles long. In thirty-two years of trapping, he traveled these lines by foot and dogsled a distance more than four times around the world. But then, abruptly, he trapped no more. Instead, he decided to write about trapping. The first thing he wrote was a pamphlet. It was entitled *Testimony of a Trapper*:

> It is sometimes said, in defense of the use of the steel
> trap, that wildlife is cruel, and that the animals to whom
> the trap causes suffering, die a painful death anyway, by
> the teeth or claws of the predaceous species. But, great
> as the sufferings are of the animals that die a natural
> death, the sufferings occasioned by the common steel trap
> are incomparably greater. It is impossible for me to esti-
> mate the aggregate number of animals tortured by the
> common steel trap. In North America there are over
> 20,000,000 muskrats caught annually. Of these, about
> 4,000,000 are caught in the tidal marshes of Louisiana,
> where I understand, they cannot be drowned, so suffer
> cruelly. When one considers this, and the millions of
> other animals and birds as well, that endure the agonizing
> tortures of being trapped, the yearly sufferings in North
> America alone, must be in excess of those that any war
> in Europe has caused the human race. Will you contem-
> plate that statement a moment? I write this in 1946, and
> I recall the long Russian front, and other battlefields
> where millions of men were wounded, the bombing of
> German and British cities . . . and yet I think the annual
> sufferings of trapped animals in North America alone are
> greater than those caused by any war in Europe to man-
> kind, over an equal period of time.

After this extraordinary statement, Mr. Conibear's *Testimony* went on with personal stories of individual animals visited on his traplines. One of them is, ironically, the lynx—the
very animal chosen by the wife of the *Vogue* publisher:

> A lynx lives longer when caught in a trap than any
> other animal. I have known two to live for three weeks in
> traps and be alive when I got there, but they were very,
> very thin. The feet of the lynx are so large that unless it
> steps fairly in the middle of the trap, it is caught by only

one or two toes and, as the days go by, the jaws of the trap squeeze tighter till they separate the joints of the bone. Sometimes the sudden jerks of the lynx breaks the last shreds and it is free. By that time, the whole of the caught foot is usually frozen, so the lynx must die from a rotten foot. Of all the deaths caused by trapping, I think that from a foot thawing out and rotting out is the most awful.

Mr. Conibear also wrote of minks, martens, muskrats, foxes and fishers. He wrote of one animal which, from experience, he knew lived three or four days and then died of hunger or pain:

> The foot is lacerated, swollen and covered with blood. The stump of the leg above the trap is swollen four times its natural size, and frozen. The shoulder, too, is all swollen. When we skin it, we will find that all that area will be a mass of blood-colored, sickly gelatin-like substance, indicating the terrible suffering it has gone through before death released it.

He also wrote of what he called the "diabolical spring pole set":

> The animal dangles, struggling in the air, the whole of its weight hanging from one foot. There is probably no greater agony than this. Its sufferings are quite beyond power to describe.

Mr. Conibear resolved to build a better trap. There were many, many traps on the market—using a wide variety of principles and boasting a wide variety of names—names like the Two-Trigger, the Triple Clutch, the Stop-Thief, and the Diamond Walloper. Some were called "humane." But some, while they may have been "humane" from the point of view of the trapper in stopping his wring-off losses, they were hardly much more. Then there were the guard-type traps, such as the Victor Stoploss and the Blake and Lamb Holdfast. Mr. Conibear considered them all, as well as all the problems. Whatever type of quick-kill trap he came up with, it could not be either too expensive, too hard to conceal, too large, too bulky or too heavy—the trapper had to be able to carry it in pack baskets, dozens at a time. It took Mr. Conibear more than ten years—an eggbeater had given him the idea—and finally, in 1958, his "Conibear" was ready for market. It met all the requirements and yet in purpose, in design, in basic theory it was not only radically different from the leghold trap, it was different from any other trap up to that time invented. Instead of merely grasping the animal by the paw or leg, it was designed to kill the animal. And to do the job quickly—by breaking its neck or back. The trap could be set on land or under water. As the animal passed through it, square spring-powered steel-rod jaws closed with tremendous force on its neck or back. Within a minute, if not sooner, the animal was dead.

Although Mr. Conibear had built a better mousetrap—the principle of his trap was the same—the world did not beat a path to his door. Today, as then, the question may well be asked—why? If the trap is both practical and efficient, if it comes in different sizes for different animals, if it is not that much more expensive than the leghold—particularly when one considers the saving from escape or wring-off—if it is easily carried, easily set, easily concealed, and finally, if it can kill the animal without prolonged suffering—and all of these it is and does—why then have the furriers not seen to it that it be used and the leghold trap be, by law, banned?

The answer is not easy to come by—particularly since fourteen countries of the world, from Denmark to Chile and including England, Germany, Austria and even Norway, where there are vast numbers of furbearers, have banned the leghold trap. And particularly too since the Conibear trap has won steadily increasing acceptance in all areas. One reason is that in America perhaps more than any country in the world, any law about any protection for wildlife is difficult to come by. Another reason is that the furriers themselves have shown little concern—and not just as we have seen in the early days of their industry, but also up to and including today. The best that can be said for them is that they are, with their vast assortment of middlemen, auctioneers, dealers, commission houses, etc., as separated from the animal as a woman who orders *pâté de foie gras* is separated from the French farmer cruelly stuffing the goose. As far back as 1947, an Interior Department memorandum stated: "Although the raw fur supply is the backbone of the industry, the trade expresses little concern about the permanency of the future supply." A report on the fur industry by Argus Archives pointed out that the industry is made up almost entirely of small firms which operate on narrow profit margins. In 1949, for example, 98 percent of all fur manufacturers had a net worth of less than $100,000, and 90 percent a net of less than $50,000. The situation is not far different today. In 1972, for example, I had lunch with the two recognized deans of the New York fur business—men who had been in the business for forty years. Both admitted to me that they had never, in their entire lifetime, seen an animal in a trap. Nor, both added, did they wish to.

Most furriers, and many sincerely, believe that by far the largest number of their animals do not come from traps at all, but are ranch raised or farmed. Eighty percent is the figure most commonly cited. Unfortunately, although the majority of furriers think they are correct when they cite this figure—again an illustration of their separation from the animals—

such a figure is simply not true. In this country, only chinchilla and mink are widely ranched (some mink are trapped) and a few fox (by far the majority are trapped). A few beavers are ranch raised in Utah, but they are raised for breeding stock to be placed in the wild. *All* chinchilla are ranched—yes. But, from chinchilla on, the furrier believing the 80 percent figure is closer to 80 percent wrong. Again, it is true that, taking the most recent season's figures, over 9 million mink were ranch raised in this country, and only 230,000 wild mink were trapped. But these figures are for mink only. Five million muskrats were trapped. One and a half million raccoons were trapped. And in that same season, 1969–70, there were almost 2 million trapped of an animal almost nobody outside of the fur business has ever even heard of—and they were trapped in one state, Louisiana, alone.

The animal is the nutria or "coypu"—which, ironically, originally started out to be ranched. A native of South America, known as the South American beaver, he is a strange-looking fellow, something like a king-sized guinea pig, with teeth like Bugs Bunny and with front and back feet which don't match. His front feet, with four digits, are paws; his back, with five, are webbed. Brought over to Louisiana in the 1930's as a ranching experiment, a group of nutria were put in an "escape-proof" pen. However, during a hurricane, they did escape, and headed for the marshes. Ever since, in tremendous numbers—for their beautiful, extremely versatile pelts—they have been leghold trapped. In contrast, in Poland, nutria are not only ranched, but extremely successfully so— as many as a million a year.

The United States both traps more *different* animals than any other nation in the world, it also traps more animals in all. It traps, for example, 17 different "principal" furs—muskrat, nutria, mink, raccoon, fox, beaver, bobcat, badger, lynx, fisher, marten, weasel, skunk, opossum, coyote, otter and ring-tailed cat. And the majority of these in the cruel leghold. The United States in fact traps about 10 million animals every year—about twice as many as, for instance, Canada's 5 million. And with such figures it should be borne in mind that, for every animal trapped which is wanted for its fur, two others are not even used for any purpose. The trappers call them "trash," and this includes everything from birds and ducks to squirrels and porcupines. The total figure of trapped animals in the United States, therefore, is larger than *25 million per year*. Although some "fun furs" are ranched—blue fox, for example, is ranched in Russia, Scandinavia and Poland, and France alone ranches almost 200 million rabbits a year (albeit most of them for eating)—practically all the other "fun furs" are trapped, from coyote to opossum. In 1969–70, almost 200,000 foxes were trapped. The "crop" of wild foxes trapped in New York State alone in 1972 was worth over $2 million. And the State of New York, which gave no figures on its major trapping to the Department of the Interior's Fish and Wildlife Service, did favor them with three trapping distinctions—that of trapping 2,793 beavers, 875 fishers and 165 otters. Minnesota was the champion beaver butcherer with 20,400, followed by Wisconsin with 10,000 and Washington with 8,000. Louisiana was the No. 1 otter killer, with close to 7,000, while Wyoming won the bobcat race with over 3,000 and Kansas the coyote stakes with over 12,000. Although California trapped comparatively little beside 50,000 muskrat—only slightly more than 10,000 other animals in all—Michigan was the outstanding offender. It trapped more than 400,000 muskrat, let alone almost 4,000 skunks and even more than 2,000 weasels.

Furriers do not like such figures as these. They point to the relatively rare laws that ban the use of "sawtooth" traps or even the kind of law that forbids the leghold trapping of bears only a few states have such a law). Furriers are also likely to maintain that there are strict laws about visiting traps within each twenty-four-hour period. The actual fact is that only sixteen states have such laws and the twenty-four-hour period, while perhaps practical from the trappers' point of view, is hardly equally so to the imprisoned, tortured animal. Georgia and Tennessee allow thirty-six hours between visits and Nevada requires a trapper to visit his lines only once a week. The plain fact is that twenty-nine states, in all of which trapping occurs and all of which use the leghold trap, set no limit at all, and have no age limit for children trapping. Furthermore, even where there is a supposedly twenty-four-hour time limit, the statute is, as admitted by those supposed to enforce it, as a practical matter unenforceable. In few states can anyone even remember that anyone was prosecuted for a trapping violation —with the one strong exception of being prosecuted for taking an animal out of somebody else's trap.*

*

If from the beginning the furriers, where their trapping was concerned, walked by on the other side of the street, what about the humanitarians? Could they too overlook what, in

---

* Mrs. Era Zistel, the same who wrote in the *New York Sunday News Magazine* of the near impossibility of anyone attempting to be a Good Samaritan to a wild animal, found that trying to aid an animal "in distress" in a trap was a literal legal impossibility. "You are strictly forbidden," she wrote, "to do anything at all except, if you like, hang around to watch the animal suffer for anywhere from twenty-four to forty-eight hours, depending upon what zone you're in, because the traps, along with whatever he has caught, are the trapper's property, which you are not allowed to touch."

prolonged pain and suffering—in actual torture—was undoubtedly one of the very worst animal cruelties of all? They
did not. Indeed, when Henry Bergh, this country's first great
humanitarian and the man who would launch this country's
first animal protection society, New York's SPCA, needed
money for his plans, it was an elderly trapper who gave it to
him. The man was in a New York hospital, dying a slow death,
the same kind, he was reminded in his fitful dreams, he had
visited on so many animals, when, literally on his deathbed,
he summoned Bergh and gave him what was then a "fur
fortune" of $40,000. Although Bergh happily took the money
and later, after the trapper's death, sponsored prizes for the
invention of a more acceptable trap than the leghold, he did
relatively little else. Actually, to the end of his life, he saw
no incongruity in prosecuting horse and dog animal cruelty
dressed from head to toe in fur—from his Russian fur cap and
his fur-lined coat all the way to his fur-topped boots. Indeed,
often he was accompanied by Mrs. Bergh wearing a full-length
ermine—a coronation robe which took the incredible toll of
three hundred pelts.

For half a century, in fact, little was done about trapping or,
for that matter, any other wildlife cruelty. In 1925, however,
a man named Edward Breck entered the field. A romantic
adventurer who had been a spy in two wars and later a historian and diplomat, he witnessed, on a chance visit to Nova
Scotia, the lingering death of a black bear held for days between the spiked jaws of a forty-pound trap. Never would
Breck forget either the moans or the last agony of that animal.
And shortly after his trip back to his home in Washington,
D.C., he founded the National Anti-Steel Trap League. At
first the very idea of attempting to alleviate suffering in the
wild brought Breck and his League only ridicule. And at first

indeed his and his League's chief weapon seemed to have been poetry. One poem ran as follows:

> All night long, gnaw and gnaw,
> Come with me, lady, see what I saw.
>
> Only a beaver suffering pain.
> God! Take that sound out of my brain.
>
> A thing of the wilds—who cares how it dies?
> God! Take that sight out of my eyes.

Another, which had wider circulation, was called "A Paradox":

> 'Tis strange how women kneel in church and pray to God above,
> Confess small sins and chant a praise and sing that He is love;
> While coats of softly furred things upon their shoulders lie—
> Of timid things, of tortured things, that "take so long to die." . . .
>
> 'Tis strange to hear the organ peal—"Have mercy on us, Lord,"
> The benediction—peace to all—they bow with one accord
> While from stained windows fall the lights on furs so softly warm,
> Of timid things, of little things, that died in cold and storm.

Still a third, by F. F. Van de Water, was entitled "To a Fur":

> The steel jaws clamped and held him fast,
>   None marked his fright, none heard his cries.
> His struggles ceased; he lay at last
>   With wide, uncomprehending eyes,
> And watched the sky grow dark above
>   And watched the sunset turn to grey,
> And quaked in anguish while he strove
>   To gnaw the prisoned leg away.
> Then day came rosy from the east,
>   But still the steel jaws kept their hold,
> And no one watched the prisoned beast,
>   But fear and hunger, thirst and cold.
> Oppressed by pain, his dread grew numb,
>   Fright no more stirred his flagging breath.

> He longed, in vain, to see him come
>   The cruel hunter, bringing death.
> Then through the gloom that night came One
>   Who set the timid spirit free;
> "I know thine anguish, little son;
>   So once men held and tortured Me."

Such poetry, dated as it may seem today, nonetheless reached millions of people, and by the time the National Anti-Steel Trap League had ended its days, it had several signal victories to its credit. Perhaps the most important of these was that its literature had found its way all the way to western Canada and into the hands of Frank Conibear. "I may have started my work to develop a quick-kill trap," Mr. Conibear told me, "primarily to prevent wring-off. But I was not immune either to what I had myself borne witness or to the literature I received, particularly that of the National Anti-Steel Trap League. Before long, I realized I was working not just for the wring-off, but also to prevent cruelty." Besides winning over Mr. Conibear, the Anti-Steel Trap League could claim actual legal victories. Within the lifetime of the League, several states —the first two being South Carolina and Kentucky, with Massachusetts soon to follow—had passed anti-steel-trap laws. And even more remarkable was the fact that the Gibbs Company of Chester, Pennsylvania, itself then the largest steel-trap manufacturer in the world, had taken an advertisement against its own chief product. The advertisement read as follows:

> The common steel-trap (so-called) as it has been used in the capturing of animals is one of, if not the most, cruel devices that has ever been invented. Not one half enough has ever been said against it. Anyone who has seen animals with their teeth broken, cut, bleeding, dying of starvation, thirst and exposure, has wished for a means of overcoming it.

The Gibbs Company solution was to have attached to the trap itself a poison capsule. Unfortunately, this turned out, like all poisoning efforts before and since, to be no less cruel and, if anything, more so. But the Anti-Steel Trap League also received help from another quarter—the powerful pens of famed animal writers. Their literature particularly moved two of these. One was Ernest Thompson Seton, who wrote memorably of all animals, but particularly so about the brutally trapped otter. "The noblest little soul," Seton called him, "that ever went four-footed through the woods." Another writer reached was the late "Grey Owl." Born in England, a man whose real name was Archie Belaney—one can hardly blame him for wanting to change it—he left England at the age of eighteen and, in the Canadian northlands, turned his back on his past and totally adopted Indian dress and ways. Giving himself his new name, he became the world's best-known "Indian writer." He himself, in Canada, was an indefatigable trapper. However, when he fell in love with a beautiful Iroquois girl, Anahareo, he changed. Anahareo too, ironically, had been a trapper, but as Lovat Dickson recalls in *Wilderness Man,* just as it was the lynx that changed Conibear so it was a lynx that changed Anahareo:

> She had come upon a lynx in a trap she had set some ten days before. The weather had not been cold enough to put him out of his misery. He had gnawed at his trapped paw until the bones were bare of flesh. Then hunger had driven him, dragging the trap to the limit of the chain, he had stripped the bark off every tree; and in the end he had kept himself alive by eating snow. He looked at her, when she came, as a rescuer, not as the one who would extinguish the spark of life he had been desperately trying to preserve. She would have let him go, but he was in too poor condition. He could barely crawl.

Quickly she dispatched him. But this was the end. She made up her mind that she would never set another trap.

Some days later, when her husband was still trapping, they came upon a female beaver who had been killed in a trap. They were about to leave when two small heads appeared above the water. At Anahareo's urging, Grey Owl rescued them and, after they had taken them home, those two beaver kittens provided the final impetus for Grey Owl's change from pro-trapper to anti-trapper. He wrote movingly of

> their almost childlike intimacies and murmurings of affection, their rollicking good fellowship with not only each other but ourselves, their keen awareness, their air of knowing what it was all about [seemed] like little folk from some other planet, whose language we could not quite yet understand. To kill such creatures seemed monstrous. I would do no more of it.

From that time on, Grey Owl became a powerful voice for the voiceless. But, to the end of his days, he wrote most often of the animal about whose trapping he felt most strongly:

> In spite of his clever devices for protection, the beaver, by the very nature of his work, signs his own death warrant. The evidences of his wisdom and industry, for which he is so lauded, have been, after all, only sign-posts on the road to extinction. Everywhere his bright new stumps show up. His graded trails, where they enter the water, form ideal sets for traps, and he can be laid in wait for and shot in his canals. Even with six feet of snow blanketing the winter forest, it can easily be discovered whether a beaver-house is occupied or not, by digging some snow off the top of the house and exposing the large hollow space melted by exhalations from within. The store of feed so carefully put by may prove his undoing, and he be caught near it by a skillfully placed trap. Surely he

merits a better fate than this, that he should drown miserably three feet from his companions and his empty bed, whilst his body lies there until claimed by the hunter, later to pass, on the toboggan on its way to the hungry maw of the city, the home he worked so hard to build, the quiet and peace of the little pond that knew him and that he loved so well.

*

Possibly the young lady whose grandfather the day before yesterday wore a beaver hat, whose mother draped herself in a beaver coat and who herself is considering a "fun beaver fur" should reread once more those words of the late Grey Owl. But Grey Owl, the reformed trapper, knew well what any reformer in the fur business was up against. Not just the furriers but the trappers themselves. "A man," Grey Owl once wrote, "who has successfully overcome the difficulties and endured the privations of the trapline can no more quit it than a confirmed gambler can leave his game."

And, where the furriers ignore the cruelty involved, the trappers simply take it in stride. The trapper, indeed, not only does not feel he is doing anything wrong, he goes a step further and feels he is a vital part of a great American tradition. Davy Crockett was a trapper. Daniel Boone was a trapper. Even today the Department of Commerce has estimated that there are over a million trappers. My estimate would be less than a tenth of that. But neither estimate is based on anything concrete. Some states do not require any trapping license. Others do not distinguish between hunting and trapping licenses. And almost all allow trapping by minors—of literally any age— without any license at all. How many trappers regard themselves as professional trappers is unknown, but it is a tiny fraction that make a living from it. A study made some years ago in

Colorado listed the figure at one percent. The same study, incidentally, listed "Students" at 26.4 percent of that total.

One thing is certain. Most trapping in the United States is done in rural areas or in communities whose rural character is giving way to suburban life. "Trappers with few exceptions," says an Argus Archives study, "are under-educated and under-employed." The report also emphasized that even fur prices mean little to them. A study of the average prices received for pelts would seem to bear this out. Taking figures for the 1969–70 trapping season, for example, in only seventeen states did muskrat, by far the most-often-trapped animal, bring more than $1 a skin—and in those states, not much more. The nutria, second largest in numbers of the trapped animals, rare as he is outside of Louisiana, brought nowhere more than $2. The raccoon, third on the list, averaged just $2. Meanwhile, in the case of the fourth and fifth animals on the list, the mink and the fox, the prices varied from, for mink, $11.40 in North Dakota to $2 in Oklahoma, and for fox, $8 in Minnesota to $3.99 (apparently a ·sale) in Arkansas. Elsewhere, if there were occasionally such prices as $32 and $27 for, respectively, an otter and a lynx in the State of Washington, there were also such prices as 49 cents for a skunk in South Dakota and, for an opossum in Michigan, exactly 5 cents. "Prices," declared W. J. Hamilton, professor of zoology at Cornell, "do not dictate the routine of the trapper. The lad or farmer in the small towns of New York and elsewhere traps for sport."

To talk to the trappers and read their trapping manuals is in itself an education in lack of education. "Mink trapping was introduced to me," says Reg Baird, "when at the age of seven one of my grandfathers took me back on the local brook and set two mink traps for me. My other grandfather always went along with me to tend the traps. My mother thought I was too young to be on the brook alone. How well I remember coming home, with water sloshing out of both boots, proudly carrying my first muskrat by the tail."

"I started trapping beaver with my Dad," states Joe Misizka, "when I was eleven years old. I have always become more interested in it every year since, not only because it is a great sport but also because of the side money a person can make."

"On the next visit to the line," writes "Major" Paul Peck, "with my 11-year-old son, Brad, one of the snares yielded a nice red fox. He had a front leg in the snare in addition to his neck, and was pretty lively."

Anyone who has ever seen any animal in a snare—a slow and horribly cruel strangulation process—must certainly give the "Major" credit for understatement, if not understanding. If there is anything that is even more cruel than a leghold trap, it has got to be the snare. A wire noose which is supposedly pulled tighter and tighter around the animal's neck as he struggles, it is actually the most fiendish instrument of torture possible to devise. Because, as the noose tightens more and more, the animal has less and less ability to struggle. One last strong pull and he could relatively rapidly strangle himself, but by that time he's too weak to do this and the wire gradually, with his increasingly feeble efforts, sinks ever deeper into his neck. If, indeed, he is lucky enough to be caught by the neck in the first place and not another area, such as the shoulder, stomach or anywhere else. Then his sufferings can be literally beyond description.

Such cruelties are to the trapper all in the day's work—or rather, we almost forgot, "sport." Pat Sedlak in *The Schoolboy Trapper*, is particularly adamant about the great trapping tradition. "I was born a trapper," he writes. "I live a trapper, I shall die a trapper." He adds, for good measure, a story of his youth:

> Coon trapping is simple. I always remember the first one caught many years ago, in a baited covey pen set for skunk. The set was made close to a trout stream. When first seeing the animal, it remained motionless and appeared to be watching me all the time. Trying to kill it with a club, I quickly learned they put up a very good fight and aren't so easy to kill.

The killing of the animals after they are trapped seems to present the trappers with so many problems that one wonders just how much experience they have had with any kind of killing—or if, in fact, their traps are so rarely visited that the animals are almost always already dead. In any case, the late E. J. Daley, of Odgensburg, N.Y., who has been described as "the undisputed dean of New York State trapping," wrote shortly before his death in *Fur-Fish-Game* Magazine what he apparently regarded as the best way to kill a fox:

> To properly kill a fox at a set, strike a light blow on the back of the neck, close to the ear, with a trowel or handle of a belt axe, just hard enough to knock the fox off his feet and stun him. Then stand on him just back of the front legs several minutes, and by so doing you will not have blood in his fur.

After such a helpful hint, I was curious to look further in the magazine. A man from Washington State asked a question. "It is illegal," he wrote, "to shoot fur animals in my state. And I would like to know how to kill the larger animals without getting hurt." He was answered as follows:

> I think you will find out it is not illegal to shoot an animal in a trap, as courts have ruled that once a trapper

has an animal in a trap, the state has lost all jurisdiction over it, and that it can be killed in any manner. However, any animal can be killed with a baseball club or the side of an axe.

The thought of what child trappers have done to animals so helplessly in their power would seem enough to end the monstrous business once and for all. Curiously, however, if the trappers are particularly vociferous about one specific thing it is what they regard as the inalienable right of children to trap. Fred Space, for example, former head of the New Jersey Fish and Game Council, recently exonerated such children from all the problems of today's youth. "These kids," he said, "aren't the ones causing all the trouble. They aren't hippies or radicals. They aren't the kind who go to those jam sessions and take dope and run around naked."

Nakedness aside, on the other hand, psychologist Henry Greenberg, testifying in Washington at the hearings for a bill to protect ocean mammals, declared that if he were the lawyer for the children who, in 1971, brutally slaughtered animals in a zoo in Harrison, New York—children who afterward admitted they were trappers—he would have the children speak on the witness stand as follows:

> It was okay for us to trap the muskrats and trap squirrels and other small animals because, after all, our parents shoot them and trap them and kill them. . . . We are just trapping and killing. Nobody bothered us about it. We killed the woodchuck all the time.
>
> So, what we did, we felt like doing something else. And we went into the zoo and we hacked up eleven rabbits and some pigeons and some chickens and we took our tokens—you know, the rabbit ears and the various other parts of the animal—and we wear them as our badges in the same way our adult models have animal heads on the mantle and wear fur coats.

Our own U.S. Government, as might be expected, puts its own good outdoor-keeping seal of approval on children's trapping. The Department of the Interior, under one of its ironically named "Conservation Notes," publishes a pamphlet entitled *Trapping Tips for Young Trappers.* "Trapping of fur-bearing animals for wholesome, outdoor recreation," this reads, "and as a source of additional income for fine youngsters, has been popular since the founding of our Country. Trapping as a means of removing a surplus is not unlike hunting—a deep-seated American tradition." Nowhere in the whole pamphlet is there the slightest criticism of this "wholesomeness"—the only injunction is to keep at it. "Anyone can set a trap," the pamphlet says, "but that doesn't make you a trapper. The expert trapper develops a 'feel' for the animal."

"Feel," in the sense, of course, of where to find it, and therefore feel, presumably, as opposed to feeling. One can only assume that very few people who are not trappers have ever written for such a pamphlet. But the U.S. Government is not alone. New York State, for example, lists under "4-H Events" and beside a picture of a beaver the heading "Interested in Trapping?" Underneath are the lines "Ever thought about trapping? Like to know more about it? Send in the coupon on page 4. If we have fifteen or more 4-H members and leaders who are interested, we will set up a trapping workshop in early March at a local Fish and Game club." And the Cooperative Extension Service of Ohio State University goes even further. It publishes a "4-H Project Book" entitled *Muskrat Trapping.* The "Introduction" quickly moves into high, come-on style:

> Have you ever dreamed you were Daniel Boone or wished you could have been around during the frontier days even if only for a short period of time? Most youth who enjoy the out of doors probably have dreamed such dreams.

Trapping is one of the few sports left today that can bring a boy as close to nature as in the frontier days. Trapping is a fine type of recreation that promotes physical fitness and can provide the successful trapper with spending money or a start toward a college education. A boy trapping in a stream abundant with fur animals can easily advance from catches worth a few dollars the first year to well over $50.00 after a year or two of experience.

Trapping is also exciting! Waiting for the first morning's catch can be just as exciting as a four year old waiting to look under the Christmas tree on Christmas morning.

From the 4-H Club! It is hard to think of any comment at all. As for people who are against trapping—against sport trapping, that is, let alone fur trapping—these, to the trappers are the "no killums," the "no trappums," the "nature no-no's," etc. "Naturally," says Pat Sedlak, again in *The Schoolboy Trapper,* "in trapping fur-bearing animals there will always be a certain amount of suffering. This is likewise true in hunting, fishing and shooting—in motoring, camping and boating—and just plain living." In a booklet with the title *Spage Age Beaver and Otter Trapping,* John Clauser first tells with pride a story of having caught a beaver with three feet "freshly trapped off." "A one legger!" he exclaims. Then he firmly handles the problem of the "no trappums." "Some people," he writes, "actually believe that trappers are cruel. Some think that animals have souls. Neither is true."

One is tempted to remind Mr. Clauser that if he, in the future, is going to some fine hereafter—for which the evidence so far would seem to be lacking—and that the animal in question is not, then that alone might be reason enough to give the animal a better break in the one life he does have. In any case, Mr. Clauser does not deserve the last word on the subject. That honor would be better reserved for another trapper. The Reverend Roy Johnson, of Hammond, New York, not only managed in his pamphlet, *Trapline Ramblings,* to combine a sermon on evolution with directions for setting leghold traps, he also managed a memorable discussion of the matter of animal souls. "If a man beats his wife every day," he writes, "she suffers because she has an immortal soul. But if he beats his hound-dog, it may yelp some but it won't suffer because it has no soul and no consciousness." And then, just as the humanitarians have in their poems invoked the Almighty, so, in his pamphlet does Reverend-Trapper Johnson:

> I would like to acknowledge God as my partner on the trapline and in all of life. Some of the catches would never have been made without His wisdom, help and strength. I said, "Lord, it is nothing with You to put a wolf in each trap the same night, if it pleases You; sure enough, one morning there was a triple catch. The muskrat catch last spring was one of the largest in the area caught with practically no Sunday trapping. Again, God must receive the glory.

*

Just how long this Mexican standoff—between the humanitarians on the one side and the furriers and trappers on the other—might have continued will never be known. Because something happened that neither side, apparently, had ever envisioned. All of a sudden, it seemed, the world started running out of animals. Actually, of course, it was not suddenly. Centuries of overhunting, overtrapping, and over-everything—from the overhunting of the over-rich to overpopulation and the overpressure on land by the underdeveloped countries, contributed. But the final, horrifying animal Armageddon was caused primarily by the market hunters and poachers working for the fur, leather and even trinket trade. Much of the time the new "modern" poachers didn't even bother to shoot the animals or, for that matter, trap them. Instead, they speared them, blowgunned them, poison-darted them, and even boomeranged them. They hamstrung them and cut them down with axes. They ran whole herds down with long wires stretched between high-powered vehicles. They poisoned waterholes and, with the ingenuity of army engineers, they ambushed them, snared them, deadfall-trapped them and blew them up with mines and grenades. Even after the African preserves, reserves, sanctuaries and parks had been set up, this poaching continued at such a sickening rate that even today, as this is written, not a single elephant, let alone any other animal, is safe anywhere in Africa. Walking around as he does, with thousands of dollars of ivory on him, his fate is all but sealed—unless man, black man as well as white man, unites to protect him.

The high-water mark of the animal Armageddon was perhaps the advertisement which appeared in the *New York Times* in 1966:

> UNTAMED . . . The Snow Leopard. Provocatively dangerous/Uninhibited. A mankiller. Born free in the wild whiteness of the high Himalayas, only to be snared as part of the captivating new fur collection by S. Breslin Baker. Styled and shaped in a one-of-a-kindness to bring out the animal instinct in you. Call Mr. Baker for your private showing.

At the time that advertisement was published, with a photograph of a model draped with several snow leopard skins, there were, in the judgment of experts, in the whole world exactly 249 snow leopards left. "The Snow Leopard advertisement," wrote William Conway, director of the New York Zoological

Society, "unabashedly used the word 'snared' to account for the capture of the snow leopard, and I doubt that a 'quick kill' snare has ever been invented."

And, if the endangered-leopard crisis could make even the New York Zoological Society for once lean toward the "protective" as against the "management" side, it could also work other miracles. Overnight, it seemed, this crisis swept through all persuasions of animal interest. Big-game hunters became little-game hunters. Trophies on the wall became museum candidates. In the furor over fur, even the poetry of the humanitarians changed tone. No longer were there sad little poems invoking the deity. Instead, the poems rang with fury—witness Vernon Bartlett's lines in *Defenders of Wildlife News*:

> Once, in a moment of great generosity,
> God has shown to me
> A leopard running free.
> How then could He expect of me,
> Born without His tolerance, calmly to see
> Those women, those bloody awful women,
> Dressed up in leopard skins, sitting down to tea.

The first of the furriers to renounce the use of endangered species was Jacques Kaplan of New York. "I have stopped selling," he declared, "all the spotted cats." Others, however, waited—to see, painfully literally, which way the cat jumped. "When and if the time comes that an embargo is placed by law," said fur designer Robert Roberts, "we will gladly stop making jungle fur coats."

The time came. The Federal Endangered Species Act named 247 individual animal species which could no longer be imported into the U.S., dead or alive, skinned or unskinned. And, when the Department of the Interior inexcusably put whole species on the list, rather than individual species, New

York went further. Its famed Mason Bill made it a crime to sell, within the state, such a skin. Other states followed with similar laws. The furriers first fought these laws every step of the way—then, even after they were passed, refused to abide by the spirit and often even begged the letter of the law. Saks Fifth Avenue, for example, sold wolf coats. One mid-day there appeared outside Saks, right on Fifth Avenue, a real live wolf. "Our wolf," said The Fund for Animals sign, "at your door." On the other hand, when, in Madrid, designer José María Pasqual was asked where he got his leopard coats, he was surprised. "Do-gooders scream about the extinction of these animals," he said, "but you can buy the pelts anywhere." He was right. Between 1968 and 1970, according to the Interior Department's own figures, the fur industry imported into this country over 18,000 leopard skins, as well as 31,105 jaguar skins and the incredible total of 349,680 ocelot skins.

The question now was, who would wear them? Ostensibly, at least, denied the use of endangered furs, the furriers embarked on a campaign of making not just coats and jackets out of fur but virtually everything else, from rugs and furniture up to eyebrows out of fur. It was a desperation effort—the high tide of the so-called "fun furs"—the "fun" of the animal in the leghold trap, of course, being conveniently forgotten. Their advertisements, in that summer of '69, featured everything from "real" fox heads to mink "mice"—pins in the shape of mice made of real mink. There were belts consisting of animal heads biting their own tails. "I *love* fur buttons," said the designer Giorgio di Sant' Angelo, who was himself described, in one writeup of his collection, as "the tawny blond Florentine who moves like a lithe cat." "I remember my mother," he said, "with all her martens full of tails."

One furrier featured, as a whole room decoration, "squirrel

rump"—"running," he emphasized, "all the way up the wall."
A columnist suggested first rumping him and then doing likewise. New York *Post* fashion writer Ruth Preston summed
up that summer's collections:

> With so many furs verboten, the variety available
> should be shrinking. Not so. Necessity has made furriers
> more inventive than ever.
> Already, in just the first few days of the fall opening,
> houses like Ritter Brothers, Ben Kahn and Alixandre
> have paraded fox streaked and spotted to look like lynx,
> badgers sliced thin and mounted on suede stripping to
> look like feathers for a fun fur that's charming, and a new
> mink mutation—some call it Snow Top, others Sand
> Drift—that's frosted a tawny beige-grey—as if the animal
> were a worrier.

After these efforts one furrier, "jokingly," it was said by another writer, noted that "any minute somebody would make
a coat out of baranduki crotches." Baranduki, it was helpfully
explained, was chipmunk. The writer continued, "At Barlan's,
coats were made of flanks, tails, and paws, and in one instance
it was specified that front paws were used." Jacques Kaplan,
the same who had been the first to renounce the use of endangered species, was given the honor of a whole individual
writeup in the *New York Times* by Angela Taylor:

> Tarzan-of-the-apes monkey, dappled hamster, mink
> pieced from heads or mink piled with sable—by next fall,
> a woman will be able to wrap herself in virtually every
> fur except mouse. The most recent bag of fur showings
> included a dignified parade of such aristocrats as Russian
> sable, by Carillon Furs, a circus party from the wild
> imagination of Jacques Kaplan, and a first-time collec-
> tion by Ellen Kourtides, a young Greek blonde. . . .
> First, there was the ermine tail skirt that Mrs. George

Plimpton wore with a black velvet ribbon crisscrossed over her bosom in lieu of a top. . . .

Then, while jugglers juggled and clowns cavorted, members of the party circuit, such as Mrs. Peter Duchin and Betsy von Furstenberg and a sprinkling of professional models did their turns wearing raspberry mink dresses, gazelle pants suits or hamster knickers.

Mr. Kaplan can be irreverent even with expensive pale minks—he adds suede cowboy fringe to a coatdress of creamy fur or scallops of caramel suede to a white mink coat—but he obviously enjoys himself most with unusual furs. The highlight of the show was a floor-length coat of golden Ethiopian monkey. . . .

Meanwhile Georges or *père* Kaplan had not been idle. His collection featured "natural" beaver and "natural" goat. Donald Brooks, on the other hand, favored "French" horse. When it was suggested to Mr. Brooks that he might perhaps have confused the French fondness for eating horse with wearing it, he replied that his coat was "stencilled" to look like giraffe. And Miss Taylor did not neglect the collection of the California-based James Galanos for Neustadter:

Although spotted furs have generally been on the decline since conservationists started a campaign to preserve leopards and cheetahs, Neustadter showed several, including the rare black leopard. This year, the company has a new pet cat—Argentine lioness, a tawny fur that blended well with a sable collar.

Nudity isn't an easy business to achieve with fur, but Galanos pleased the girl watchers with a skinny jumpsuit of black broadtail, slit below the navel. The other hit of the show was a white mink evening coat flowered in shades of brown mink. Prices are $1,000 to $40,000.

Loretta Young, in a pleated white dress and bubble hat, went to the Biegeleisen & Schour showroom to cheer the designs of her friend, Jean Louis.

"Oh, that's beautiful," she said, when a bright red broadtail coat with a black fox collar emerged.

In this "fun" era the furriers were particularly determined to befur the American child. "The fall and winter coat collection," reported fashion writer Marilyn Bender, "now being assembled for toddlers to pre-teen girls and boys are replete with fur." Ms. Bender emphasized that these were not "touches of fur," as in collars and cuffs, but rather "whole coats, or at least parkas, of rabbit, raccoon, lamb, seal, fox, Mongolian cat and even mink." And she also added a word of caution:

> The last two furs are potentially troublesome. Some children are allergic to cat fur and others break into tears when they recognize a household pet on the hanger.

"The same holds true," Ms. Bender continued, "for pony." There were still children, it seems, she suggested, who preferred the idea of riding one to wearing it. But not all furriers agree: "Children are fashionable, honey," Edith Bloom, sales manager of Weather Winky, told Ms. Bender, while Helen Lee, who was described as "a children's designer who has long been an Establishment darling," told Ms. Bender she had no objection to what she called "the growing subtrend of putting little boys in fur coats." "I see no reason," she said, "why they shouldn't be cozy, too." Brooks Brothers, on the other hand, apparently on chauvinistic grounds, disagreed. "We really have to say 'no,'" said William Oakley, a merchandise manager. "Our buyer was tempted, but then he and I had a heart-to-heart talk." Meanwhile, Mr. Fred, of Fur and Sport, summed up the dilemma. "Some kids," he said, "won't buy rabbit coats because of conservation, so we're putting them into what I call 'fib fur.' At least that way they can get used to the cuddliness about the body, and then, when they're a little older, and can think for themselves, we hope they will grow out of it and into a little more mature coat with real fur."

As if all these excrescences weren't enough, the fur business really outdid even its own tastelessness when it came to the matter of advertising summer fur storage. Real furs are, of course, as anyone who has ever tried to sell a secondhand one knows, a poor buy at best. And, without special summer care to prevent everything from moths to just plain warmth, many a fur will all but disappear. As a result, come summertime, the furriers really put the pressure on. In Washington, D.C., for example, Woodward and Lothrop advertised Woody's Fur Storage . . . a home away from home. "It's Fur Storage Time," the advertisement read. "Time to get your pet fur to Woody's." Above was a picture of a teddy-bear-looking cat in a porch chair sipping a cooling drink with a straw. Ohrbach's advertised their cold fur storage under a picture of a back room in the broiling sun. "What a small favor," the advertisement read, "to do for your furry friends that have kept you warm and looking great all winter long." As for Gimbels, in its advertisement it showed a reclining teddy-cat figure smoking through a long holder a cigarette. "Each fur," the copy read, "is individually placed to avoid crushing, and allow 'breathing' room." Finally, New York's Bonwit Teller showed in its advertisement an igloo. No animals were visible, but two balloons, cartoon style, emerged from the igloo. "I'm so glad," said one, "I'm spending the summer in Bonwit's Fur Storage. Heat does terrible things to my hair and can even age a beautiful young mink like me. How do you feel, Mr. Sable?" The other balloon said, simply, "I love you."

*

Ever since the demise of the National Anti-Steel Trap League, the furriers have had relatively ineffective organized opposition. Although local humane societies and some national groups, such as the Animal Welfare Institute, the National Catholic Society for Animal Welfare and the Humane Society from time to time wrote pamphlets about the evils of trapping, all of them, hard-pressed with other problems, could give the furriers only so much of their attention. In 1967, however, The Fund for Animals was organized and from the beginning dedicated itself to a war on the leghold trap. Furthermore, since from the beginning it went in heavily on its national board for movie and TV personalities, it was also resolved to use these personalities on its fur firing line. The Fund's campaign, however, did not go into high gear until 1970, and meanwhile, to another group, the Friends of the Earth, went the honor of initiating what was called a "fashion revolt." On November 18, 1969, in San Francisco, in a remarkable press conference at the Friends of the Earth office, a group of San Francisco women not only pledged "to stop buying the thousands of fashion and home products made from the skins, fur and feathers of wild animals" but also called on "men and women everywhere to join us in an 'international boycott.'" "It is up to the people who set fashion styles and establish taste," they said, "to assume the responsibility for the world's endangered wildlife."

Mrs. John Fell Stevenson, daughter of architect Nathaniel Owings and then daughter-in-law of the late Adlai Stevenson, was the spokesperson for the group. Others included Mrs. William Matson Roth, whose husband was the Johnson Administration Deputy Special Representative for Trade Negotiations; Mrs. William Hamm, a member of the Milwaukee brewing family; Mrs. Walter Landor; Mrs. Harold Brown and Ms. Joan McIntyre. Their statement read as follows:

> At stake is the survival of many species of wild animals throughout the world. At least 861 species and races of

mammals, birds and reptiles are known to be in danger of extinction. All wild creatures are subject to increasing pressures from different sources: the loss of space to live in; the loss of life itself through pollution, direct poisoning and hunting; the taking of specimens for zoos, the pet market, and large-scale research. If you add to this already unbalanced equation the incredible demand for skin, fur, feather, and horn, prompted by the fashion and interior decorating market, then the outlook for wild creatures is very grim indeed.

It is much easier to kill animals than to count them. While biologists painstakingly compile data on endangered species these same animals appear in advertisements as desirable acquisitions. The exploitation is fierce and the line is long. Last year in a ten-month period alone, reports from a single source show over 4,000 timber wolves killed, over 300,000 wild foxes slaughtered for their pelts. It takes 12 baby ocelots to make a coat, 10 lynx, 25 opossums, up to 40 raccoons. Shoes are made from turtles, lizards and many species of snakes. Rare colobus monkeys are manufactured into rugs; nearly extinct snow leopards into coats; and leopards into purses, belts and hats. Endangered timber wolves decorate ski parkas, and baby seals and Canadian fishers are skinned to make "fun furs" for men.

"So it appears," said Mrs. Stevenson, "that our only course, if we wish to save the lives of wild creatures, is to dissolve the market—simply to make it unfashionable to decorate our bodies or our bedrooms with the skins or pelts of wild animals, whether it is exotic leopard or once common wild wolf, cobra lampshades, sealskin toys, alligator shoes, or the precious oil of the fast-disappearing great sea turtles. These are now luxuries none of us can afford."

Press and public reaction to the "fashion revolt" was prompt and favorable. The story was carried in newspapers throughout the country and was perhaps best summarized by *Women's Wear Daily,* a newspaper which, to its credit, though beholden to the fur trade for both advertising and news, has been remarkably fair to the animal side of the controversy. "A group of San Francisco social kingpins," the paper said, "knocked the first props from under the fur industry."

A Friends of the Earth news conference was followed by two advertisements, one in this country and the other in England, advertising their pledge. In this country, the advertisement bore the heading "IMPORTANT MEMO TO THE FUR INDUSTRY." And after the words "We will no longer buy anything made from the skins, fur or feathers of wild or endangered animals," it included one hundred names which ran the gamut from society to show business, and included such names as Mrs. Leonard Bernstein, Mr. and Mrs. William Buckley, Herb Caen, Truman Capote, Mrs. Johnny Carson, Ossie Davis, Dave De Busschere, Ruby Dee, Mrs. Jacob Javits, Danny Kaye, Mrs. Pat Lawford, Mr. and Mrs. John V. Lindsay, Ali MacGraw, Pete Seeger, George Segal, Mr. and Mrs. Neil Simon, Mrs. Gianni Uzielli, Mrs. George Plimpton and even Betsy von Furstenberg—the same who had, a year earlier, been modeling gazelle pants suits and hamster knickers.

The London version of the Friends of the Earth pledge advertisement was stronger. It showed two natives bearing on poles an upside-down tiger. Over it was the headline "MADAM, YOUR NEW TIGER SKIN COAT IS ALMOST READY." Underneath were the lines:

> This tiger was lucky. He was poisoned by weedkiller.
> If he'd been a leopard, a red hot steel rod thrust up his anus would have done the job instead.
> So there wouldn't be any unsightly bullet holes in Madam's fur coat.

Seals get off lightly. They're just clubbed to death.

Even if this slaughter was humane, it would still be unforgiveable. Because it's wiping out whole species from the face of the earth.

And the rules and regulations that might stop it are riddled with loopholes.

You still buy furs of endangered species like tiger and leopard in London.

You still buy vicuna wool in Regent Street. Even though trade of any kind in vicuna has been banned in Peru (its home) for the past two years.

And, of course, you can still buy the furs, skins and feathers of wild animals that won't get put on the danger list until they're almost extinct.

The thrust of the Friends of the Earth pledge had still been primarily the endangered issue. The biggest challenge to the furriers and the fur business of all, however, would embrace not just the endangered issue, but the matter of cruelty—specifically the matter of the leghold trap. This came about through the visit, to The Fund for Animals office in New York, of an advertising-agency woman representing the E. F. Timme Company, manufacturers of fake-fur material. She asked The Fund if, through its offices, it would be possible for Timme to get, as she put it, "society names" to say they would not wear endangered fur. She told The Fund she was empowered to offer each of such women $200 and a fake fur coat.

The Fund, impressed as it was with the Timme Company's concern, was not impressed with the agency's idea of limiting the deal to endangered fur—they felt even "society women" knew not to wear such fur. The agency representative was advised to try the World Wildlife Fund. "They," she was informed, "give awards to furriers who promise not to break the law and make fur coats out of something there isn't any more of." This reception evidently took the agency representative aback. What, she inquired, did The Fund suggest? The Fund suggested that the advertisement feature five well-known actresses on its national board, who would urge that *no* wild fur be worn. The Fund even promised to get these board members for nothing, provided the Timme people upped their original ante from $200 to $2,000—a sum which The Fund well knew each of these ladies would happily donate to the cause.

The advertisement as published included Mary Tyler Moore, Doris Day, Angie Dickinson, Jayne Meadows and Amanda Blake, all of them pictured together wearing imitation fur coats. The advertisement also included quotations, made from actual taped interviews with the actresses, on how they personally felt about furs: These intervews were as follows:

DORIS DAY: Killing an animal to make a coat is a sin. It wasn't meant to be and we have no right to do it.

At one time, before I was aware of the situation, I did buy fur coats. Today when I look at them hanging in the closet, I could cry.

It's so wrong for a man to think that the biggest thing he can do for his wife is buy her a fur coat at Christmas. It's the most *evil* thing he can do. Buy her a fake fur. They're so beautiful, so lovely, so warm, so pretty to look at.

A woman gains status when she refuses to see anything killed to put on her back. Then she's truly beautiful.

AMANDA BLAKE: The wearing of any kind of skins—even the kind that are supposedly raised for fur, like mink or sable—is something I just don't believe in. Killing animals for vanity I think is a shame.

I feel very guilty about having worn fur coats. As for the women who know about our vanishing wildlife and continue to buy fur coats—I wonder how *they'd* like to be skinned?

I have noticed that the reaction to real fur coats is becoming nausea on the observer's part. If a woman wants to wear something that looks like an animal, fake fur is the only way to go.

People are putting the whole real fur thing down and I thank God . . . thank God.

JAYNE MEADOWS: I don't see how you can wear a fur coat without feeling, literally, like a murderer. It is, I believe, against God's law. Against His whole plan for the universe.

I feel very sad for women who continue to purchase real fur coats. They are lacking in a woman's most important requisites, heart and sensitivity.

Bravo for the women who are wearing fake fur. It's the only way to go. It's warmer and everything else. And you are happy because you don't feel guilty in it. You don't feel like a murderer.

ANGIE DICKINSON: Although I don't feel I have the right to tell other people what to do, my respect for an animal's right to live doesn't let me approve of the killing of animals for coats.

If a woman can help an animal or a child, that's the most important thing.

MARY TYLER MOORE: The killing of an animal for the sake of the appearance of luxury doesn't achieve anything. I have seen so many coats so much more attractive than

fur—some fake fur, some fabric. It's in the design, not
necessarily the fabric.

I am aware that there are specific ecological problems,
but for me all animals have a right to humane treatment.

That advertisement, which was called the most influential
anti-fur statement in humane history, appeared three times in
the *New York Times,* twice in *McCall's,* twice in *Newsweek*
and once each in *Esquire, Look* and *New York.* It was also
scheduled to appear in *Vogue, Harper's Bazaar* and *The New
Yorker.* But all three of them, because of the effect on their
pro-fur advertising, turned it down. The decision was an
especially dubious one in the case of *The New Yorker,* which
for years ran the late A. J. Liebling's articles on "The Way-
ward Press," and which has, through the years, never hesitated
to criticize the integrity of newspapers, television and radio,
let alone its fellow magazines. The statement by Gordon Morford of *Vogue* about the advertisement was that it was "especially in poor taste"—a curious comment from a magazine
which had, up till then at least, never considered the tasteful-
ness of wearing fox heads, mink paws, marten tails and so on.

The furriers raised a special furor over the advertisement.
Letters, telegrams, phone calls and even personal visits beset
the actresses involved, but it was soon realized that the stars
not only meant what they said but were perfectly willing to
go, where fur was concerned, further. Mary Tyler Moore, the
leader of the group, afterward stated that she didn't think her
statement was "anywhere near strong enough." Later, in fact,
for a *Reader's Digest* article entitled "Must We Use Torture
Traps to Get Fur Coats?," as well as for a public-service television announcement, Miss Moore was even more emphatic.
"Behind every beautiful wild fur," she said slowly, with a

delivery that showed she meant every word of it, "there is an ugly story. It is a brutal, bloody, barbaric story. The animal is not killed—it is tortured to death. I don't think a fur coat is worth it."

All of the actresses were amused by one letter which apparently went to all of them, and was signed "The Fur Workers of America." "Why," it asked, "don't you fight the filthy, perverted, pornographic film-making emanating from Hollywood?" And Doris Day had a particularly unnerving experience. On the day she gave her interview for The Fund for Animals advertisement, and as she talked about the animals gnawing off their own paws in the traps, her eyes filled up with tears. Photographers crowded around. Some weeks later a movie magazine appeared. "DORIS DAY," the headline on the cover screamed, "NOT INVITED TO OWN SON'S WEDDING!" And to go with that cover story—which wasn't true in any case—was a cover picture of Miss Day crying. It was, unmistakably, one of those taken when she had been talking about the animals in traps.

The third major blow to the furriers came from, of all places, a country which had literally been settled for fur—Canada. From the beginning the problem in Canada was considerably different from that in the States. Whereas in the States the number of professional trappers had been estimated at 2 percent of the total "trapping population"—the rest being part-time trappers, children and people who trapped for sport —in Canada the ratio of professional to total trappers was over 20 percent. The fur trade in Canada, while considerably smaller than that of the States, was far more important economically from an export point of view. Nonetheless, the anti-fur furor had reached that country, too. And, as Frank Conibear had earlier, another well-known trapper from the

Canadian West had after many years of trapping seen the light. His name is Ed Cesar. Instead of developing a humane trap, however Mr. Cesar had gone to work on a film. Years before, the great Scottish humanitarian, Dr. Harry Lillie, had made a film called *Traplines*. This memorably depicted the actual agony of the trapped animal, but in black and white only. Cesar went further. He pictured it all in color.

A small but vigilant organization in Canada, The Canadian Association for Humane Trapping, which The Fund for Animals had for some time worked with, heard of Cesar's film and bought the rights to make a short documentary from it. They added a fashion show filmed in Italy. The title of the completed work was taken from the last line of the first verse of one of the Anti-Steel Trap League poems:

Of timid things, of tortured things, that "take so long to die."

The film was called *They Take So Long to Die*. The Canadian Association mailed a copy to the office of The Fund for Animals in New York; from there it went to the offices of CBS *Evening News*. On the night of March 21, 1972, the final seven minutes of the program were devoted to The Fund's campaign to abolish the leghold trap. Walter Cronkite introduced the film in these words: "If you have young children watching," he said, "you just might want to send them away from the television set for the next few minutes. On the other hand, particularly if your children are just a bit older, you may want them to see this film." He said this, of course, in reference to the fact that the program made clear that most of the people who set leghold traps, as CBS's Ike Pappas put it, "are not professionals. They do it for sport." Pappas also emphasized that a large number of them were children.

That evening an estimated twenty million people, including,

ironically, many thousands in the fur business itself, saw for
the first time animals actually killed in traps. It was called
the most moving animal film ever shown on network TV, and
few people who saw it will ever forget it. Few people indeed
may have thought an ermine was anything but a coat, until
they saw that brave little white animal covered with blood,
fighting and biting to its last breath. The film also showed another animal in a jump trap on a branch. The animal seemed
to be crucified, hanging by a paw until dead. Just as bad, or
worse, was the coyote caught in a snare, in its seemingly endless death throes. And, as if this were not enough, all the
"trash"—the animals and birds not even the trappers want—
a squirrel, a fieldmouse, a whiskey jay, even a particularly
pathetic little porcupine. But the high point of the film was
the startling back-and-forths—on the one hand, a haute couture
fashion show with the aloof, nose-in-the-air models, parading
down the runway to *thé dansant* music, on the other, pictures
of the animals which made those very coats, dying in leghold
traps accompanied by screeching music.

I appeared on the program, demonstrated the Conibear
trap, and pleaded for, "at the least," as I put it, "in simple
decency, a quick death." I was followed by Gerald Walkup,
president of the National Trappers Association, who was
asked by Mr. Pappas what his emotions were when he saw
an animal in a trap. "What are my emotions?" Mr. Walkup
repeated. "It's a harvest, just like any other harvest. If there
is an excess of them, that's all I will take—the excess. I
always leave some seed for next year. Same way with every
other trapper. He wants something for next year, and the
years after . . . and the years after . . . and the years after."

*

Meanwhile, the furriers and trappers, reeling from the three blows—the Friends of the Earth news conference, The Fund for Animals' advertisement and the Ed Cesar film—took stock. There was no question that they had been hurt. Fur historian Reuben Papert perhaps most clearly told the story. His article "And the Fat Years Shall Follow the Lean," written early in 1972, was reprinted not once but twice in *Fur Age Weekly*:

> The causes of this havoc and devastation are well-known and a simple recital will suffice: A general economic depression and the collapse of the stock market; the gloomy atmosphere created by the Vietnam war; the revolt of the younger generation, making unseemly any display of luxury or affluence; campaigns by humane societies against the use of furs; the increasing popularity of "imitation" furs.

Fur figures, we have seen, are not always reliable—they come, after all, from the furriers themselves, and they are obviously not averse to announcing good news in order to boost sales. By the same token, however, when they do admit bad news, it is probably news you can go to the bank on. And in this period, make no mistake, bad news there was. At first, spokesmen for the fur industry confined their efforts to attacks on the attacks. Some of these took the form of satire. Art Littman, for example, of Littman's Fur Factory in Milwaukee, entitled his attack "Don't Wear a Dead Animal . . . and for Goodness Sake, Don't Eat It!"

> Join the Social Animal Protection Society. The S.A.P.S. needs you! Many movie stars have already joined! But please don't ask them to discard their sexy looking buckskin, sheepskin or calfskin leather or suede outfits. Don't call Mary Byler Boore to join! She told us to drop dead. . . .

I like the S.A.P.S. slogan also—"Save the Bald Headed Eagle." I see the government has allocated millions of dollars for this. They took the money from the slum clearance program! Say, what the devil does a Bald Headed Eagle look like? Why don't they have the furriers make raccoon hats for them!

They threw a lot of makers of fake furs out of S.A.P.S. last year. It seems they were not selling their fake furs, so they put REAL FUR on the collars, cuffs and borders this year.

Dear: don't let the kids eat so much hamburger, you know how expensive the animals are now.

So, as you slip your new calfskin shoes, your sleek new leather and suede ensemble, tighten your buckskin belt, and then slide across the sheepskin seats of your car, remember the S.A.P.S. slogan. It's all right to eat animals, but don't wear 'em. Wait now! I'm confused!*

A member of the S.A.P.S.
Mrs. Doris Dingel
3131 Bird Drive

Mrs. Doris Dingel was supposed to be, of course, Mrs. Doris Day. And, for "Mary Byler Boore" Harold High, a chinchilla rancher from Peosta, Iowa, had a suggestion:

> There are constructive things that can be done with this money. They could have a campaign to educate people not to run over animals with their automobiles. They could erect signs in wildlife areas where wild animals cross highways, for motorists to be alert for such.

---

* The furriers' charge that wearing furs is no different from wearing leather is an oft-repeated one. Both involve a death of an animal—yes. But, in the case of leather, the animal is first eaten and then its "hide," literally, is used. The basic question, of course, is *how* the animal is killed. The Council for Livestock Protection, in Braintree, Mass., under the leadership of Malcolm Ripley and John Macfarlane, is supported by the American Humane Association, the Humane Society, Humane Information Services, the ASPCA, the Mass. SPCA, The Fund for Animals and the Animal Welfare Institute. Perhaps the furriers would like to help too.

Perhaps Mary Tyler Moore would like to stand at a deer or skunk crossing and see that the animals cross safely.

Tom Parent, who, *Fur Age Weekly* reported, gave up "a promising career as a novelist" to crusade for the furriers, wrote a column declaring it was time for the fur people to engage pro-fur celebrities to launch a counterattack:

> My first candidate was Ann-Margret, whose extensive wardrobe of furs has received some publicity—and some adverse reaction to that. Or Catherine Deneuve, named by some magazines as the most beautiful woman in the world today, who has been quoted as saying she's absolutely mad about furs. Or Connie Stevens, Carol Baker, Liz Taylor, Faye Dunaway, Diana Ross, Sandra Dee, Ursula Andress, Claudia Cardinale and the Gabor girls— each of whom has been extensively publicized wearing a considerable number of fur wraps.
>
> Unfortunately, none of these befurred beauties has as yet to my knowledge come forth with a public statement in defense of the beleaguered industry they all so generously support with their purchases.
>
> I did hear one mild word of encouragement on the radio from Maureen O'Hara. This lovely red-headed colleen has been a top Hollywood star ever since her film debut at the age of 19 as Esmeralda in "The Hunchback of Notre Dame." She is beloved and respected by her peers in the film industry.

Bob Harrowe, editor and publisher of *Fur Age Weekly,* took on fake furs directly. "In knocking furs to promote cheap pile fabrics," he wrote, "Timme reminds me of a pushcart manufacturer tearing down Rolls Royce in the hope of getting business from the 'carriage trade.' " Tom Parent, then took up the battle:

> I don't think the fake fur people fool anyone with the asinine attacks they sometimes make against the industry

they imitate. It's easy enough to see that the fur industry zealously protects its own stock in trade. Did Cleveland Amory ever pay a veterinarian to treat a sick mink? Fur ranchers do it all the time.

Next he asked himself a question:

> Were potential fur coat customers dissuaded by even that ludicrous Timme ad of August 1971? The only people influenced by that pitch were already on the side of the pseudo-ecologists. How many people believe that rabbits are an endangered species or that wolves are sweet, adorable pet dogs? Notwithstanding the main point of that Timme ad, I think that there are very few ladies who can afford natural fur and yet settle for plastic imitations. What woman wants to walk around wearing a big sign announcing: "My husband is too cheap to buy me a real one!"

Bob Harrowe and Tom Parent obviously wanted stern action. This began with a letter published in *Fur Age Weekly,* and written by one Frank Donalson, who was described as "a very prominent raw merchant of Anchorage, Alaska." He wrote the editors of *Fur Age Weekly* complaining about all the endangered-species bills:

> Enclosed is a clipping from the "Anchorage Daily News" on the latest anti-fur bill to be introduced into the Congress (S. 3199, called the "Endangered Species Conservation Act of 1972").
>
> This is not the last similar bill to be introduced, as there are more and more coming. The ultimate aim is a complete outlawing of all fur in the United States, including ranch mink and the various lambs.
>
> And, this bill and the similar bills which will follow are all certain to pass by an almost unanimous vote, because it is currently politically expedient to vote for such legislation.

Bob Harrowe published the letter and then, for his own column, picked up, in capital letters, on the words, "POLITI-CALLY EXPEDIENT."

> Our own congressmen, senators and State legislators are flooded with anti-fur mail. I wonder how much mail they receive from furriers.
> Despite the way we make it seem, furriers do indeed vote. Furriers' families vote. But, voting alone doesn't do the trick. You have to let your legislators know that you vote, and you have to make your vote count by throwing your weight around with those for whom you vote.
> WRITE LETTERS TO YOUR LEGISLATORS. Have your family members write letters. Then, when our representatives in Congress weigh their mail, the scales won't show the seemingly overwhelming tendency toward some of these absolutely ridiculous laws they're passing almost unanimously.
> MAKE IT "POLITICALLY EXPEDIENT" FOR CONGRESS-MEN TO SEE OUR SIDE OF THE ISSUE. WRITE . . . WRITE . . . WRITE . . .

Bob Harrowe also demanded action about anti-fur advertising, taking on, in particular, an ad by the Animal Protection Institute. Said Harrowe:

> It says, in the ad, that contributions are tax deductible.
> I wonder how long the U.S. Government is going to continue to permit people to form just any organizatio' they please, to serve just any purpose that they themselves see fit—and claim tax deduction.
> The gimmick, of course, is that the organizations themselves are non-profit—but there are usually, if not always, officers of the group who draw salaries and expenses.
> This has reached the point of complete absurdity. I could probably set up a "foundation" tomorrow, alleging brutality on the part of people who happen to step on ants. I could even prove that ants serve a constructive

purpose on earth—just about everything (except people, it would seem) serves some purpose.

I could solicit contributions . . . and receive them from gullible bleeding hearts, declare the proceeds tax deductible—and draw a salary greater than I draw from my "for profit" taxable position as editor-publisher of *Fur Age Weekly*.

How long are we going to permit the Government to grant such tax deductible status to these people, while we are forced to share our meager incomes with the City, State and Federal Governments?

Soon indeed the fur industry had its very own foundation. It was called The Fur Conservation Institute of America. "There was a time," said Robert Ginsberg, president, on September 28, 1972, "when we would not pay enough attention to the force operating against us—a time when I'm sure we all thought 'Leave it alone and it will go away.' But, as you know, the forces operating against us didn't go away and they aren't going to go away unless we do something about it." Speaking in the Gold Room of the Statler Hilton in New York, Mr. Ginsberg continued. "Alice Herrington and her group, 'Friends of Animals,' never had any unified opposition before. Cleveland Amory and his 'Fund for Animals' went around the country making ridiculous claims. He continues to do this. But, now at least, both of them know that there is a solidified group that says, 'No! No lies, here is the truth!' " By 1973, The Fur Conservation Institute of America had what they called a "campaign fund" of $750,000—for 1973 alone. Said *Fur Age Weekly*:

The FCIA made its campaign multi-purposed. In addition to the original purpose of combatting anti-fur activities through advertising publicity and legislative actions, the FCIA set up the American Fur Industry advertising campaign, aimed exclusively at making fur garments more desirable. This is presently being accomplished through national advertising in six well-known magazines and in 12 Sunday newspaper supplements, for the balance of 1973 alone.

The matter of correcting misinformation in the minds of the public and legislators is being taken care of by a speakers bureau that includes Dr. Richard Van Gelder, curator of Mammalogy at the American Museum of Natural History; Margaret Nichols, an editor of *Field & Stream* magazine; Allen Ternes, editor of the official publication of the American Museum of Natural History; Ed Ricciutti, naturalist and wildlife writer; and Dr. Ward Stone, chief of Wildlife Pathology of the New York State Dept of Environmental Conservation.

These were all to a man, of course, men who believed in the use of animals for man—i.e., management men. With the exception of Margaret Nichols, who apparently earned her stripes by an article in *Field & Stream* attacking both The Fund for Animals and Friends of Animals. Besides forming this group, the Fur Conservation Institute also formed its own "environmental" group. This was called The Foundation for Environmental Education or, as it quickly became known, FEE. Lewis Regenstein, executive vice president of The Fund for Animals and author of *The Politics of Extinction,* was equally quick to point out what FEE was. "FEE," he wrote, "is somewhat different from other ecological groups around the country: it was created and is being financed on a tax deductible basis with the help and generosity of the U.S. fur industry." Mr. Regenstein continued:

FEE can appear to speak for conservation, while at the same time serving the industry's interests. FEE was the subject of a recent seminar for furriers entitled "The Fur Industry Fights Back." The seminar was organized by

The Fur Conservation Institute and its New York public relations firm, Bell and Stanton. The basic theme of the meeting was announced in the opening sentence of the seminar's position paper: "The American fur industry is now one of the nation's leaders in animal conservation." The paper flatly admitted that the industry "created" and "established" FEE. . . .

The furriers campaign also involves the aggressive distribution of a book entitled *Animals and Man—Past, Present and Future*, written by Dr. Richard Van Gelder of the American Museum of Natural History, and published by FEE. The book contains a general defense of wildlife management, particularly trapping and hunting ("I have the impression, based on field observation, that many shot animals do not especially show feeling or pain. . . .") ("There are no 'rights' in the natural world— to the victor belongs the spoils") ("It is hard to know what people mean by 'cruel' or 'inhumane.' . . .") Etc., etc.

Mr. Regenstein noted that a special FEE seminar brochure entitled *Tips on Working with Your Local Press* was made available to the furriers. These "tips" included, "Meet the managing editors, the women's and fashion editors," and also advised, "Ask them to lunch separately over a period of time, to better acquaint them with the facts about furs, about animal management and conservation." Furrier-conservationists were also, Mr. Regenstein noted, exhorted to "offer your services as a speaker for conservation, Earth Day or other school programs" and reminded that "your wife and children . . . can easily be converted into positive spokesmen. . . . This is especially important with your children because of the growing interest in ecology among youth." Mr. Regenstein concluded:

And so this season the slaughter of raccoons, wolves, lynxes, otters, seals and other valuable wildlife will con-

tinue as usual. Fashion highlights will include such unusual "fun furs" as kangaroo, skunk, monkey, pony,
zebra, wildcat heads, and even fox and mink paws, tails,
heads, sides, bellies and gills.

Only this year it will be done in the name of conservation.

It was, in truth, almost incredibly ironic. Here were the
furriers, now patting themselves on the back for saying they
were not using endangered animals when the real reasons they
were not using such animals were (1) there were not enough
of them left to use even if the furriers wanted to, (2) it was
now against the law, and (3) it was a law which virtually every
single one of these same furriers had fought, tooth and nail,
every single solitary step of the way.

And, in fact, they fought all such laws. Take, for example,
the question of the Federal law banning the shooting of animals
by airplane—for the passage of which animal societies had to
fight at every turn all the "management" people, from the Department of the Interior to Seventh Avenue. Finally, in 1971,
the law was passed. The very next spring people read in amaze-
ment that that one winter, in one state alone, South Dakota,
twenty thousand foxes were shot from the air. How, one might
well ask, is such a thing possible? It's all, it seems, in that
wondrous word "management." By a last-minute amendment,
states had been allowed to grant permits for aerial hunting in
the case of depredation by predators. That winter there was
a 60 percent jump in furrier prices for fox pelts. At once the
good citizens of the sovereign State of South Dakota managed
—you will pardon the expression—to find the most extraordinary amount of depredation—all caused by foxes, of
course—since the days of Attila the Hun. Permits were issued
hand over fist and the state's Department of Game, Fish and

Parks dutifully announced that "the species is not endangered by the airborne fox hunting." For once, though, the farmers, as well as other decent people, had a surfeit of the cruelty and stupidity. One farmer, Jerome Sturm, wrote a letter to the Governor, protesting. "The foxes are shot so bad," he said, "that there is nothing left to control the jackrabbits, which are eating all the bark off the trees. Have you watched a plane run down a fox? The animal doesn't have a chance." Another farmer, Julius Olsen, told writer Robert Lindsey that he had befriended a family of five foxes. "They got so tame I could get real close to them, but when the winter came, the planes shot them." Mr. Lindsey's account follows:

> "You fly about as high as a rooftop," explained one of the airborne hunters, Cecil Ice. "You aim a 12 gauge shotgun out the window and fly the airplane with your knees. The foxes will dodge and dodge and jump and run into their hole if you're not quick. It's tricky shooting."
>
> The hunters explain that at that altitude the damage to the pelt that is shot is minimized and few of the pelts are rejected.
>
> Mr. Ice and three partners brought in 191 foxes after one busy weekend recently—for a two-day income of almost $3,500.

As if the foxes were not enough, there was more to come. In October, 1971, Reuters reported from Paris that Christian Dior had launched a collection of budget-priced, ready-to-wear furs. "They featured," it said, "such democratic pelts as African monkey." A few months later, however, when the Dior firm brought to this country its winter fur collection, to be shown at the French Consulate in New York, more than a quarter of the collection never reached the consulate. It was banned because the Dior designer, Frederic Castet, had included furs which were on the Federal Endangered Species list—specifically, leopard, jaguar and tiger. When questioned about the use of these animals, Mr. Castet replied, "In France, women are not concerned with such things as endangered animals."

Hard on the heels of the Dior controversy came, early in 1973, perhaps the most outrageous story in the outrageous history of the fur business. This story began when an alert Air Transfer agent at Kennedy Airport in New York noticed, hanging from a large crate marked "Leathers," on a Pan American plane bound from Brazil to Canada, a striped furry tail. That tail, it turned out, led to the U.S. Government's exposure of an operation on the part of what was described as "a ring of furriers" which involved close to a quarter of a million skins, worth many millions of dollars, most of which were from endangered species. One fur company alone, Vesely-Forte, pleaded guilty in Brooklyn to a fifty-count criminal indictment charging that between December 11, 1970, and April 10, 1972, the company purchased and received a total of 5,975 margay, 2,984 ocelot, 2,723 otter, 419 jaguar, 78 puma and three giant otters. Additional dealings engaged in by Vesely-Forte from January 3, 1971, to May 31, 1972, involved $5 million worth of skins, including such staggering figures as 46,181 margay, 30,068 ocelot, 15,470 otter, 5,644 leopard, 1,939 jaguar, 1,867 cheetah, 468 puma and 217 giant otter. At the same time thirty-two other defendants, meaning fur companies as well as individuals, in a related civil action, signed a consent injunction, enjoining both the companies and the individuals from any activities in illegal skins "anywhere throughout the world forever." The signers included a host of well-known furrier names, all the way from Joseph Poser, president of the American Fur Merchants Association, and Benjamin Ritter, of Ben Ritter, Inc., to the Intercontinental Fur

Corporation and the Mid-European Fur Buying Corporation.

Nathaniel Reed, Assistant Secretary of the Interior, personally announced the fateful news. He charged the furriers specifically with violating the Lacey Act, which states that any furs shipped in interstate commerce that have violated any state or foreign law are also in violation of Federal law—in other words, he charged that the furriers had not only broken endangered-species laws of Mexico, Brazil and other South American countries, which had embargoed such furs and where most of the skins had come from, but that they had also broken American law. Secretary Reed also noted that gathering in Washington shortly would be delegates from 74 countries, to attend the first World Convention on Endangered Species. "I hope the Government action yesterday," he said, "will persuade the delegates to agree on a system of controls and permits to end the harvest of destruction."

The furriers' answers to all this were hardly less extraordinary than the charges. "DEPLORE GOVT. TIMING," read the banner headline in *Fur Age Weekly*. "J'Accuse," said Bob Harrowe. "I accuse Secretary Reed of 'grandstanding.' . . . The charges themselves are so petty as to be laughable. . . . But for a United States Government official to use these flimsy charges as a means of inciting a conservation group is like having a policeman yell 'Kill Whitey' at a demonstration of black militants." The answers, he told his readers, are "all over this issue of *Fur Age Weekly*." He particularly recommended that they read a telegram from the Fur Conservation Institute's executive vice president, Irvin Hecht, and Joint Council Manager George Stofsky.

He could at least have spared his readers that trouble. Less than two weeks later George Stofsky was one of seven leaders of a furriers' union indicted on charges of conspiracy, extortion and threats of violence in "a pattern of racketeering activity." Four of them, including Mr. Stofsky, were later convicted and sentenced to two to three years in jail. Mr. Stofsky, incidentally, was one of several furriers with whom I have from time to time debated about the fur industry on television and radio programs. In one such debate, Mr. Stofsky said that I was interested in fake fur, that fake furs were made from natural gas and that the country was running out of natural gas. I replied that, as long as Mr. Stofsky was on the air, the danger was slight.

*

In any history of the fur business, *Fur Age Weekly* deserves a profile of its own—if, for nothing else, its furry fury in defense of the indefensible. Its advertisements alone are worth the price of admission. "THE PAWS THAT REFRESHES," reads one, "WE'VE GOT THE RUSSIAN'S GREATEST INVENTION— RUSSIAN SABLE!" reads another. A third runs, " 'PUSSY' KATZ TURN INTO 'WILD' KATZ WHEN THEY VISIT IRVING KATZ' COMPANY." The editorial matter is hardly less enticing. "TORONTO EDUCATOR," one headline recently read, "REFUTES ANTI-FURS." The man turned out to be Sidney Schipper, past president of the Fur Trade Association—his "college," the Ontario Fashion Institute. "If King Charles I had banned furs," he said, "Canada might not have been developed for centuries. . . . To suggest that people not wear furs is to threaten the livelihoods of thousands of Canadians and leave a natural resource to be ravished by over-population, disease, neglect and savage death by predators." Along with such features run some extraordinary letters to the editors. F. J. Graf, of Graf's Fur in La Jolla, California, for example, noted from Canada that the publisher of Canada's *Fur Trade Journal* had talked about the glue on postage stamps being made from fur-bearing animals. "It occurred to me," he wrote, "that information of this sort could be used effectively in our conservation argument."

Perhaps for a direct mail campaign. In any case, the dean of the Seventh Avenue damn-the-torpedoes crowd is surely the same Mr. Parent who was introduced as having given up "a promising career as a novelist." Whether true or not, one can surely understand the helpfulness of Mr. Parent having a solid grounding in fiction. Week after week, he manages to find something good about almost everything in the fur business; he even went into ecstasies over seeing, on the New York streets, a sheepskin-covered automobile. Owned, possibly, by another fur-business "educator." Only once, it seemed, has Mr. Parent been brought up short. This was when he suggested that the reason Europeans use more furs than Americans is "because they have more appreciation for things that are genuinely beautiful." This was hard cheese, apparently, even by Seventh Avenue standards. In an article entitled "I Stand Corrected," he pointed out that the real reason American women didn't wear more fur was that the U.S. crime rate was so high. He then told a touching story about a woman who was so "foolish" as to "go window shopping unescorted in New York City wearing a mink coat." "She was," he wrote, "suddenly flanked by two men and, at gunpoint, ordered to shed the wrap." It was this sort of thing, he maintained, "plus fur pilfering from theatre seats, restaurants, checkrooms and private homes," that made the American woman so backward about fur. The second reason, he noted, was that the insurance rates were so "outrageous." "Many a young lady," he said, "has declined a proper gift of costly fur simply because she couldn't afford to pay premiums on same."

Mr. Parent also had stern words for Women's Lib's not measuring up to his fondest fur hopes:

> Women's Lib has its negative effect on the U.S. fur trade. It might at first seem that the newly independent woman would be more inclined to indulge herself in the luxuries ladies love. The working wife, with her own income to spend, would seem more likely to treat herself to fur than the stay-at-home, full-time mother. But it has worked just the opposite. The cost of the needed second car takes her fur coat money and, I was told, the salaried female proletarian is a more practical budgeter, who places many other things ahead of fur. It is the whimsical male, especially in a still patriarchal European household, who lavishes expensive luxuries on his hausfrau.

For the energy crisis, however, Mr. Parent had nothing but praise. All furriers apparently hate sliding back and forth on the front seat of an automobile and the resulting wear and tear on their furs. And in the energy crisis, Mr. Parent found it great good news that women would be buying new furs instead of new automobiles.

As for Mr. Harrowe, he found much solace in hunters. "LEGISLATORS CALL HUNTERS LEADERS IN CONERVATION," he headlined one issue. He particularly praised National Hunting Day. He also found the field of furs for men a fertile one. Tom Parent also went to work. Henry the Eighth, he wrote, wore furs, and, to be sure that his readers got the point that Hank was no sissy, he added that he was "as virile a bull as ever fathered a multitude of bastards." Then, wanting to be sure he mentioned an intellectual type, he told us that Voltaire, too, wore furs. And even that "the statue of Thomas Jefferson standing under the dome of the Jefferson Memorial wears a sculptured fur-lined coat." Indeed, he pointed out, furs for men were both so virile and at the same time so intellectual that "it wasn't until the Twentieth Century that women wore fur coats per se." But the 1920's, he tells us happily, saw men, women and children too wearing them—even, he adds, in that "prosperous and uninhibited decade, high school kids." But then, alas, came bad times:

> It was a pitiful thing during the Depression to see a man in a fine sable-collared cashmere overcoat standing in a breadline, holding on to that one precious souvenir of bygone affluence. Or ladies in mink trying to get even the most menial employment. Perhaps it was the Depression that made furs verboten for men for well over a generation. A man wearing an expensive wrap, even though he'd bought it before the '29 Crash, would be likely to be resented by the starving hoboes and corner apple-peddlers he now rubbed elbows with. He'd also be likely to be robbed of his finery. So his good old coonskin went into mothballs up in the attic—until his house was repossessed.

John Gilbert, he recalls sadly, "the idol of the silent screen," was "laughed at" when he appeared in an elaborate fur coat in the early Garbo talkie *Queen Christina*. And thereafter, he mourns, only comedians were seen wearing them. Summing up, however, he pulls no punches:

> A man wasn't considered merely dated or eccentric if he wore fur. He was just plain sissy. The stigma was not so much an implication of fetishism or transvestism, even then, as it was that he needed his security blanket against a cold, cruel world of the 1930's and World War II. He was refusing to face the bitter fact that he was no longer a carefree, Ivy League undergraduate. . . .
> We can now see, in historical perspective, that the restoration of the fur coat to the well-dressed gentleman's wardrobe is simply returning things to the way they'd always been. It was the 1932-1967 stigma against furs

for men, rather than the few who dared ignore it, that was abnormal.

At the end Mr. Parent pays tribute to Alan Case and Bill Blass for pioneering what he calls "the successful revival" of men's fur coats in 1967. But he adds much credit is "justly given" Joe Namath in 1968 "for ending the notion that wearing fur was effeminate." Although he admits that "Broadway Joe" had tough sledding at first and recalls the widespread remark "All he needs now is a purse," he declares that "one doesn't call an eminently heterosexual quarterback a sissy for very long." He is not so kind when it comes to Liberace. "Liberace's white beaver coat," he declares, "which preceded Joe Namath's mink, didn't really help a whole lot!" Nonetheless, again he ends on an upbeat note:

> A man in a wolf coat might be bad-mouthed for his extravagance or because of all those poor, innocent wolves that were slaughtered. But call him a sissy! No way! The guy's hip, that's all, he's, like, with it!

Besides furs for men, *Fur Age Weekly* also recommended fur bedspreads, fur blankets and even fur sheets. "WHY DOFF YOUR FURS WHEN YOU COME INDOORS?" asked an advertisement for "The Fur Pad" at B. Altman's. And Mr. Parent, after his trip to Europe, was quick to take up this cause in an article entitled "How to Sleep in Your Fur Coat." "Wolf and the less expensive colors of fox fur," he said, "are excellent for blankets and throws." He also recommended as something that "would constitute a work of bona fide pop art," as he put it, "a bedspread of civet cat." Then he got down to bedding basics:

> Fur bedspreads have many advantages over fur coats from a business point of view. First of all, they are a non-seasonal commodity—just what the fur business has always desperately needed. It is unlikely that anyone in

the fur bedspread income bracket lacks air conditioning. Customers will still be using their opossum blankets when their mink and beaver coats are locked up in your vaults. Author-interviewer Rex Reed sleeps in his fox fur blanket the year round. What you don't get in summer storage fees, of course, you'll more than make up in cleaning and re-conditioning of fur bed coverings. . . . Fur bed coverings would lend themselves very nicely to the old Spring Maid sheet approach. Or, as one manufacturer of a recent sensational invention maintains, "Two things are better on waterbeds. One of them is sleeping . . ." Perhaps a person who might be timmie-timid about wearing real fur in public, fearing the censure of myopic, misguided pseudo-ecologists, might feel more comfortable covered with fur in the privacy of the bedroom. Sealskin sheets, anyone?

Mr. Parent chided furriers for not advertising in home magazines which had featured fur-furnished bedrooms and even bathrooms. One issue of *Architectural Digest*, he noted, featured a private ski chalet at Aspen. "In the master bedroom, a gigantic wolf fur spread trails on to the wall-to-wall carpeting." He also noted a number of celebrities who were bed befurred: Ursula Andress (silver fox), Jane Fonda (red fox), Liberace (alpaca), Rock Hudson (alpaca), Herb Alpert (chinchilla), Steve McQueen (brown fox), and Derek Sanderson (French rabbit). He concluded:

If Europeans go in so much for fur couvertures, why wouldn't the transplanted Europeans on these shores? Or Afro-Americans, for that matter. Like Wilt Chamberlain. Or Walt Frazier, who recently ordered a mink spread for his circular bed. Or Sammy Davis, Jr. who, in his current hit, "If My Friends Could See Me Now," boasts of owning "a bedspread made of three kinds of skin." . . . Let's put furs in the bedroom where they belong! It can bail the entire industry out of its current doldrums. And Americans will be able to sleep a lot better at night.

Occasionally, of course, *Fur Age Weekly* takes up the question of the killing. "How," asks Mr. Parent, "do you rate an animal's God-given right to live against Man's God-given prerogative of killing it?" He noted that no furrier would now use tiger. But, he also noted, "The tiger will not hesitate to exercise his prerogative to kill a human . . . even now, in northern India, tigers are a major danger." "The point is," Mr. Parent briefly concludes this unpleasant subject, "you've got to draw the line somewhere. Or do you think it's okay to kill a mere mosquito because it can't look up at you with soulful puppy-dog eyes just before you administer the death blow?"

One thing *Fur Age Weekly* dearly loves, understandably, is nostalgia. The fur industry, Mr. Parent notes in an article entitled "The Winter of '42," really "did its part" in the war effort of 1941–45. Society women, he reported, donated their "used fur," and members of the fur industry "donated gratis" their "time and labor" to make vests for the American seamen who had "to plough the frigid northern route to supply our Soviet allies with Lend-lease equipment." The Germans, too, he noted, pitched in. "Goebbels," he said, "beseeched the German hausfraus of the Third Reich to donate their fur coats—new or used—to keep their sons and husbands from freezing to death at Leningrad or Stalingrad."

The furriers, it seemed, were everywhere. And when these boys say nostalgia, they really mean nostalgia. Not content with the winter of '42, Mr. Parent in an article entitled "The Noblest Industry of Them All" goes right back to the caveman:

> Primitive Man, with his many innate physical deficiencies, could compete successfully with the other carnivorous predators that shared his pliocene environment only because he was considerably smarter. Any wolf or leopard could tear apart a slain deer and gorge on the raw

meat. But how many beasts had the wit to peel off the skin with a sharp stone and use it to cover their own bodies against the cold?

This "wit" in the business continues to the present day, in Mr. Parent's view, to make "mankind what mankind is." And the use of fur, he points out, "played no small part in bringing this great marvel about." Meanwhile, back at the cave:

> The first tool, as anthropologists use the term, was not the first stone to be hurled or the first stick to be wielded. Lesser anthropoids can do that. The first precision tool requiring nimble fingers was probably a bone needle used to sew hides together. . . . Thus it is not unreasonable to assert that the fur industry is largely responsible for the extraordinary adroitness and coordination of the human hand—particularly that crucial, uniquely human device, the fully opposable thumb. The ability to stitch rabbit pelts together ultimately became the ability to assemble transistor radios, perform delicate surgery, and play the music of Chopin.

"Homo sapiens," Mr. Parent feels, "might well have been long since extinct but for fur." All in the quest for fur, he points out, "new lands were discovered, new civilizations contacted, new cultures hybridized." And, while other businesses and industries were subjecting the American Indian, the Eskimoes and other primitive peoples to "a most sorry and ignominious fate," not so the fur industry. "In the fur trapping regions today," he declares proudly, "the land is still precisely as God made it." Mining, lumbering, petroleum, even agriculture have in sharp contrast, he points out, been nowhere near so full of nobility. In contrast to the great fur industry they had, he declared, "tragically despoiled the wilderness." In a peroration, he sums up:

> The fur industry, in its prehistoric origin, helped to shape Man into what he is—at least anent his more com-

mendable aspects—dexterity, skill and intelligence. And ever since, Man's better characteristics have retained that natural affinity for the fur business. Few industries can boast such long-standing merit and consistent virtue.

Be cognizant of your heritage, Mr. Trapper, Mr. Trader, Mr. Rancher! For no commercial enterprise in Man's checkered history is more blameless than the fur trade. Few other commercial endeavors have, over the centuries, done more to benefit Man and at the same time, done less harm to his natural environment.

Hold your head high, Mr. Furrier! For your craft is rich in the finest traditions of that grace, the long tapestry of the story of Man. From the first enterprising Neanderthal furrier, whose resourcefulness saved Mankind from extinction, to the elegant salon couturier who creates the ultimate in loveliness out of animal hides, workers in fur have always been among the most respected and useful members of society.

Wear your fur coat with pride, Mrs. Customer! For it is the end product and the raison d'être of the noblest industry of them all!

*

The "Toronto educator" whom *Fur Age Weekly* quoted at least did not use the usual furrier nonsense about the percentage of ranched furs being 70 or 80 or even 90 percent of the total—a percentage, incidentally, that always seems to increase in direct proportion to how much pressure the fur industry was getting at the time from opponents of the leghold trap. Instead, the Toronto man said merely that "most pelts today originate on fur ranches." Actually, as we have seen, only chinchilla and mink are widely ranched—and, even at that, hundreds of thousands of mink are still trapped. But the Toronto man, emphasizing the solicitous care given mink on ranches, declared they "must be protected from disturbance, even undue noise, or they won't breed." Yet just six months before the United States Air Force, "cooperating" for some strange reason with the fur industry, subjected farm-raised mink on Mitkof Island near Petersburg, Alaska, to "intense sonic boom." The mink were boomed, the experimental data revealed, when 40 percent of the females had whelped, "a time when mink are believed to be easily disturbed." They were boomed three times in one day—at 10:58 A.M., 11:44 A.M. and 12 noon—at 5.05 pounds per square foot, or roughly comparable to the intensity of a thunderclap. The test showed, the data concluded, no adverse effect on behavior or reproduction or on the subsequent growth of the kits.

So much for the solicitous care. On the question of how they are killed, the Toronto man maintained that ranch-raised animals were "more humanely killed" than farmyard sources of meat and poultry products. This is a truly extraordinary statement. Although the Humane Slaughter Act for livestock was passed as long ago as 1958—and without the help, to anyone's knowledge, of a single furrier—there are literally no humane slaughter standards or even similar practices, let alone laws, obtaining on the ranches. The animals are, in fact, killed any way the ranchers choose—all the way from wringing their necks with their hands to individually "snapping" them—and although this is far better than an animal killed, after being held in torment, in a leghold trap, it could still stand vast improvement. "The killing of animals on fur farms," says the booklet *Facts About Furs*, distributed by the Royal Society for the Prevention of Cruelty to Animals in England, and the Animal Welfare Institute in this country, "presents a big humanitarian challenge because the number of animals killed annually is over 24 million, of which over 23 million are mink." Besides the primitive hand killing all sorts of other methods are used—from gassing to injection to what is called

a neck breaker, which is not unlike a nutcracker. The best
method is the injection of sodium pentobarbital, the same drug
used by veterinarians for the humane destruction of dogs and
cats, and a method which is infinitely preferable to the common practice of injecting nicotine or magnesium sulfate (Ep-
som salts) into the heart. Nicotine, in fact, according to Dr.
P. G. Croft, kills by paralysis without producing prior uncon-
sciousness. Other "reasonably humane" methods are carbon
dioxide, carbon monoxide (provided it is cool) and chloro-
form. Strychnine is probably the worst—it causes convulsions
and agonizing muscle cramps throughout the body during
heightened consciousness. Cyanide inhalation has also come
in for severe criticism, because, in almost exact contrast to
barbiturates, it poisons the lower brain centers before the
higher ones, which are concerned with consciousness. The
matter of electrocution—a method used, ironically, in an
effort to be more humane at the world's largest chinchilla
ranch, located in Anza, California—is controversial. Says
Facts About Furs:

> Humane electrocution necessitates expensive appara-
> tus, such as the following:
> Electrodes must consist of stainless-steel clips lined
> with saline felts and used wet. A small, lighted electrode
> must be placed on the ears and a larger one on the root
> of the tail, not on the genitals from where it is more likely
> to be dislodged. Voltage 500 V. A. C. 50 c., should be
> supplied from an earth-free source. A resistance bridge
> must be used to measure the inter-electrode resistance,
> and there must be a current meter in the circuit. The
> animal should be in a transparent box with doors having
> switch interlocks to prevent current flowing with the
> doors open.
> Without this apparatus, or one designed with equal

scientific accuracy, the method is most inhumane. In particular, the mouth to anus method of electrocution should never be used because it does not ensure that a current of electricity sufficient to stun passes through the brain. Death results from cessation of heart beat, and this is preceded by severe pain.

Many fur ranchers sincerely believe that ranching is the answer to the endangered-species problem—the final management, so to speak, by man. "Even the Dodo bird would still be in existence today," declares chinchilla rancher Wade Watson of Texas, "if man had found some use for him as an end product and had had foresight enough to raise him in order to harvest a crop from him. Shall we," he asked, "have 500,000 live and healthy chinchillas on fur farms or shall we have zero chinchillas both in captivity and in the wild state? These little animals thrive in captivity and are practically extinct in their native wilds in South America."

Such an argument has its points. But it brings up another question. What about other animals that "thrive" in captivity? In Seattle, a zoologist actually proposed the ranching of ocelots and leopard cats, and Jim Fowler, of *Wild Kingdom* fame, and vice president of The Fund for Animals, was personally approached by a man on the subject of raising cheetahs. He did not even have to reply—the horror on his face answered for him.

But the question remained. If wild animals, why not domestic? In Coro, Venezuela, the Pied Pipers of Coro, a group made up of four doctors and a banker, backed by something called the "Regional Development Bank" announced a plan to make fur coats out of house cats. They also announced it would be a most profitable venture. They would only receive, they noted, on the American market, fifty cents a pelt for each cat, but it would cost them next to nothing. They would, they also said, breed mice. And the cats would eat the mice and the mice would eat—except apparently for the skins—the cats. And, as if this were not enough, in Johannesburg, South Africa, a man named Van de Sandt de Villiers Smit—who certainly sounded like someone to be reckoned with—announced a plan to make fur coats out of dogs. "What's wrong," he asked, "with your wife wearing a nice Dalmatian—or a spaniel?"

There was, it soon turned out, plenty wrong. And the *cause célèbre* soon turned out to be more than even Van de Sandt de Villiers Smit had bargained for. One dog lover in England went so far as to offer, for Mr. Smit's skin, $39,900. And, while this was a case of fact imitating fiction—the fiction being Dodie Smith's novelette *The Great Dog Robbery*, and the story of Cruella de Ville, which became Walt Disney's *101 Dalmatians*—the facts won out in the end, when dogskin coats indeed turned up in New York's Saks Fifth Avenue. The Saks manager, faced with humanitarian Max Schnapp and a delegation from Beauty Without Cruelty, protested that the skins were "Chinese coyote." But it was no use, and, before the day was out, Saks agreed to cease and desist from putting on the dog. The real irony in the whole furor was, of course, that the fur industry has, as *Fur Age Weekly* noted, "long made extensive use of dog skins." And once again Mr. Parent rose to comfort all furriers engaged in the traffic in Chinese and Manchurian dogskin:

> The objection to collie coats certainly can't be for the same reason as the objection to leopard coats. Domestic dogs are one of the few mammalian species that have increased right along with man, as a stroll in any fashionable part of New York City makes obvious. Nor can it

be ascribed to Fido's genetic relationship to man. If that were it, the real objection would be to using monkey fur.

No, it's purely the sentimental syndrome of the pet-owners. Just be glad that foxes and wolves, despite their considerable intelligence, have been successfully domesticated by very few people.

Probably the oldest fur-ranching business of all is the very worst of all. This is the so-called "Persian lamb," or karakul, business. For centuries, the fat-tailed karakul has existed in the Bukhara region of Central Asia; later they were introduced into Afghanistan and comparatively recently—1907—to Southwest and South Africa. However, since they first reached the outside world through Persian traders, the skins were called Persian lamb. Millions of these skins are produced every year and, to produce them, every single lamb must be killed within five days of birth—usually less than that and often when only one day old. This is because, at that time, the baby lamb still has its tight, lustrous, usually black curls. As far back as 1934, a documentary film was taken in Southwest Africa, and although it showed the slaughter of the newborn lambs in the presence of what were described as their much-distressed mothers, and was shown to the National Council of Women of South Africa, nothing, to date, has been done about it.

Cruel as is Persian lamb or karakul or "swakara"—as the skins produced in Africa are called—even more grotesque is the so-called "broadtail." This is an Asiatic product only and is the skin from an unborn, premature or aborted, lamb. It is made by killing an old, pregnant ewe and then extracting the fetus or taking a younger ewe and inducing abortion, in some cases by beating. The only good thing possible to say about this whole horrible industry is that sometimes, because of the harshness of the climate, nature herself induces the abortion. Indeed, in Central Asia, when the winter is unusually severe, broadtail production goes up.

*

Neither the question of fur farming nor fur business propaganda has ever been able to obscure for the humanitarian the basic, immediate goal—to get rid of the leghold trap. In this country, the outstanding individual effort was made by a young New Jersey housewife. Her name is Valerie Maxwell, of Oradell, New Jersey, and although she and her husband, Tom, have been active in many animal causes, her anti-trapping effort was started, ironically, by her six-year-old daughter. One day in 1967, young Miss Maxwell returned from school in tears—she had seen boys chasing and throwing rocks at some Canada geese living in the river behind the Maxwells' house. Mr. and Mrs. Maxwell started an investigation—one which took a full year and a half, but resulted in the town of Oradell's adopting a strict "anti-molestation" ordinance. During this investigation, however, the Maxwells found half a dozen geese with missing feet, and they soon learned that these injuries were almost certainly inflicted by leghold traps.

Once more the Maxwells started an investigation—and this time it took four years. When they were through, however, the investigation had resulted in the sovereign State of New Jersey having banned, in its first- and second-class counties—virtually all highly urbanized counties—not only the leghold trap and other cruel trapping devices but also trapping by any means by children under the age of fourteen. Mrs. Maxwell had originally opted for the age limit being under eighteen, but that, at the last moment, was brought down to fourteen.

How Mrs. Maxwell and her cohorts went first from person

to person, then from town to town, then from county to county and at last to the State House is a stirring story. But the hearings themselves were also stirring. From start to finish, they were attended by large crowds and packed balconies. They took place in the New Jersey State House Assembly Chambers in Trenton on March 30, 1971, before the Agricultural, Conservation and Natural Resources Committee, and over and over again the chairperson, Assemblywoman Josephine Margetts, had to call for order.

Senator Joseph Woodcock spoke first. "I don't see trapping as a sport," he said. "I think trapping, at best, is a bloody business. And I really don't think we ought to leave that type of occupation in the hands of the younger people of this State." Assemblyman Kenneth Black next spoke against the bill. "I believe," he said, "that the sponsor of the bill, Senator Woodcock, is sincere in his beliefs that the passage of this bill is necessary. I do believe, however, once again, that he is unaware of the explosive damage, ecologically, physically, medically, sociologically, the passage of this bill could have across the State. If you take away trapping . . . we won't need roads, we won't need tires. We'll just be able to take the tires off the cars and just run across a nice furry blanket because we'll have wall to wall muskrats."

Assemblyman Black then addressed himself to the number of trapped pets, most of them in illegally set leghold traps, hundreds of which had been documented by Mrs. Maxwell and other proponents of the bill.

> And when we talk about the hundreds or thousands of cats and the hundreds or thousands of dogs that are caught in traps each year in the State of New Jersey, why don't we really do the pets a favor and discontinue all automobile travel in the State, because I'll wager there's a

devil of a lot more killed by automobiles than there are by traps in this State.

The next speaker was Robert Perkins of the Wildlife Preserve Society. He noted that for twenty years he had been directly involved in the preservation of sanctuary areas, totaling about seven thousand acres. "During that time," he said, "I personally have picked up well over 1,000 traps from these areas, all of which, of course, were set illegally." He also declared that the number of animals in those traps not being sought often considerably outnumbered the number sought, then added:

> I would also like to point out that the problems that landowners have or anybody having a sanctuary or any member of the general public who is involved with wildlife are just not taken into consideration at all by the present legal situation. In other words, the present situation is virtually a hundred percent in favor of the trapper and really giving no consideration to the general public which does, under our system of government, own wildlife as opposed, for example, to England where the wildlife is owned by the landowner.

I was the next speaker and addressed myself specifically to the question of the cruelty of the leghold trap. I compared it to other animal cruelties I had personally witnessed and stated that none of those cruelties, not even all of them together, could compare with the cruelties inflicted on wild animals in leghold traps. The next speaker was Robert Hughes, chairman of the Endangered Species and Wildlife Committee of the Atlantic Chapter of the Sierra Club. Mr. Hughes started by quoting George Alpaugh, chief of the Bureau of Wildlife Management of the State of New Jersey, who had stated, "At the present time we do not have any way in which to estimate the number of fur animals taken." Mr. Hughes mentioned "innumerable instances" of American and golden eagles being trapped and then addressed himself specifically to the question of the New Jersey Fish and Game Council:

> We understand the Fish and Game Council is opposed to these bills. It is unfortunate the Council is not representative of the State's population and interests and needs. Law requires that the Council's membership be made up of 11 persons—three farmers, six sportsmen recommended by the Federation of Sportsmen's Clubs, and two commercial fishermen. There are also geographic qualifications.
>
> This Council makeup is most unfortunate. The members are interested in game preservation and they do, by the nature of their interests and the limitations of their funding, tend to ignore the broader wildlife and environmental problems.
>
> This obsolete system needs immediate revision so that funding is on a broader basis and the Council is representative of all the people of New Jersey. Such a Council must have ecologists and non-sportsman conservationists within its membership.
>
> We consider the Council's opinion to be that of a special-interest group reflecting as it does the very narrow interests of the hunter-trapper. We do not consider the Council a suitable spokesman for all the citizens of New Jersey.

Mr. Hughes was asked by Assemblyman Robertson how frequently leghold traps were checked. Mr. Hughes replied that, although the law said they should be checked every twenty-four hours, this was highly unenforceable, and, as he put it, "in the case of some of the kids and those less concerned, I am sure they may go unchecked for a week or more."

Mrs. Maxwell herself made an extremely effective witness:

More than 600 documented cases reported to me personally and now in our files testify to the variety of suffering to which leghold trapped wildlife, pets and birds, have been subjected in this State. In the majority of these cases, traps were set illegally, out of season, left for days and even weeks unchecked or set on private property without the owner's permission. In not one case, to our knowledge, was a trap identified with the owner's name and address, as required by State law. These are hard-core facts which illustrate that the persons who set these traps were ignorant or contemptuous of the law, and indicate that in a large proportion of cases, probably the trappers were youngsters. . . .

Trapping is a privilege, not a right, and it is incumbent upon this state to strictly control this activity and to require, as far as possible, the most humane trapping methods available be used. We must reduce use of the unselective and cruel device that mutilates and kills wildlife which, by law, belongs to all the people; a device that maims and kills, in a most dreadful fashion, great numbers of pets also.

That these measures might cause inconvenience to some people must not override the consideration that use of the leghold trap is unethical and must be condemned for the simple reason that it is barbarous, while in no manner necessary to the welfare of man.

This bill before you is a moderate approach to a serious and widespread problem. We respectfully urge this Committee to release the bills unamended.

Following Mrs. Maxwell came Fred Space, chairman of the New Jersey Fish and Game Council. "I am Fred Space," he said, "Agriculturist, Ecologist, Naturalist, Zoologist and most of all, Realist. My schooling consists of forty years in the outdoors." Mr. Space spoke of his own view on the trapline:

Every morning up at 5 A.M. to travel the fields and swamplands from November 15 to March 15—rain,

snow, below zero and all—then I have to skin and prepare the pelts after school only for token amounts of
money. These activities helped teach my youth responsibility, which they certainly lack today. . . . Don't discourage them from this beneficial rodent-controlling
outdoor activity. If kept from these outdoor activities,
the kids will spend their leisure time on the street corners,
bait for the dope pusher. I have never seen a dope pusher
in the marshlands or mountains.

Nor, presumably, a streaker.

*

Hard on the heels of the New Jersey hearings came an even
greater victory. In 1972, the Florida Game and Fresh Water
Fish Commission became the first regulatory game agency in
North America to ban the leghold trap. Although the commission's ban provided for a special permit which could be
issued to landowners for up to five traps for the purpose of
trapping predators when "necessary for the protection of private property"—the usual kind of loophole all animal measures
seem to end up with—the fact remained that the fur business
had suffered a severe blow. And one of the commissioners,
O. L. Peacock, Jr., of Fort Pierce, left no doubt where the
commission stood. He termed the leghold traps "cruel and barbaric" and said they were "probably one of the worst devices
ever conceived by man for catching animals."

Still a third blow awaited the furriers—and again the leghold
trap was the basic issue. In the summer of 1972, representatives of the Canadian Association for Humane Trapping met
in the offices of The Fund for Animals in New York and laid
plans for the first international humane-trapping conference.
This conference, held in November, was attended by furriers
and trappers, by representatives of the Hudson's Bay Company

and the Canadian Department of Indian Affairs and Northern Development, as well as all by the major Canadian, American and international animal societies, ranging from the International Society for the Protection of Animals, headquartered in London, to the Association for the Protection of Fur-Bearing Animals in Vancouver, British Columbia.

From the beginning as we have seen, the problem in Canada was considerably different from that in the States—principally in the far higher percentage of professional trappers. As a result, its vice president Neal Jotham made clear, the Canadian Association for Humane Trapping was not out to abolish trapping; it was merely out to abolish cruel trapping methods, specifically the leghold trap and snares. Since 1961, he pointed out, his association had exchanged some $40,000 worth of Conibear traps free to trappers throughout Canada—one to a customer and one Conibear per leghold received. "As long as use of the leghold trap continues," Mr. Jotham declared, "CAHT will point out the suffering it causes, particularly since there is no question that it is a cruel device. It is CAHT's belief," he went on, "that an informed public will be concerned enough to insist that their respective legislators take the necessary action to correct an intolerable situation—a situation which has also created an increasingly bad image for Canada and its fur industry."

Specifically, the meeting heard the story of and actually saw in action, at the University of Guelph and McMaster University, the Humane Trap Development Committee. Engineer Harlan Lunn, chairman of the Research Subcommittee, stated that it was the objective of the committee to establish humane standards for the evaluation of humane traps, and to develop suitable humane traps for commercial production, in order, he said, "to ameliorate the suffering of fur-bearing animals presently trapped by a variety of inhumane devices and procedures." He also stated that to achieve their objective the Humane Trap Development Committee was involved in "the first systematic evaluation of traps ever undertaken in this country and, as far as is known, elsewhere." Using everything from electroencephalographic machines and cardiographic units to high-speed cameras, underwater test flumes and computer banks, the Development Committee was determined to study every possible humane trap from the point of view of (1) its primary characteristics (impact energies, speeds of closure, clamping and prying force), and (2) its secondary characteristics (trap geometry, location of impact, resistance to opening, ease of setting, safety, size, weight and bulk, mechanical reliability, effect on pelt, cost of production, durability and maintainability and, finally, flexibility in usage). The high-speed photographic studies on live animals were to be, it was pointed out, made under strict humane control to determine the exact power of the blow necessary to kill an animal in the shortest time with the least stress and the quickest loss of consciousness.

"I think," Lunn told me, "we can come up with hard answers, even in such an unclear area. But wouldn't it be ironic if we finally got an absolutely perfect trap—one that always kills immediately, with no panic or pain—and then found no need for it because people had decided not to trap animals for fur?" I had the feeling it was an irony he wouldn't mind at all.

One specific about the leghold trap to come out of the Canadian conference was the agreement, on the part of all the U.S. conferees, to have Tom Garrett, head of the Friends of the Earth Wildlife Committee, work with the office of Senator Birch Bayh in Washington to come up with a practical bill to abolish the leghold. Although Senator Bayh had previously introduced a trapping bill, his new effort was the first practical one from a hearings standpoint. What the new bill did in brief was to (1) instruct the Secretary of Commere to set up criteria for establishing which traps "capture painlessly or kill instantaneously" and establish a list of approved traps, (2) provide a seven-member commission to help in determining which traps shall be approved, (3) halt the entrance into interstate commerce of all traps which are not approved traps, (4) halt the use of other than approved traps on public lands, (5) impose labeling requirements for interstate shipments of hides, furs, feathers, etc., and (6) provide penalties and aids to enforcement by citizen participation and action.

While humanitarians pressed the Senators and Congressmen with the power to call trapping hearings—Warren Magnuson and Philip Hart in the Senate and, in the House, John Dingell and Leonor Sullivan—state by state the war on the leghold trap went on. An army of humanitarians from Maine to California, including such individuals as Gretchen Wyler, Regina Frankenberg, Steve Seater, Patt Mitchell, Guy Hodges, Virginia Handley, Gladys Sargent, Sandy Rowland, Doris Dixon, Carol Koury and Jennifer Johnson took on all comers. For some the fight was a lonely one. Hope Sawyer Buyukmihci, founder of The Beaver Defenders and owner of the Unexpected Wildlife Refuge in Newfield, New Jersey, found that not even thorough posting of NO TRAPPING signs did any good. She had to thread the trails on her property. Then, even at night, she had to patrol, and when she found a thread broken, she knew she had to find the trapper or his traps before one of her semi-tame beavers found them. For other humanitarians, the fight was a public one. When, for example, a reporter called The Fund for Animals office in New York about a trapping story and asked with what appeared to be sarcasm why The Fund objected to it. "They die of thirst, they die of hunger, they die of cold and they are tortured to death," Marian Probst, my assistant, replied slowly. "That is why we don't consider it a 'humane' death." In Palm Beach, along Worth Avenue, in February, 1974, paraded, wearing fake fur coats and REAL PEOPLE WEAR FAKE FUR buttons, two of Palm Beach's best-known socialites, Mrs. Allen Manning and Mrs. John Volk. Both members of the board of directors of The Fund, they marched boldly into the showroom of Ernest Graf, president of Ben Kahn Furs, who was showing, among other things, lynx, fox and swakara. "Really, ladies," Graf protested, "this is not fair to my business." He told them that he was on the board of the "American Conservation Fur Institute"—a name which he apparently did not know well enough to state correctly—and then added that the lynx and other so-called "fun furs" which he was showing were not taken by leghold traps. Which, of course, they were. Mr. Graf also stated "the fox is over-populating its environment and infecting livestock with mange and other diseases." He also told the ladies that they were "idealists." "No," Mrs. Volk replied, "we are realists."

But the other side too was not idle. Indeed, armed with $750,000 per year from the Fur Conservation Institute alone —a sum given by fur ranchers as well as the wild furriers— they began a brand-new fight. Edwin Reid, in *Fur-Fish-Game*, sounded the alarm for the trappers:

> The nature "no trapums" are all over the place, spreading their sticky propaganda against trapping innocent little, harmless animals. If they weren't innocent, little and harmless, the story might be in the reverse. Let them form their small refuges. This is quite noble of them. But when they try to transform an entire state into

something resembling an animal paradise of untouch-
ables, that's something the trapper better wake up to.

Where *Fur-Fish-Game* led, the outdoor writers were quick
to follow. Stewart Bristol, in the Vermont *Times,* was perhaps
the most remarkable. "After seeing an anti-trapping ad," he
wrote, "to begin with there are very few animals that receive
the abuse mentioned in the ad. Just as there are but a handful
of cats and dogs being mistreated, in comparison to the great
numbers which have good homes and are well cared for." The
Atlantic City *Press* published an irate letter from Charles
Kosten of Pomona. "Since these anti-trap people have so much
time and money to devote," he wrote, "why don't they use
it to help hunt down and trap the human predators who club
crippled old men, women and others over the head so they
can run off and buy more dope?" Caine Pieffer, secretary-
treasurer of the Northeast Ohio Fur Takers, wrote The Fund
for Animals,

> I read with disgust the paper you put out in your
> "So You" series, entitled "So You Want to Do Some-
> thing About Trapping." Don't you realize that trapping
> with leghold or steel-jawed traps has been proved to be
> necessary for control of animal population for "manage-
> ment and economic reasons" by the U.S. Department of
> Interior? . . . If you want to fight us, do it openly, not
> by sneaking around looking for evidence.

Meanwhile, from one end of the country to the other, came
a rash of articles telling of the joys of trapping. The Des Moines
Register featured a half-page article on Dick Erb, art teacher
and wrestling coach of the Nishna Valley High School, who
was billed as "Mat Coach, Art Teacher and Trapper." "You
can either let the animal tell you where he'll be caught or you
can tell him," Erb was quoted as saying. "When a guy goes

out and gets his tail wet and wades in mud up to his knees, he's not doing it for the fun." The Pittsburgh *Press* featured teen-age trappers. "We always get up an hour earlier than we have to to catch the school bus, so we can run our traps before school," one youngster was quoted as saying. "Then we take another look at them after school, so we don't take a chance on a rat [muskrat] chewing his way out of the trap." The Asheville *Citizen-Times* favored its readers with a half-page article entitled "Beats Baby-Sitting" about a thirteen-year-old girl trapper, Johanna Nowak. "I can skin a muskrat in four minutes, twelve seconds," Miss Nowak said, "and I hope to make it three minutes." "One wily muskrat," Bob Satterwhite wrote, "would chew the bait stick until the apple would drop into the water and float clear of the trap. Johanna puzzled with the problem a while, then set an unbaited backup trap. When the muskrat chewed the apple clear and headed for it, he was zonked by the second trap. . . . Johanna's love for nature and wildlife comes naturally. Her father studied geology, archaeology and anthropology at the University of South Carolina and the University of Michigan Graduate School."

Side by side with the outdoor writers were the fashion writers. "FUR IS IN—NO LONGER A SIN," headlined the Los Angeles *Times*. "Pleas for the poor, endangered animals," wrote Eugenia Sheppard, "budget prices and an incredible amount of publicity have all failed so far in luring women into preferring fake furs to the genuine thing." Miss Sheppard, who is rarely at a loss when it comes to saying good words about furs, was even able to find encouragement in the energy crisis. "If the energy crisis has been good for anyone," she wrote, "it's the furrier. Psychologically women are more anxious than ever to be sure of comfort and warmth." Even the *Wall Street Journal* got into the fashion act. "YOUNG

BUYERS HELP FUR INDUSTRY BOOM NOW THAT ECOLOGICAL ISSUE IS SETTLED." Although here and there were dissenters— Bill Cunningham in the Chicago *Tribune,* for example, noted that many designers, "fearful of the crusade against the wearing of fur," were causing furriers to "produce cloth coats and hide the pelts inside"—the majority jumped on the furrier's bandwagon. The most incredible article was perhaps one by Helen Harris in *Town & Country* on which hundreds of letters of complaint were received. This the editor, Frank Zachary, now knows, was based on Fur Conservation Institute propaganda. Ms. Harris' most amazing statement came early in the article when she declared that the buying of a fur "may turn out to be a woman's wisest, most practical purchase." The fact is there are thousands of animal people in this country who bought real furs before they knew better and who would now like to get rid of them. Unfortunately, they can't. As an investment, they have found, fur ranks with the Edsel automobile. Indeed, as anyone who has ever tried to sell a secondhand fur knows firsthand, there is almost no market for them at all.

As if the outdoor writers and the fashion writers weren't enough, the humanitarians also had to cope with renewed propaganda on the part of virtually all the states' governmental agencies—which, instead of following the lead of the Florida Game and Fish Commission, seemed to redouble their efforts to promote the leghold trap. From Washington State to New York, fish and game departments vied with each other in extolling the trap as a management tool. "We know," wrote the State of Washington's Department of Game, "that the wild furbearer will die whether we harvest it or not. Death will occur whether we see it or not. There is no justification for preferring the unobserved 'natural' death to the observed, trapping death."

New York State and its elaborate magazine *The Conserva-tionist*, the official publication of the state's Department of Environmental Conservation, devoted, in its February-March, 1974, issue, not one but two articles to the virtues of trapping. The first of these was entitled "Trapping: Sport, Art and Live-lihood," and bore the come-on subhead, "Nearly 15,000 New Yorkers annually match wits with the furbearer." Complete with a picture captioned "Beaver Trap and Raccoon Trap," the article offered also a "raccoon lure" (1 ounce honey, ⅛ ounce beaver castor, ⅛ ounce muskrat musk, 10 drops anise oil and the gall from one coon). The article also stated, "Trap-ping is an art and the trapper is an artist. . . . Yet trapping as an outdoor sport that pays its way, or as a livelihood, is threatened constantly by well-intentioned but misinformed peo-ple who promote legislation that would outlaw trapping or the use of wild furs, even of animals whose over-population causes starvation and disease."

The second article was entitled "The Case for Trapping," and was written by Ward B. Stone. Dr. Stone is identi-fied, in the "Contributors" section of the magazine, as head of the Wildlife Pathology and Physiology Section of the Department of Environmental Conservation. He is not, how-ever, identified as a member of the Speaker's Bureau of the Fur Conservation Institute, one of the very people designated to, as the Institute puts it, "correct misstatements by humani-tarians." Dr. Stone, *The Conservationist* says proudly, "sug-gested Tom Gebo as a source for our article on trapping, with the excellent result the reader will find." Dr. Stone's article first concerned itself with the terrors of rabies and then moved on to the business of fur promotion. "New York City," he wrote, "is the national center of the fur industry. In 1970, they had 52,000 people employed in various capacities . . . They produced an income of approximately $425,000,000 at the retail level. The volume of business for 1973 is expected to be greater because of the increased fashionability of furs."

For a person on the one hand to be paid by the New York State Conservation Department and to have a part in deciding how many animals to trap and, on the other hand to be an announced speaker for the fur industry—this was, even by our war-on-wildlife standards, a bit much. In company with Malcolm Ripley, Marion Schaefer and Dede Kline, president, vice-president and secretary, respectively, of the New York State Humane Association, I paid a call on the heads of the New York State Conservation Department in Albany. The work of Dr. Stone was the first order of business. But we also reminded the department, as well as the Governor's staff, that if they didn't represent the animals, they did at least represent, as well as the people who wanted to trap animals, the people who did not.*

Over the country in general, however, the furriers were still very much in the saddle. When, for example, in January, 1954, the Museum of the City of New York celebrated its fiftieth anniversary, it literally sold out to the furriers. The American Fur Industry made a contribution of $10,000 and in return was graciously permitted to provide a wide variety of wild furs

---

* In May, 1974, Stone was back at the old stand beating his drum. Said *Women's Wear Daily:* "Stone, who believes in the fur industry 'because it's good for conservation,' sees 'plenty of room for the harvest and utilization of certain species. There are more raccoons, skunks and red and gray foxes present in the United States today than there were before the coming of the Europeans.'" Stone may be credited here with originality. The usual phrase is "since the days of the Indians." In any case, his thesis seemed to be that if we don't wear fur coats we'll all get rabies. Words like "rabies," "feral dogs," "bite cases," etc., have become through the years to animal workers code words for animal haters. The fact is, of course, you have about as much chance of being killed by rabies as you have of being hit by the Comet Kohoutek.

for the occasion. Dozens of show business personalities, all of whom by then, even if slow learners, should have known better, were awash in animals. Mrs Joshua Logan, co-chairman of the event, wore the cruelest fur of all—broadtail. Maggi McNellis wore the cruelly trapped white ermine. Meanwhile, Kitty Carlisle, one of the major offenders among fur-wearers on TV game shows, chose sable. In contrast, out in Los Angeles, Susan Saint James and her husband Tom Lucas engineered a contract with NBC's "McMillan & Wife." This provides that, if any wild fur is worn anywhere on the set, Miss Saint James, regardless of the scene being shot, is permitted to leave. Needless to say, no wild furs are worn.

Elsewhere, the news was grim. At Hide and Fur, of Paris, Texas, the largest fur-buying company in the Southwest, where the fur of mink, nutria and beaver begin the trek north to New York and then across the Atlantic to European dressers and on to designer showrooms, '75 business is booming. The fur market was the best it had been in years, and times were prosperous for the Texas trappers, too—$20 for a bobcat pelt, $13 for beaver and $6.50 for, as it was described, the "common raccoon." The use of imitation fur, declared Elmer Whitaker, the owner, had backfired. "Women want the real thing," he said, "a real piece of fur, rather than an imitation." Elsewhere, from one end of the country to the other, advertisements signed merely "The American Fur Industry" not only ignored the trap but also even common taste. "HOW TO SAY 'I LOVE ME,' " read one of these, and underneath were the lines "This winter say 'I Love Me.' Out loud. And outside. With fur." There was even the line "If you want to spend a bundle on something to bundle up in, broadtail's for you." (Never mind, of course, the "induced" abortion.) Or another advertisement suggested, "HAVE YOU EVER CAUGHT THE LOOK ON YOUR FACE WHEN

YOU'RE WEARING FUR?" Underneath this was the line "How about . . . yards and yards of sexy, silky fox." (How many foxes in how many traps does it take to make "yards and yards"?)

And then, in *Women's Wear Daily*, there was a more modest ad—of a "sale":

SALE

We are pleased to offer the following
approximate quantities of Wild Fur for Sale:

FRIDAY -FEBRUARY 8th, 1974 -9:00 A.M.
50,000 BEAVER

1,750 LYNX   **300   LYNX CATS**

SUNDAY -FEBRUARY 10th, 1974 -6:00 P.M.
10,000 CANADIAN SABLE   1,200 WOLVES
3,000 OTTER

MONDAY -FEBRUARY 11th, 1974 -8:30 A.M.
35,000 RACCOON   2,500 FISHER
8,000 WILD MINK   12,000 FOX
200 BEAR   175,000 MUSKRAT
SUNDRY OTHER FURS

Beaver on Show: Feb. 5th. All Other Goods: Feb. 6th

This is an exceptionally fine offering of salable goods
and it is to your interest to attend or be represented.
Hotel reservations made on request.

ONTARIO FUR TRAPPERS ASSOC.
A. Shieff, Manager

Box 705, North Bay, Ontario, Canada (705) 474-3177

Read those figures once more—175,000 muskrats; 50,000 beaver; 35,000 raccoon; 12,000 fox; 10,000 Canadian sable; 8,000 wild mink; 3,000 otter; 2,500 fisher; 1,750 lynx; 300 lynx cats; 1,200 wolves; and 200 bear! All for *one* sale, of one fur trappers' association.

TRAPPERS—HUNTERS—FARMERS FISHERMEN!

IT IS TIME TO STAND UP AND BE COUNTED

DO YOU KNOW THAT TRAPPERS AND HUNTERS ARE AN ENDANGERED SPECIE?

Do you know about the Committee to Outlaw Steel Traps in Missouri? It has said that Coyotes would be removed from the open season status as far as trapping is concerned.

These anti-trapping and anti-hunting groups insinuate that trappers and hunters are cowards and bullies and that they have affected minds.

If the trapper is stopped, this will be a foot in the door, and hunting will be next. Will the fish hook be third?

A guest on a national TV program boasted that all trapping and hunting will be stopped in this country.

The support for such groups is coming from the areas where people are ignorant of the true facts.

Join with us in helping to Fight!—Fight!—Fight!

Stand up and be counted before it is too late! Write to and support our Department of Conservation. Let the people who are trained make the decisions.

Write to: MISSOURI DEPARTMENT OF CONSERVATION
P.O. BOX 180
JEFFERSON CITY, MISSOURI 65101

There are more fur bearers in the State of Missouri now than there was one hundred years ago.

We NEED the leg hold steel trap for the control of predators and fur bearers.

Missouri Trappers Association

Last but not least, the humanitarians were now squarely up against not only the furriers and the trappers, the outdoor writers and the fashion writers, the Fur Conservation Institute and the state governmental machinery; they were also up against the hunters. *Michigan Out-of-Doors*, an M.U.C.C. publication, sternly warned of an anti-leghold-trap bill. "DNR Wildlife biologists say," the publication said, "the bill would almost effectively wipe out trapping as it is now practiced. The activity generated about $30,000 annually for the Fish and Game Protection Fund." Protection, presumably, from humanitarians. Stanley Patterson, testifying on a Missouri anti-trapping bill, was asked, as is almost anyone who testifies against trapping nowadays, "Mr. Patterson, are you opposed to hunting?" Mr. Patterson said he was a hunter. If he had not, the chances are he would have been asked if he was against fishing. The Missouri Trappers Association asked not only hunters and fishermen to help them, they also asked farmers, as witness the poster on the facing page.

And indeed in *Fur-Fish-Game*, in November, 1973, an advertisement was taken by the Woodstream Corporation of Lititz, Pennsylvania, the largest manufacturer of traps in the country, for—what else—the National Rifle Association. (See p. 282.)

The furor over fur had achieved one dubious distinction. It had united the trapper, the trap maker and the hunter. But despite the power of the opposition, the bottom-line fact still remained—the cruelty of the leghold trap. I spent many days in western Canada with Frank Conibear, the world's most famous trapper. For forty-two years he has kept records and statistics—the most complete in existence—of the "survival hours" of trapped animals. I have also talked to scores of other trappers. Until the leghold trap is outlawed, any woman who

wears a wild fur, meaning, in the U.S., any fur not mink or chinchilla, has on her back at least 150 hours of torture.*

*

If man's relationship with the furbearers of the land has been suspect, what of his relationship with the furbearers of the sea? Let us begin with the seal.

* The writer wishes to make clear that, while Mr. Conibear agrees with these facts he does not agree with the writer's opinion on trapping. Indeed, Mr. Conibear's opinions on trapping are widely different from the writer's. "I believe," he told me, "that we should try to encourage the trappers to

For centuries man has slaughtered seals—for fur, for blubber, for fun fur, even for fun.

Men have shot them, knifed them, clubbed them, netted them, trapped them, quintered them, gaffed them.

They have quintered them by first clubbing them, then putting a hook through their jaws and then reeling them in like fish. They have gaffed them by driving the gaff, or spike, through the seal's eyes.

Men have also just plain kicked them to death.

Ironically, clubbing, over which the fight to save the seals began, and by which victory will surely someday be won, is not the cruelest of these deaths. It is, however, brutal and it is the cruelest-*looking*. Shooting, for example, can be worse— a seal is a difficult animal to kill with one shot.

Also ironically, the fight to save the seals began over a type of seal which is not used for a sealskin coat. He is called the harp seal and he is a hair seal whose pelt is distinctly different from the luxurious fur of his cousin the fur seal. The harp seal is so named for the grayish-brown marking on his back and sides distinctly resembling the shape of a harp. When newborn,

---

use humane ways of trapping. I think it is a big mistake to antagonize them by saying that all trapping should be banned and that artificial furs only should be worn. Statements like these only get the trappers' backs up and make it more difficult to outlaw the leghold. It is my contention that the surest and quickest way of taking the suffering out of trapping is to appeal to the trapper, pointing out that there are humane traps which perform on the whole more efficiently than legholds and that the time has come to phase out the leghold by legislation. When that time comes—and I think it is not far away—it will be no worse to wear furs than it is to eat ham and eggs or wear shoes. It is a known fact that every year nature produces many time more fur-bearing animals than those for which she provides food. . . . If the overpopulation is removed, the remaining animals enjoy a better life and produce more numerous and sturdier young. It is just as important that the suffering of animals occasioned by overpopulation be prevented as it is to prevent the suffering caused by leghold traps. Trappers using humane traps could prevent both of these evils!"

the harp seal is pure white with huge soulful eyes and is called a "whitecoat." The pelt of the adult is used for making ski parkas and boots. The pelt of the whitecoat, unbelievably, is used only for lining of gloves, boots, etc. and for trim on coats and parkas.

A harp seal, even as an adult, is a timid creature. He has practically no means of defense and, as a practical matter, is inclined, even when cruelly attacked, to run away. Fast in the water, he is on land extremely clumsy. As a baby he cannot swim at all—and although his mother, who has only one pup per year, will try to defend him, for her too on land it is a hopeless job.

Since his "whitecoat" matures at the age of three or four weeks into a less-desirable brown coat, he has long been hunted as soon as possible—at an average age, indeed, of just ten days. At that incredible age, with his mother at his side, he wiggles forward, waggling, since he has no tail, his whole backside. He goes to meet, in a curious, friendly, playful way, the first human being he has ever seen—and is, by that human, bludgeoned to death and then skinned.

Until 1964, he had only one defender—the weather. There was always the danger of storms on the ice floes of the Front of Newfoundland and Labrador and the Gulf of St. Lawrence. In 1852, for instance, some 40 sailing vessels were lost. In 1868, the sinking of the *Deerhound* took 28 lives. In 1872 the loss of the *Huntsman*, 47. In one year alone, 1914, the S.S. *Newfoundland* was lost with 77 men, the S.S. *Southern Cross* with 173. And in 1931 the *Viking* sank with a loss of 24 men —including, of all ironies, a group of newsreel men who, for the first time in history, had come to film the cruelties of sealing.

By the 1930's, however, the weather was no real ally—

because by that time airplanes and helicopters had made the seal's breeding grounds easy to pinpoint, and he was more than ever at the questionable mercy of man.

The Canadian Seal Hunt, as it is called, is in fact the Canadian and Norwegian hunt and takes place each year during March and April. It is really two hunts, one which takes place in the Gulf of St. Lawrence and another off the coast of Newfoundland and Labrador called for sealing purposes "the Front." Only native Canadians carry out the hunt on the Gulf and most of these are local people who for a pittance obtain a license and walk out on the ice to club seals. Since 1971, large commercial vessels have been banned and only small ships, less than sixty feet, are allowed to participate in the Gulf. But landsmen in the Gulf account for only about 30,000 of the 250,000 seal quota of recent years. The vast majority of seals killed are killed on the Front by large Norwegian and Canadian vessels equally. The vessels plow their way through the ice to where the seals congregate and then the hunters disembark onto the ice to club the seals. The Canadians use a club that resembles a baseball bat, but the Norwegians use a device called a hak-a-pick. The hak-a-pick is a gruesome-looking club that resembles a pickaxe with one blunt end and one pointed. The Norwegian sealer stuns the seal with the blunt end of the hak-a-pick and piths its brain with the sharp end. This, the Norwegians say, precludes the possibility of skinning the seals alive and, as gruesome as it is, may be more humane than the Canadian club.

*

In one way, the fight to save the seals, at least as a public issue, might be said to have had its beginning with Rudyard Kipling's memorable story, "Kotic, The White Seal." The first man actually to film sealing, however, was the great Scots humanitarian, Dr. Harry Lillie—the same man who had made the pioneer film on trapping, *Traplines*, and who had signed on for this purpose as a ship's doctor aboard one of the sealing vessels.

Unfortunately, as in the case of *Traplines*, Dr. Lillie's film was ahead of its time and failed to reach a large audience. But on a dark and stormy day in March, 1964, something happened which would change sealing history forever. On that day, a small Montreal film studio, Artek Films, having already completed a series of hunting and fishing television features, decided to finish the job with a short feature on sealing. At first, the company had no intention of getting involved with commercial sealing—but simply planned to take a few short shots of individuals killing seals. By chance, however, the film schedule was delayed by bad weather, and by the time the weather broke, the commercial seal hunt had begun. The very first day, Artek filmed four scenes of live skinning, including scenes which showed baby seals stunned by a rubber-booted kick, then slit open and skinned while alive—while the mother seals close by were clearly aware of what was going on. In some cases, the film showed the mother seals charging the sealers; in others, after the skinning, it showed the mothers returning to sit by the carcasses of their babies.

Twelve days later, back in Montreal, the editor of a local Montreal weekly called a reporter and asked him to cover a press showing of the film. The reporter, Peter Lust, protested that he was a political analyst, not an outdoorsman, and suggested a sports writer. The sports writer, however, was sick.

So, when he saw the Artek film, was Mr. Lust. "In my newspaper work," he remembers, "I had seen life at its worst and I believed myself shock proof." He also recalls that his first reaction was one of anger. "Canada is a civilized country," he exclaimed to the Artek film makers. "We have to tell the public of this outrage. Their indignation will stop it in short order."

The Artek men smiled. They told Mr. Lust that he was an optimist, that seal hunting had gone on for centuries and that sealing conditions had changed hardly at all in all that time. All right, they told him, he could get his article to the public, and a few members of that public would probably get angry—for a little while. Some, they admitted, would even write the Minister of Fisheries. And what answers would they get? That such things didn't exist, that the story was made up. As for the film, they would be told, of course, that it was staged —a phony.

Mr. Lust was determined to try anyway. "In the early morning hours," he remembers, "I wrote my report. It was short, as newspaper stories go. It contained nine paragraphs. I timed myself while writing it: eleven minutes, eighteen seconds. I drew a payment of $3.54. Little did I know at the time that my story would eventually reach more than 300 million readers":

> The Magdalen Islands in the Gulf of St. Lawrence are far removed from Canada's urban centers. They could be among nature's beauty spots, but instead they have become a place of agony. Terror stalks the island.
>
> A huge helicopter slowly circles the ice floes near the largest island. . . . From the ice below come hundreds, thousands of death cries. Two men watch, from above. They look at a scene of horror—small figures covered with blood convulsing on the ground in their death throes. Tiny bloodstained beings scream their death cries into the air. Among them walk men in parkas and corduroys— long wooden sticks and knives in their hands—and commit murder after murder.
>
> Are they killing people? The horrible wails would indi-

cate it. Actually, they are murdering tiny, innocent helpless babies. The victims are not human. They are baby
seals. A group of humans who have lost all semblance of
humanity skin these poor, helpless animals while they are
still alive. . . .

That story, first published in a local weekly, went around
the world. Before long, three hundred German, Austrian,
Dutch, Swiss, Belgian and Scandinavian papers had reprinted
the story; so had smaller papers from Alaska to Australia.
Even Japanese and Indian journals picked it up. Some em-
bellishments were made, and some of these were remarkable.
A Salzburg paper assured its readers that the Magdalen Islands
were "a popular resort frequented by top Government brass."
Another weekly declared that seal hunts were conducted as
"entertainment" by the rich sporting bloods of Montreal and
Ottawa; the paper helpfully compared it to "the popular British
sport of fox-hunting."

Curiously, West Germany, where, after Norway, most of
the harp-seal fur is processed, was as angry as any other country about the clubbing of the baby seals. Bernard Grzimek,
world-famous zoologist and head of the Frankfurt Zoo, leapt
to the defense of the seals. So too did the wife of then West
German President, Heinrich Luebke. "I condemn the cruel
treatment of Canada's seals," she publicly stated. "I consider
these hunts to be utterly inhumane." But the reaction of the
Canadian Government was, in its ways, just as curious. In the
beginning, the Department of Fisheries decided to ignore the
thousands of letters of protest which either reached them
directly or were forwarded by the Prime Minister or Canadian
ambassadors on the simple theory, apparently, that if they
ignored the controversy it would go away. Then, when it became obvious, even to bureaucracy, that it would not go away,

the Canadian Government first protested that no seals were ever skinned alive, and then promptly passed an amendment to the Sealing Act, stating, "It is forbidden to skin seals while they are still alive." And, finally, when all else failed, just as the Artek men had predicted, they stoutly maintained that the films were faked. Indeed, five full years later, Fisheries Minister R. J. Robichaud was stating before the Canadian House of Commons, "We now have evidence that film taken in 1964 was taken three days before the opening of the sealing season."

Mr. Robichaud had indeed evidence there was a film that had not been shot during the sealing season—but, unfortunately for him, it was not the Artek film. Indeed, this film, as was the only other Artek film ever made—in 1965—was genuine. No trick of any kind was used to make it, as Serge Deyglun, who narrated it, later stated. Ironically, the only film that was faked was shot by the prestigious Canadian Broadcasting Corporation itself—whose film crew arrived in the spring of 1964 not before but after the sealing season. CBC staffmen, to have something to show, bought a live baby seal from an islander (who, of course, had no right to sell it) and had him clubbed for the camera.

"It is impossible," Deyglun has stated, "to 'stage' such a massacre," and as one who has seen this massacre on a number of film clips, I would agree. But I also know that no matter which film of the baby-seal clubbing you cite, it will be *called* fake. When I showed, for the first time on American television, on the old Dick Cavett *Morning Show*, the horrors of the baby-seal slaughter, that film too was promptly called fake, although it was shot on the scene, during the annual scheduled killing, by a friend of mine on the ice. The plain and simple fact of the matter is that no matter how awful the clubbing scenes may

appear to be on film—and that can be very awful indeed—
they are, in reality, incredibly worse. Nor is there any real
question as to whether or not seals were, in those days, skinned
alive. The only question is how many were so skinned. The
very first veterinarian with whom I spoke on my first visit to
the ice floes in Canada was Dr. Elizabeth Simpson, a lady
who, just back from the ice, was firm on this score. "On landing," she wrote, in her official report of the 1966 hunt, "the
first thing I saw was a baby seal being skinned alive."

Nor was it, in those days, difficult to come upon documented
firsthand stories of the cruelties of the hunt. Here are some of
them from Mr. Lust's book *The Last Seal Pup*.

> Pierre T., a crewman on a vessel based on Halifax:
> "Live skinning? I saw some cases of live skinning. Killing
> a seal is tough, because it's so cold. Just try to swing a
> club in sub zero weather, with a 15 mile an hour wind
> hitting you head on. Your arms get stiff, your hands
> frozen, so you cannot aim properly. This is why so many
> cases of live skinning occur. No, we aren't deliberately
> cruel. It's so cold, so we do as well as we can. All right,
> put it this way: Sealing is a cruel, nasty business."

> Sven H., also crewman for a vessel based on Halifax:
> "We've gone sealing for the past 14 years. No one really
> wants to skin live seals. These cases are accidental but
> sometimes you cannot avoid them. It is cold, the wind
> blows, it starts snowing. You try to get seals, the club
> freezes in your hand, gets heavy. You aim and miss. You
> aim again—you hit it, not too well. The thing starts wail-
> ing. The wind blows snow in your face. You hit three,
> four times. You are sure it's dead now. So you turn it,
> open it and start tearing the skin off. Suddenly it rolls
> its eyes at you and screams its head off. Yes, it happened
> to me more than once this trip. I am not proud of it,
> but it happened, so there you are."

Eric N., a crewman of a Norwegian sealer: "I did see something you fellows might like to print. One of my shipmates deliberately blinded a mother seal with his gaff, to see it stumble on the ice. I killed the poor thing."

An observer: "1:42 P.M. I met a group of three men and witnessed the killing of a mother seal, a practice forbidden in this area by the Sealing Act. Usually the mothers flee when the hunters arrive, and return only after the hunters have gone away. This mother seal departed from the normal behavior pattern. She stood in front of her pup and tried to charge the killers who approached it. One hit her with a club. The other gored her right eye. 'Don't blame me! I acted in self-defense,' he told me later when I asked him whether he was worried that the Fisheries inspector would call him to task. The mother animal was writhing in pain on the ice, screaming terribly. The two men ignored her while they killed and skinned the pup in front of her.

Despite the documentation of such stories, the Canadian Government refused to believe them. In fact the lengths to which this government would go to discredit people who fought to save the seals was hard to believe. Brian Davies, president of the New Brunswick SPCA, was subjected to a hearing by the Fisheries Committee of the Canadian Parliament—which has been called the most unfair hearing in its history. Mr. Davies, like myself, favors total abolition of the hunt. He is also a Canadian and served his country with distinction in the Canadian Army. But "during the hearing," wrote eyewitness reporter James Quig, "Mr. Davies learned a lot":

During a five hour period in the witness stand, he learned that parliamentary committees can and do ask a witness any question that comes into their minds— regardless of how irrelevant it is to the question being studied or how embarrassing it may be for the witness.

He learned that evidence based on rumor and hearsay may be used against him—and was.

He learned that the committee has unlimited powers, need answer to no one for its action and truly is above the law of the land.

He learned that the committee has the power to destroy a man's reputation and get away with it if it so desires and he feels that in his case the House of Commons' standing committee on Fisheries and Forestry so desired.

And he learned that there was not a damn thing he could do about it.

The general procedure of the committee, many of whose members represented areas where the seal hunters lived, was to start off a question with something on the order of "Mr. Davies, you admit that your film was a fake," and then, at the end, with the reporter's pens busily scratching, ask an innocuous question like "And what time of day did you make it?" If Mr. Davies, for his part, tried to refute the statement first and then answer the question, he was cut off abruptly and told to confine himself to the question; that he was not—and this sarcastically, of course—"addressing the annual meeting of the SPCA."

Gordon Petrie, a Fredericton, New Brunswick, lawyer who represented Davies at the hearing—but who was not allowed to speak—said afterward, "I didn't believe that sort of thing could happen in Canada." He pointed out that while Mr. Davies was put under oath, another witness was not. "I think this was just another effort to embarrass and discredit him," Petrie said. "I think that was their purpose from the start."

On the specific matter of Mr. Davies' film, another Montreal film maker named Henri Stadt was brought in to say, "I think the film and I think the man who did that film not only sold himself but all of us in all of the country," and yet Davies was given no opportunity to cross-examine nor even to question the relevancy of Mr. Stadt's testimony or very presence at the hearings.

In the end, however, Canada found that world opinion was not so easy to "sit on" as Mr. Davies. Letters of protest about the killing of the seals poured into Government offices from every corner of the globe. Canadian embassies were flooded with calls. In Washington and New York, pickets appeared. On the world fur market, the price of baby-seal fur plummeted. Canada found out the hard way that millions of people cared about seals.

Desperately, the Canadian Government tried to stem the tide. At one time, in a truly remarkable example of tortured logic, the Government maintained that the clubbing of the baby seals was necessary to the Canadian fishing industry because the seals "ate a terrific amount of fish." At another time Jack Davis, who had succeeded Mr. Robichaud as Minister of Fisheries, made the memorable statement that six thousand people would lose their livelihoods if baby-seal clubbing were discontinued. At this, two Los Angeles women, Mrs. John B. Breaks and Mrs. William G. Ensfield, wrote a joint letter to Mr. Davis. "It makes one wonder," they wrote, "if Canadian authorities would frown on the cessation of the dope traffic, as undoubtedly such an occurrence would wreak real hardship on those whose means derive from the selling of dope."

At long last, shortly before the 1972 hunt, Canada gave in. The clubbing of the six-day-old baby seals was banned. Sealers were ordered not to kill the seals until they were, instead, three weeks old—at which time they are no longer whitecoats but brown-coated "beaters," i.e., seals which have learned to swim and are attempting to "beat" their way north. Also, sealers were ordered not to use clubs, but rifles—an almost incredible decision because, as we have already seen, the rifle shooting of a seal is, if anything, even more cruel than clubbing.

And the Government did not give in to these changes gracefully, poorly thought out as they were. Both Fisheries Minister Davis and Prime Minister Pierre Trudeau himself publicly declared that the killing would be just as cruel for the three- to four-week-old seals, but that nobody would care. "Mother has left," Mr. Davis said, "and the animal is no longer as cute as it was." Mr. Trudeau's statement was equally callous. "Those who protest," he said, "won't be shown those same photographs of baby seals with their big blue or brown eyes."

As to the killing being just as cruel but that nobody would care, once again the Canadian Government was wrong, this time on two counts. The new killing was not just *as* cruel— it was more cruel. And it would have been horribly more so had the seals actually been beaters, and had rifles in fact actually been used. Fortunately, neither of those situations obtained. Because pupping was unusually late, the seals which were killed were still whitecoats. They could not swim, and so they were clubbed with their mothers near them just as they had been in previous years. Although slightly older than before, they were, in fact, just as hapless and helpless at eighteen days of age as they had been at six days. However, being that much older, they obviously sensed that much more accurately, as the sealers approached over the ice, what was about to happen to them.

As for the other count, that nobody would care, on this score the Canadians were almost triumphantly wrong. If anything, more people cared, and cared, well, more. Although the Canadian Government did not make it easy to observe the hunt—one of the regulations, for example, forbade the landing of a helicopter or other aircraft less than half a nautical mile away from any seal herd—I found that even some of the sealers themselves were divided on the subject. One matter-of-fact old-timer had just returned from an entire day of bludgeoning baby seals. "I don't mind seeing an animal's insides," he told me, "for money. Nothing bothers you if you make money out of it." And another old-timer felt the same way. "I only wish to God," he said, "there were more of them." I had seen that particular sealer, on the ice itself, while a friend of his was being filmed in the process of clubbing a seal. "Hey, Joe," he had called out, "you're going into the movies."

On the other hand, many of the younger sealers felt very different. Peter Norwood, nineteen, of Halifax, told me he was proud he hadn't killed a seal as yet and that he had no intention of doing so. "All this," he said, waving his arms at the four thousand pelts already on board his ship, and the gunwales literally running with blood, "is no way to make a living." Chris Bushnell, also of Halifax, had killed twenty-five seals. "And that's all," he told me, "I will ever kill." He was later, of his own volition, demoted to mess boy on his ship. "It's pitiful," he said. "It's just downright pitiful. It's not just they're so helpless. They're so darn harmless. The last one just looked at me before I killed him. And that was it. No more. And if I ever see one of these guys start to skin one before it's dead, I'll club him."

Actually, by the time of the 1970 hunt there was little chance of that. For one thing indeed had been improved about the baby-seal hunt—the supervision. To the vast credit of the Fisheries Patrol and its chief operating officer, Stan Dudka, all

the regulations, from the size of the club allowed to the pro-
hibition of the use of the gaff, were strictly enforced. Dudka
himself, in addition to assigning two Fisheries Patrol officers
to every sealing crew, patrolled in a helicopter in all kinds of
weather. On one occasion, he was stranded for thirty hours
in a temperature of ten below zero. On another, he went on
board a ship whose men had used illegal-sized clubs, and
barred them from the ice. The captain ordered two of the men
to throw him off the ship. Dudka looked at them. "You may
be able to do it," he said, "but if you do I will be back, and
that time I will seize your ship." The captain gave in.

At first, of course, regulations about cruelty were nonexistent. In time, however, even Canadians unopposed to the
hunt, such as Tom Hughes, executive director of the Ontario
Humane Society, not only saw the necessity of them but tried
to get more vigorous regulations. Hughes, for example, pointed
out to me that it was far easier to regulate the sealers operating from ships than it was to handle the landsmen who walk
to their clubbing over the ice. And recently, owing to the regulations, the number of landsmen has dropped appreciably—
and almost all the sealers have come from ships. It is also due
to Hughes that the parish priests of the Magdalen Islands now
preach, before the start of the annual seal hunt, at least one
sermon on the subject of cruelty to animals.

Still another society which deserves credit for some improvement in the conditions of the seal hunt is the International
Society for the Protection of Animals, or ISPA. ISPA has
had, for example, an "official observer" of the activities, not
only in the Gulf of St. Lawrence but also on the "Front"
further east, where Norwegian sealers hold forth.

But there were ironies too—and especially among all the
"conservationists" and "ologists" of various kinds who came

to see baby seals being clubbed. Keith Ronald, for example, a professor of zoology, told me he was on the ice as "a representative of the Canadian Federation of Humane Societies." Yet, when I asked him about the Canadian Federation of Humane Societies, he knew, what seemed to me, remarkably little about it. He did tell me, however, that he had been observing the hunts for fifteen years—and that this was the first year that he was affected, as he put it, "by the messiness of it."

Talking to the Magdalen Islanders themselves also produced diverse answers. Some in the quaint village made no bones about their resentment that outsiders now make almost all the money from sealing. And most cannot see anything wrong with sealing and frankly cannot understand what all the fuss is about. Why, I asked one of the latter, were there so few dogs on the island? "Dogs?" he questioned. "What good's a dog? What can you do with a dog?"

Cruelty is not the only issue of concern for humanitarians and conservationists observing the Canadian seal hunt. The other issue is the diminishing numbers of harp seals returning to Canadian waters each year. Several Canadian biologists, including some employed by the Government, have expressed concern that the quotas on the harp seal are far too high and that the seal herds won't be able to sustain the slaughter. What should happen of course—an idea fostered by a wide variety of humane societies, including both The Fund for Animals and Friends of Animals—is the possibility of turning the entire area, in the Gulf of St. Lawrence, into a seal sanctuary. To this would come each March, instead of killers, tourists—tourists who would be able to view on a vast scale, in the midst of a true winter wonderland, one of Nature's greatest spectacles: the birth of one of its most beautiful animals. The possibilities would exist, indeed, of reintroducing, if necessary, other creatures menaced by "management." Meanwhile, however, and until all this happens, there is one way everybody can help in the fight to save the seals. This was best expressed to me one morning at breakfast in the Bellevue Hotel, a tiny hostelry in the heart of the Magdalen Islands, by Celia Hammond, a beautiful British model and actress who is also a leader of the English humane group, Beauty Without Cruelty. Miss Hammond had, the previous day, seen the clubbing of the seals for the first time.

"I'll never forget it as long as I live," she told me. "It may be no good trying to stop men hunting, but I do not believe there is a woman alive who could go out on that ice and see all the killing and ever buy anything made out of seal again."

*

There is one thing, however, that Americans should not do —and that is to belabor Canada and Norway for clubbing seals without realizing that America too clubs seals—each summer, in the Pribilof Islands of Alaska, in the Bering Sea. They are not baby seals, it is true; they are four-year-old adult seals, but they are fur seals and their skins are used, specifically, for fur coats.

Furthermore, unlike the Canadian clubbing, there are at least three things about the American clubbing which makes it, despite the fact that the seals are adults, in some respects even worse than its Canadian counterpart. The first of these is that the seals selected to be clubbed are first sorted out and driven along the land as much as a mile—a long, fearful, painful journey for a seal—and then are grouped, albeit all the seals are supposed to be bachelor seals, for the final clubbing. The second thing is that while the Canadian operation is at least farmed out and not directly, or at least exorbitantly, profitable to Canada, the American operation is run directly by the United States Government and is indeed exorbitantly profitable—in fact the United States Government grosses several million dollars on the deal.

The third and final thing is that all the clubbing—of 40,000 or more seals each summer, a figure incidentally, down from 120,000 in the early sixties—is done by just five men at a time out of a rotated total of eight men in all.

These men are Aleut Indians, descendants of those originally landed on the Pribilofs as slaves of the Russian Empire for the specific job of killing seals. There are about six hundred Aleuts in two Aleut communities. Although visitors are fond of making for them the usual case for primitive peoples, the fact remains, of course, that they are nowadays not so primitive. There are, for example, eight automobiles on the island of St. Paul, and in 1970 these managed, among other feats, the remarkable one of having a head-on collision.

The United States Government has an answer, of course, to the thousands of people who have already written or petitioned them on the subject of why it is engaged in sealing. Man has, as I have said, an infinite capacity to rationalize his own cruelty. In years of dealing, or at least trying to deal, with the Department of Commerce in general and the National Marine Fisheries Service in particular, I have learned these answers well. The Government contends, in a word, that it is forced to club seals—that it is bound by an international treaty dating back to 1911. It also contends that if the United States did not club seals, the seals would be subject either to shooting or pelagic sealing (i.e., "fishing"), both of which would be more cruel, on the part of the other signatories to the treaty. These signatories, incidentally, include not only

Canada, which gets 15 percent of the American "harvest," and Japan, which gets 15 percent, but also Russia—which, in turn, gives Canada and Japan 15 percent of the harvest from those islands in the Bering Sea under its jurisdiction.

The trouble with the Government's argument, of course, is that the treaty has already been voided for at least one period —that begun by the Japanese attack on Pearl Harbor— without any lasting harm to either the seal population or the economy of the Pribilof Islands, and there is no real evidence that the United States has ever made any genuine effort to sit down with Canada, Japan and Russia and discuss the basic immorality of sealing. One American animal society has in fact already discovered in conversation with the scientific adviser of the Russian Embassy in Washington, that a proposal to end the killing of seals entirely would be quite open to consideration by the Russian Government.

In any case, it should be evident to all governments that the whole question of sealing belongs in the United Nations. The seals themselves are clearly neither American, Canadian, Japanese nor Russian, and the United Nations is an organization which has not had such a signal success with people that it could not profit from a little practice with animals. It is, after all, one thing to slaughter an animal for food, and quite another to slaughter it, cruelly, for something to wear—and a luxury item, at that. "We cannot," says The Fund for Animals, "give every animal on this earth a decent life. But we can and do fight to give it, at the least, a decent death." And, entirely apart from the basic immorality of sealing to begin with, death by clubbing is clearly indecent.

To this, the United States Government answers that it has spent a good deal of time, money and effort—lately through, among others, the Virginia Mason Institute—to find alternative methods to clubbing. Shooting, for example, has been tried; so has gassing and the use of electric shocking. In shooting, it has been found that even explosive bullets do not explode when they hit the delicate skull of a seal. In gassing, it has been learned that not only is it a difficult and cruel job to get the seals in the carbon-dioxide chambers to begin with but that afterward, when the chambers were opened, out would stream the seals, screaming and gulping in anguish, but still very much alive. As for electric shocking, even a giant scissorlike device, with two electrodes, one to be fastened to each side of the seal, produced no effect. Seal fur, it seems, is an almost total insulation.

Clubbing, the Government has therefore concluded, is still the best way to kill a seal—and, from the Government's point of view, it undoubtedly is. From the seals' point of view, however, I suggest that it would be impossible to find five men to club, humanely, forty thousand ducking, bobbing, crying seals—even if the Government could find, among the Aleuts, five Ted Williamses and Mickey Mantles.

And, as a matter of cold but not cold-sober fact, it has not found them. In 1971 and 1972, summer absenteeism among the clubbers due to partying the night before a clubbing was one of the main problems in the Pribilofs.

One obvious difficulty is that the Government continues to argue on this question out of both sides of its mouth. On the one hand, it says it must kill the seals to honor the treaty. On the other, it declares that even if it didn't have to kill them, even if there were no treaty, it would continue to do so because it is such good "conservation." It points out, for example, that before the treaty of 1911 the seal population was down to about 200,000 seals in the Pribilofs, or almost at the extinct danger line, but that now, with 40,000 bachelor seals killed each summer, the population is flourishing. Again, one wonders. As late as 1948, the herd numbered 3.8 million, so while it has increased since 1911 it has obviously severely decreased since 1948. Man always seems to be concerned about the necessity of killing just the animals he wants to kill in just the amounts he seems to need. That, indeed, is from the Government's point of view almost a standard definition of "good conservation." And it certainly is, if nothing else, remarkable, that each year the United States Government comes up with the number of seals to be killed as 40,000, or very close to it. Even if there were a remotely accurate way of counting all the seals in the ocean—which there isn't—the figure would surely vary from 100,000 one year to none another year. And it is even more remarkable that at least one official of the National Marine Fisheries Service whom I asked if the seal killing would go on for "conservation" reasons even if there were no end product involved, looked at me as if I were berserk. "Why, no," he said, "not if nobody made a *profit*."

Not the least amazing of the Government's claims is its belief that tourists to the Pribilofs each summer, who witness the clubbing, do not find it inhumane. There are, however, good reasons for this belief. One is that the tour buses make sure to stop some distance from the clubbing. Another is that the guides in the buses are hardly impartial. Among other duties, these guides are responsible for having the tourists fill out questionnaires, and they are particularly anxious to receive a correct answer to the "inhumane" question. One recent summer a tour guide regularly pointed off in the far distance to the clubbing. "Now, that isn't so bad," he urged, "is it?" And "Be sure to fill in the questionnaire, won't you?" Frank McMahon, of the Humane Society, was especially indignant at this. Victor Scheffer, in *A Voice for Wildlife,* reported that the agent in charge of the sealing workers had issued sweatshirts with the words SEAL PRUNER. "By this device," said Scheffer, "he was trying to show the public that only 'surplus' seals are subtracted from the herd, for its own good."

In the final analysis, the Government case contains two great and incontrovertible ironies. One is that the United States Government supports the entire Aleutian Island community and all the six hundred people in it entirely for the dubious purpose of killing seals. The other is that the Government also gives to just one American fur company, the Fouke Fur Company, of Greenville, South Carolina, a virtual monopoly on the skins of the seals killed. Then this company takes full-page advertisements in dozens of newspapers and magazines to say that it too is part of a "great movement to save the Alaskan fur seal." And these ads are, in reality paid for by the people of the United States, because of a Government contract with Fouke calling for "compensation for promotion and advertisement."

However one attempts to rationalize it, the killing of the seals, to anyone who cares anything about animals, has become the *cause célèbre*—the fight that has to be won. In 1971, for example, I sent a new agent to the Pribilofs, one who had never seen sealing before. Her name is Marjorie Stockton, and she has lived in Alaska—a land in which, unfortunately, the mistreatment of animals seems sometimes almost a way of life. This was her report:

> After spending a week at St. Paul Island I am truly sick to realize that my Government makes $5,000,000 each season from the brutal killing of innocent seals. Let me tell you something about this. In the first place the Aleuts do not either eat seal or wear seal. In the second place, 95 percent of them are not supported by sealing

at all. Almost all of them are on welfare all year and the ones who are supported by seal killing are so supported for only six weeks.

As for the sealing itself, from the beginning, when the Aleuts beat on empty five gallon tins to awaken the seals, who are asleep in their rookery, which the Department of the Interior calls a sanctuary, to the bitter end when, already exhausted by the lung-bursting overland journey, the seals are bludgeoned to death making last, feeble attempts to help each other, it is brutal, bloody business. And when one sees a thousand to fifteen hundred seals bludgeoned per day, the words "sanctuary" and "conservation" become a mockery.

In 1971, humanitarian forces gathered in Washington for an all-out fight on the clubbing of seals. At the height of the controversy in June, 1971, a letter was sent to President Nixon and later another letter, saying virtually the same thing was circulated to all members of the House and Senate which declared:

> An organized press and television campaign is under-way to solicit support for banning the taking of certain marine mammals. . . . The undersigned national conservation organizations believe such a step would interfere with . . . scientific management. . . . Total protection, as is being urged, would halt a number of management programs. . . . Total protection also would make it impossible to manage any population of marine mammals.

This incredible document, designed as a last-minute effort to sabotage an extremely moderate ocean-mammals bill, whose chief provision was perhaps the one which forbade American citizens to have any traffic with the products of baby seals clubbed beside their mothers, would, in the old days, have worked. But in the new day, with a new wind blowing, it failed. The organizations which, to their lasting shame, did sign one or the other of the infamous documents are listed here:

American Forestry Association
Citizens Committee on Natural Resources
International Association of Game, Fish and
    Conservation Commissioners
Izaak Walton League of America
National Audubon Society
National Rifle Association of America
National Wildlife Federation
North American Wildlife Foundation
Sport Fishing Institute
Trout Unlimited
Wildlife Management Institute
The Wildlife Society
World Wildlife Fund

The Marine Mammal Protection Act was finally passed in 1972. With the exception of the continued clubbing of seals on the Pribilof Islands—an exemption granted the fur industry in general and the Fouke Fur Company in particular—this bill prohibited the killing of seals, whales, dolphins, porpoises, walruses, sea otters, sea lions and polar bears by U.S. citizens, and the import of any products there from into this country. The bill, despite it exemptions, was a landmark. For the first time in animal history, man had stopped doing something to a species not because there were not enough of them left, but because it was cruel. Sealing would go on but the handwriting was on the wall. A Seals and Sealing Committee, set up by the Canadian Ministry of Fisheries—even one dominated by the management philosophy—had, as of 1973, made two important recommendations: (1) phase-out of the Canadian and Norwegian Atlantic seal hunt by the end of 1974, followed by a minimum six-year moratorium on hunting, (2) no increase in the exploitation of seals in any other area of the world, especially in the Antarctic. Finally, in the spring of 1974, I talked with Dr. Harry Rowsell, veterinary pathologist and member of this committee—a man who has studied every method of seal killing from the Norwegian hak-a-pik to the American pole. "It's a hell of a thing," he told me. "It's a particularly hellish thing when you've got what amounts to an open-air slaughterhouse. What you've got to do is stop telling people just to write letters to Canada, Norway, etc. Tell them instead to start a world-wide campaign against the wearing of furs."

*

Unfortunately, sealing is not confined to Canada and the Pribilof Islands. South Africa and Peru kill fur seals, and our old friends, the Fouke Fur Company, each year seeks a special exemption from the Marine Mammal Protection Act to import the skins from South Africa for tanning. And there is a whole new frontier being opened up for the taking of seals. It began in 1971—a year which will live in animal infamy. The animals of an entire continent were sold out. Antarctica was opened to "commercial" sealing—i.e., bloody clubbing. Antarctica, a continent which, except for whaling operations, was the last pristine ecosystem on the face of the globe, the last place, literally on earth, where animals roamed free, unharmed by man.

In that year, hard on the heels of the news that Canada had, at long last, bowed to world opinion and had placed at least a partial ban on baby-seal clubbing came the news that our own State Department had agreed to be part of a twelve-nation conference in London. At this conference, it was a foregone conclusion, the Antarctic south of 60 degrees would be opened up.

This was the same Antarctic which, in a treaty ratified by the U.S. Senate in 1961, had been guaranteed for peaceful uses only—guaranteed in fact in a treaty which specifically spoke of the "preservation and conservation of its living resources." This was a treaty which the nations only signed, of course, not to save the seals but rather because the seals north of 60 degrees were gone. Starting in 1775, when Captain Cook visited South Georgia, the Antarctic suffered almost two hundred years of bloody butchery. As far back as 1820, in the South Shetlands, 250,000 seals were killed in a single year. Relatively recently, when the fur seals were annihilated, the sealers turned on the Southern elephant seal, which was rendered for oil, and then for good measure also decimated several species of penguin.

The worst cruelties of all were inflicted during the pelagic expeditions—when the seals were fished from open water. Only one animal in three killed was ever retrieved, let alone the thousands upon thousands of wounded left to die. And then, at long last, came the treaty.

And now this was to be broken by a new treaty. Why? Had Canada stopped its clubbing because of an under-the-table agreement to open the Antarctic? No one knew. But one thing was certain. Great Britain, the host of a conference to discuss it all, was determined to keep out even the "conservation" people, let alone the humanitarians. So one man, Tom Garrett, representing Friends of the Earth and The Fund for Animals, was in the position of being the sole representative of millions of people over the globe who had protested the massacre of seals.

In the entire eight days of the conference, not a single soul mentioned the word "cruelty." "I honestly think," Mr. Garrett told me, "they regard anybody who even thinks in those terms as being just as strange as you and I regard anybody who doesn't."

The British, who do not kill seals themselves but process a very large percentage of all the world sealskins, were hopeless. So were the Norwegians, who told Mr. Garrett they would seal in the Antarctic in '72 with or without the treaty. There was, however, one piece of good news. The Argentinian and Chilean delegations both believed that the seals should be protected. Australia proposed a compromise—that the quota of Weddell's seals to be taken be cut in half and all other quotas reduced by one-fifth. Despite the scathing reaction of the British, this was accepted by the Norwegians and temporarily by other delegations, until the Soviets suddenly demanded the restoration of the full quota of crabeater seals. When the quota of crabeaters was raised, a last-minute effort by the U.S. and Chilean delegations to trade this increase for a total exemption of Weddell failed.

The other delegations couldn't have cared less. A brief disputation arose and the Japanese, who were expected to be intransigent on all questions, yielded with surprisingly little resistance and were soon backing a ban on all taking of seals in open waters. "This," Garrett told me, "was a particularly pleasant surprise, since a portly science advisor to the Japanese delegation, during, if I may so put it, the bulk of the proceedings, slept peacefully in his chair."

The final result was an incredible treaty—one by which, on the one hand, a majority of nations cannot halt abuses without the consent of the abusers, on the other a majority can at any time raise quotas and further weaken controls, and cannot be prevented from doing this by a minority.

Yet this was the treaty initialed for the U.S. by a man who bore the title Coordinator of Oceanic Affairs for the State Department. "I remember thinking," Mr. Garrett told me, "that even if I had been ordered to initial it, I could not have done it."

*

No chapter concerning man's exploitation of mammals for profit would be complete without mention of those leviathans of the deep—the great whales. These gentle giants are among the earth's most intelligent creatures, not excluding man, and yet if man has not the intelligence to stop their slaughter at once, they most certainly will be gone forever.

Many books of late have told the whales' sad story. Earlier ones, of course, from *Moby Dick* on, had glorified man's savagery toward them. Indeed, whole American towns, such as Mystic, Connecticut, and Sag Harbor, Long Island, still bask in the gory glory of yesterday. Actually for centuries man has hunted whales. It started in the twelfth century, in the Bay of Biscay, with the Biscay "white whales." In the past fifty years more than two million whales have gone into oil, soap, shoe polish, candle wax, pet food, margarine, fertilizer and cosmetics—not a single product for which there is not an adequate substitute. Farley Mowat, the great Canadian writer, has told in his book *A Whale for the Killing* the story of a whale trapped in a cove, and of how when he tried to enlist the aid of Canada's leading mammalogist in an attempt to rescue it, the man said he couldn't help—that he had to go to a meeting at the American Museum of Natural History to study incredibly, whale skeletons.

One man who is no longer a whaler is Aristotle Onassis. But some years ago he was indeed—with a vengeance. He started his whaling fleet in the late 1940's, and it was then probably the most modernized one ever—complete with nineteen "units," a "mother ship," sixteen "chasers" and two tankers, not to mention a helicopter, radar equipment and explosive harpoons. This murderous flotilla, which cost $60,000 a day to operate, was apparently under orders to harpoon every whale it sighted. And, in so doing, it ran afoul not just of outraged humanitarians but of entire governments. At one time the Peruvian Navy, feeling the fleet had violated Peru's offshore limits, attacked the flagship and seized the fleet. At another time, the Norwegian Government tied up a shipload of whale oil. The Norwegians, according to George Carpozi, charged Onassis with exceeding whale quotas, catching whales out of season and violating limitations on their minimum size. Onassis settled by paying $435,000 to the Norwegian whaling industry and then finally sold his fleet in in 1956 to the Japanese for $8 million. The bar stools on Mr. Onassis' famous yacht, *Christina,* were covered, he once told me proudly, with the skins of whales' private parts.

The great blue whale, the largest animal ever to have lived on this earth, is probably already past the point of biological extinction. George Small, in his book *The Blue Whale,* has best written its epitaph:

> The tragedy of the blue whale is the reflection of an even greater one, that of man himself. What is the nature of a species that knowingly and without good reason exterminates another? How long will man persist in the belief that he is the master of this Earth rather than one of its guests? When will he learn that he is but one form of life among countless thousands, each one of which is in some way related to and dependent on all others? How long can he survive if he does not? It might be easier for man to acknowledge his dependence on

other life forms if he could recognize his kinship with them. Whatever the nature of the Creator, he surely did not intend that the forms on which he bestowed the gift of life should be exterminated by man. Survival chances for the human race will be greatly enhanced when man concedes to the Earth and all its life forms the right to exist that he wants for himself. The only homage he can now pay to the blue whale is to learn the lessons of dependence on and kinship with all life. If he does not learn them the great blue whale will have died in vain—having taught nothing to his only mortal enemy.

Who still kills the great whales and why? The who is much easier to answer than the why. The Japanese and Russians are, for the most part, responsible for the killing, taking approximately 85 percent of the annual catch between them. Norway, Iceland, South Africa and a few other countries share the rest. The United States, to its credit, protects the whales via the Endangered Species Act, and Americans may not kill whales or import any products made from whales. Furthermore, at the twenty-fifth International Whaling Commission meeting in London in June, 1973, the U.S. delegation, headed by Dr. Robert M. White, fought long and hard for a ten-year moratorium. And, even though the moratorium failed, the United States did succeed in convincing some of the previously borderline nations to support reduced quotas. The Russians even voted against the Japanese for the first time on one quota issue. And no delegate could doubt that the commission saw firsthand the beginning of a new statute for the private citizens of the world who had gathered to save the whales. In this country, this effort was headed by Project Jonah and by Project Monitor in Washington, D.C., the latter a coalition of environmental organizations largely put together by Dave Hill —and a score or more of regional groups such as Phoebe

Wray's ESP in Boston and Tony Mallin's SOS in Chicago. The Fund for Animals is proud to have been the first to suggest a boycott on Japanese goods. Indeed, at the whaling commission meeting in 1973, Patricia Forkan, The Fund representative not only roused the delegates with a speech for a moratorium on whale killing immediately, she even received congratulations from the Russians.

Still, as far as Japan was concerned, it was not enough for them apparently that the United Nations Conference on the Human Environment had gone on record for a ten-year moratorium on whale killing by a vote of fifty-three to nothing. Before the Whaling Commission meeting in June, 1974, the presidents of Audubon, Sierra, National Wildlife, and The Fund for Animals—representing seventeen environmental groups with a membership of 5,000,000—paid personal visits to the Japanese and Soviet embassies. It was to no effect. There was no moratorium. After meeting in London, the Japanese and Russian delegations even voted against the Australian compromise which set three categories of whale management with a new concept of optimum population. Indeed, as this book goes to press, only one thing seemed to be working—the boycott. Witness the letter written by the president of the Nissan Motor Corporation, makers of Datsun, to the Japanese Consul in Los Angeles, in the early days of the boycott on February 28, 1974:

> I know you are aware of the tremendous amount of adverse publicity which Japan has received in connection with the harvesting of whales. At this time, however, I am obliged to call your attention to public pressure now being directed at Japanese companies doing business in the United States.
> Our company has received hundreds of letters from

concerned people who are saying they will not purchase
Datsuns or any other Japanese products until the exces-
sive killing of whales is stopped.

Such a boycott of Datsun products is especially ironic
for our company. As you may know, we originated the
"Drive a Datsun—Plant a Tree" promotion in 1972
and as result, planted 250,000 trees in United States
National Forests. This idea was subsequently used in
Japan and other countries and many more trees were
planted around the world. Nissan has always advocated
ecology and has always tried to be a good citizen in countries where it does business—hence, the irony of being
threatened now in connection with an ecological issue
over which we have virtually no control.

I feel that the concern of the people writing to us is
real. These concerns should now be fully made known
to the government of Japan and we are asking that you
please convey these latest developments to the proper
people.

United States citizens, however, are still far from faultless in
the killing of one kind of whale—which is, ironically, perhaps
the greatest of all the creatures of the deep. This is the dolphin.
In the course of the taking of tuna fish, the U.S. tuna industry
kills a staggering number of dolphins. Indeed the kill numbers
between 200,000 and 300,000 dolphins. This industry, which
until recent years caught tuna one at a time, discovered a few
years ago that it could be much more efficient if it used a
large purse seine or net to catch tuna by the school. For
reasons no one yet fully understands, schools of yellowfin tuna
accompany schools of certain species of dolphin. The latter,
traveling above them and leaping out of the water as they do,
are far easier to detect than the tuna. Thus when the mastheads-
man of a tuna clipper spots the dolphins, he knows there are
tuna present and immediately launches small high-powered,

high-speed power boats. The huge purse seine is then shot over the stern and the dolphins are herded into the net with the tuna following them. Unhappily, the dolphin, which is a small, air-breathing whale, when netted and held underwater drowns. The industry has no use for the dead dolphins, and their killing is entirely a waste. For many years, nothing at all was done about this. In 1970, however, the Detroit Audubon Society, under its able leader, Joe Bartell, initiated a tuna boycott. The National Audubon Society, to its vast discredit, refused to back it. Nonetheless, Bartell and his small group persisted. And they played no small part in the fact that when the Marine Mammal Protection Act was passed in 1972, it gave the tuna industry only until March of 1974 to find a way to stop killing the dolphins. The industry, dragging its feet if not its nets, asked for an extension, to approach, as the act stated, "zero mortality." Again, as we went to press, dolphins were still being killed in incredible numbers. And here again one may ask, as I did in the case of the raccoon, if man will not lift a hand to save the dolphin—a creature which, in countless documented cases, has actually rescued and saved man—what chance can there be for lesser creatures?*

*

If the United States is still at fault where dolphins are concerned, it is even more so in its contribution to the virtual

---

* Michael Greenwood, a man who worked for ten years as a senior researcher on dolphins for the Navy, quit in 1973 and blew the whistle on use of dolphins and "killer" whales in Navy "research." The first way the Navy uses them is as a "swimmer deterrent system," which is Navy euphemese for killing enemy swimmers, and was actually used in Vietnam. In this the dolphin is fitted with a nose cup to which is attached a lance to which, on the other end, is attached a syringe. When the dolphin rammed the "target," the syringe released high pressure gas, which caused collapsing of stomach and intestines. The second way is a "back-pack system," in which the dolphin wears a saddle over his dorsal fins and carries anything from an

extermination of another of the world's most fascinating creatures—which exists some six thousand miles from our nearest shore. This is the kangaroo. For countless centuries, this creature has captured the imagination of people around the globe—carrying as it does its young in its pouch, boxing playfully with its joeys, or babies, and hopping from place to place with incredible speed and grace. Yet not only has the United States taught Australia, as it has other countries, the horrors of its so-called "management," in the case of this animal it has gone further and actually provided Australia with its major economic incentive for the massive slaughter of these creatures. Until 1973, indeed, the United States market accounted for 75 percent of kangaroo exports. And we annually imported the incredible total of one and a half million kangaroo pelts. These were used not only for such items as football, baseball, basketball and other athletic shoes, as well as riding boots and ski equipment, but also for furniture and, inevitably, fur coats. Everything, indeed, from can openers and kangaroo-paw bottle openers to kangaroo-tail soup. The most ironic use of all was probably fur for the stuffed souvenir koala bear, an animal which in Australia is totally protected.

Finally on January 11, 1973, primarily owing to the work of a handful of kangaroo defenders in Australia and one twenty-six-year-old American housewife in Washington, D.C.,

---

instrumentation system to, theoretically, explosives. This is better than the nose cone system from the Navy's point of view because it doesn't inhibit the dolphin's sonar capabilities. Its disadvantage, like the nose cup lance, is that it can be seen. The third use of the dolphin is converting it into a super spy by hiding whatever it's carrying inside the mouth and suturing it to his fore-stomach or, by major surgery, placing it deep in its stomach. The fourth and final way is using him in a tow system—with a ring over his nose such as you've seen at Marineland, etc. The next Pearl Harbor, Mr. Greenwood says, may well be just a silent swish in a crowded harbor— one signifying a school of dolphins or "killer" whales carrying either deadly bacteria or hydrogen bombs.

by the name of Marian Newman, Prime Minister E. Gough Whitlam announced a ban on the export of all kangaroo pelts. But two questions remained. As Martha Hodge Amory reported, after a firsthand study, it could have been too late. Seven out of fifteen species of kangaroo had already been wiped out, and in Queensland, infamously known as "the slaughter state," the average annual kangaroo kill was over a million animals. In October, 1972, when a State Parliamentary delegation journeyed seventeen hundred miles to the northwest part of the state, though they traveled both by day and by night—the kangaroo having been forced by the slaughter to become a nocturnal animal—they found not one single live kangaroo. Mrs. Newman herself, on a five-week trek through "kangaroo country" saw only forty-two 'roos.

The second question was, would the ban, which after all affected only the export market, have any influence on the continued domestic slaughter? According to Professor Harry Messel, the Australian Government's top wildlife scientist and the architect of the export ban, it would—but only if the U.S. Department of the Interior would place the kangaroo on the Endangered Species list. As of the summer of 1974, this department had, unfortunately, still deferred that decision. Meanwhile, Professor Messel informed Mrs. Newman and The Fund for Animals that he sorely needed letters from American defenders. A.W. Bickerton, Minister of Flora and Fauna for western Australia, had gone so far as to propose a plan to poison over a million kangaroos—by putting arsenic in waterholes—unless the ban was lifted. One American letter, Professor Messel told The Fund, to the Honorable Lionel Murphy, Minister of Customs and Excise, would do more than ten letters from Australia.

Colin Simpson, author of *The New Australia,* has best told the story of the great Red Kangaroo and his beautiful smoky-blue doe, the Blue Flier:

> One of these graceful animals, when pursued by a horseman, across a dusty plain where the tracks were checked afterwards, made ten leaps of 37 feet, then cleared an 8 foot fence with a leap of 42 feet. But kangaroos will not ordinarily jump a fence more than five feet high. Some are able to travel, when pressed, at thirty miles an hour. . . . But kangaroos are not hunted by horseman and dogs anymore. The jeep type vehicle that goes out to get night-feeding kangaroos has spotlights and telescopic sighted rifles on padded gunrests. The light-blinded kangaroo has no chance—not even of instant death if the shooter is more interested in skins than meat. It has to be shot in the hip, which marks the hide less than a chest shot. When the shooting is over, the kangaroo is finished off. Does are of good value— they may have a joey in the pouch.

Charles Baines, the fearless Australian head of the Save a Kangaroo Committee sums up:

> It is up to the people of America then to take heed. Remember that Australia is a unique country. It has unique marsupials and strange birds. It has strange people too. They are the only race on earth who exploit their national emblem. But you can help to save the kangaroo from extermination by resolving never to purchase articles made from his leather or fur.
>
> If the Commonwealth Government yields to the pressure of vested interests and revokes the proposed export ban even before it is implemented, not only will it be the bitterest blow yet suffered by those who have fought so hard and long on behalf of the persecuted kangaroo, but the Government on which so many dedicated conservationists had pinned their hopes will lose all

credibility. The long twilight of the kangaroo will deepen into the darkness of complete oblivion while the gluttons count their pieces of silver.

Like the unicorn, the kangaroo, betrayed by his people, will remain just a memory—a fabulous figure on a coat of arms—a constant occurring reminder of the political idiots who brought about this extermination.

And we, perhaps even more than the Australians, will have been responsible.

III: For Revenge

The Most-Persecuted List

To single out the most-persecuted animal on earth is not easy. Man has persecuted them all, and with almost equal abandon. Whatever species one chose, someone else would probably choose another. The snake, of course, would have to be one candidate. Another would be the skunk, albeit for a different reason. The names of both of these animals have, in any case, becoming epithets for us. Yet these lowly creatures are, in their way, as indeed is the very tallest animal of all, the giraffe, not only kinder than man but, in one way at least, smarter. As Heini Hediger of the Zurich Zoo has pointed out, bull giraffes can smash the skull of a lion with one blow of their forefeet. When they fight with other giraffes, however, they use only their forehorns, which are covered by a padding of thick skin. And rattlesnakes, which, with their deadly venom, can kill animals a hundred times larger than themselves, do not use it for fighting with each other. They do not even bite; instead, they settle their contests seemingly on points, according to an agreed-upon ritual. As for skunks, they too squirt their secretion only at other predators—not at other skunks.

Now take man, and all his marvelous weaponry. What has

he learned? Perhaps some day, when he has finally renounced biological and nuclear warfare—and, for that matter, thrown away his guns—then it will be time to compare him with his betters. Then at last one may be able to say that he has the brains of a giraffe, the sense of a rattlesnake and the decency of a skunk.

Meanwhile, let us continue our search for the most persecuted. I have often said that if I could decree the end of all cruelty to just one animal, I would probably choose the donkey—that most abused of all the beasts of burden. But there are so many others to be considered—the horse, the dog, the cat, the rabbit and so on. And, since we have already brought up the subject of zoos, almost any animal in at least some zoos is subject to almost total persecution. And certain animals in even good zoos would qualify. Take, for example, the story of an elephant named Ziggy, whose address is the Brookfield Zoo, Chicago.

Ziggy is the biggest (13,440 pounds) and oldest (54) elephant in captivity. At the age of two, in 1922, he was bought from the Ringling Circus by the late showman Flo Ziegfeld, as a present for his six-year-old daughter, Patricia. Ziggy was taken to the Ziegfeld home at Hastings-on-Hudson in New York. Unfortunately, despite his name, within a matter of months Ziggy proved too much for the Ziegfelds, and had to be sold back to the Ringlings, who promptly resold him to Singer's Midget Circus. Here, in traditional circus fashion, Ziggy was "taught" to play "Yessir, That's My Baby" on a harmonica while smoking a cigarette out of a long holder and dancing on the top of a drum. Once, while engaged in this obscene activity, while the circus was on a tour in Spain, the entire stage collapsed under him. Ziggy was never the same again. In 1936, when the circus visited the San Diego Exposition, Ziggy curled his trunk around a stray musician and hurled him across the ring. After that, he was sold to the Brookfield Zoo and put in the charge of animal trainer George Lewis. The latter in time, introduced him to a female named Nancy.

On April 26, 1941, when Mr. Lewis was taking Ziggy for a walk in the area where he had hoped to find Nancy, Ziggy, becoming infuriated at not finding Nancy, threw Lewis across the yard and then, between his six-foot tusks, pinned him to the ground. Fortunately for Lewis, the tusks stuck in the ground—one is now broken off—and he was able to escape.

For this crime, Ziggy received thirty years' solitary confinement indoors, chained to one spot. Finally, in 1971, after $50,000 had been raised—partly by the schoolchildren of Chicago, partly by Buick-Opel dealers—a special sliding-door outdoor area was built and Ziggy was paroled. Man's revenge was over. For the first time in thirty years, Ziggy saw the light of day. He stayed out exactly one hour, and then moved back inside.

Although the aftermath of the Ziggy story is a happy one—in the spring of 1974 he was given a second female for company—the story for other zoo animals is all too often not so. Take, for example, the case of two orangutans at the Los Angeles Zoo. This zoo was built as recently as 1966 at a cost of $9 million. Nonetheless, from the point of view of the animals it was so inexpertly designed that almost immediately $7 million more had to be spent. And yet still, as we go to press, there is no decent home for many of the animals that man has chosen to imprison there. "Seven years ago," wrote the Los Angeles *Times*'s Mike Goodman, "two orangutans were put in a padlocked cage inside a gloomy, barn-type structure out of public view. . . . They are still there today." "We realize," said Michael Crotty, curator of mammals, "these aren't the most attractive facilities. But you humans can't put yourself in that animal's place."

Maybe not—but we wish *his* humans would give it a try. The whistle was blown on the Los Angeles Zoo, incidentally, by Michele Pugh, an eighteen-year-old zoology student. "This zoo kills giraffes," she told a Fund for Animals meeting in the summer of 1973—and it was the truth. In five years, the zoo has lost four out of a total of seven giraffes. The reason— "slippery floors." And yet as reporter Tom Thompson discovered, there was, as early as 1968, evidence of complaints about the "slippery floors."*

If you think the Los Angeles Zoo is bad, try the Racine, Wisconsin, Zoo. Here, under a tiger cage, you can read the sign "SIBERIAN TIGER—-USEFULNESS: PELTS FOR DECORATIVE PURPOSES." Under a bear cage there is the sign "SYRIAN BROWN BEAR—USEFULNESS: HIDE FOR RUGS, MEAT FOR FOOD." And, finally, under an African lion, "USEFULNESS: PELTS AND RUGS."

You know, humane education. And even the Racine Zoo is not by any means as bad as the so-called roadside zoos— which, despite the able efforts of Defenders of Wildlife, still abound. Nor is it, for that matter, as bad as a zoo which has the largest number of visitors of any zoo in the world—New York's Central Park Zoo. Not long ago this zoo was called by Richard Sweeney, founder of the American Association of Zoo Keepers, "a menagerie for people and a jail for animals."

---

* A 1974 postcard from Ms. Pugh, from San Francisco, is at hand. "Dear Cleveland," she writes, "The San Francisco Zoo makes the L.A. Zoo look like a paradise! There are a few good enclosures but way too many bad ones, leading to the discomfort and deaths to many of their animals. This zoo does not have a non-feeding policy and they have no security day or night."

Unfortunately, it has not turned out to be a safe jail. A few years ago in the Central Park Children's Zoo, two "children" leaped over the wall and, when a playful duck waddled forth to greet them, they strangled it to death. In 1974, after five fallow deer in the zoo were brutally beaten with heavy sticks, zoo officials were forced to string barbed wire across the open tops of the animal pens. In between, in 1971, Skandy, a gentle polar bear, was tormented by a man—one who had already been warned away from other cages for tormenting other animals. When the man stuck his arm into the cage, Skandy grabbed it. A policeman came up and, after firing two warning shots, shot Skandy dead. A newspaper reporting the incident headlined the story "COP SHOOTS VICIOUS BEAR." The zoo bought two more polar bears.

The Central Park Zoo was not alone. A mother polar bear at the Detroit Zoo was so tormented by teen-age visitors that she went into her den and killed her own cubs. At the same zoo, a bowhunter shot a duck, while someone else stoned to death a baby wallaby—one who had, for a moment, left the protection of his mother's pouch. Still other vandals hurled firecrackers at a pregnant reindeer; the animal had convulsions and miscarried. Not long after this, visitors to the alligators were caught dropping cigar butts on their backs, then laughing when the alligators reacted to the burns. Finally, when a hippopotamus came over to a man for peanuts, the man, who thought he was very funny, rolled a tennis ball down its throat. The hippopotamus choked to death.

Obviously the time had come for zoo keepers to let the animals out and put the people in. And, in a sense, this is just what did happen in the zoo world—with the emergence of the Lion Country Safari concept. The animals would run free, and people, caged in cars, were not allowed even to roll the windows down. Even the greatest of American zoos, the San Diego Zoo, soon followed suit. But this concept too could lead to cheap imitations—when the animals, obviously to be seen better, were fenced right on the road. Only if it was a true "running free" concept could it meet the demands of a concerned animal-caring public. Such a public was no longer asking, but demanding, that animals be protected. In America, in Africa and everywhere else. The name did not matter. Call them large zoos or small reservations. What mattered was real protection.

In Africa, indeed, there is a story of a kind of protection visited on at least one animal. The incident occurred at a South African park outside Durban. The story is related by Gualtiero Jacopetti:

> In Queen Elizabeth Park, as in every other African national park, the principle was in force that the visitor literally could not even move a stone. It was obligatory, among other things, to keep the car windows closed in the park, even if it was 100 degrees in the shade. Nevertheless, a regular visitor to Queen Elizabeth had a close friendship with an elephant. He went to visit it almost every day, and brought it delicacies. The animal was spoiled and associated the idea of an automobile, from which the arm stretched out food, with food itself. So the elephant began to molest every vehicle that came close to it. When it didn't see any food forthcoming, it would reach out its trunk and shake the car, maybe hoping that some nuts would fall out. Well, this animal was brought before a judge because it had damaged a dozen cars. Get this: it was a real trial with a judge, a public minister, a defending lawyer, and witnesses. All the newspapers in West Africa followed that trial with detailed reportage. Public opinion was aroused . . . and when the elephant was absolved, everyone breathed a sigh of relief.

Even the most manlike of all animals—monkeys—belong on the most-persecuted list. Monkeys live a long time—from twenty-five to forty years—if they are lucky. Most monkeys, unfortunately, live for only a fraction of this. It has been estimated that there are 750,000 pet monkeys in U.S. homes today, most of whose owners don't admit that they have them. Yet, statistics show that nine out of ten monkeys die within one year of purchase.

The really sad thing is that monkeys make terrible pets to begin with. If you don't believe it, take the word of Michael Corradino, who runs the Florida Monkey Sanctuary. Though a working newspaperman, he devotes all his spare time to it— and his wife, Janie, practically all her time. They started it in 1968 with eleven monkeys on a city lot, and they now have, on ten acres, seven miles from Venice, Florida, over 130 monkeys. Almost all of these have come from homes that could no longer keep them. The Corradinos make the flat statement that all monkeys become aggressive, and even potentially dangerous, once they reach puberty, and can inflict serious wounds. They also warn that humans cannot, even under the best conditions, supply the monkeys' emotional needs. Monkeys are highly personal animals—the male monkey will love the wife, hate the husband; the female, vice versa. On top of this, there are very few humane shelters anywhere that are properly equipped to take monkeys. Then, too, the pet trade and the animal laboratory trade have brought many kinds of monkeys to the brink of extinction. All in all, the Corradinos figure that, at the most, again under the best conditions, monkeys can be kept as pets only for eight years. Remember, this out of that twenty-five to forty-year lifespan.

*

Even in an animal Utopia of the future, there will still undoubtedly be animals on which man will, as the saying goes,
"turn." Indeed, of all the animals on what one might call the
Most-Persecuted List, there is one whose very name is synony-
mous with "turning." It is, of course, the wolf. In fable ("Little
Red Ridinghood"), in art (the victims being thrown out of
the Russian troika in "Pursued by Siberian Wolves"), in song
("Who's afraid of the big bad wolf?"), in history (the Romans
gave five drachmas for a dead male wolf), even in the Larousse
dictionary his persecution goes on: *Wolf: A member of Canis,
a genus of large, fierce carnivorous mammals of Europe, Asia
and North America, which hunt in small groups and prey on
deer and caribou, etc.; (popular), a man who tries to pick up
women and seduce them; in music, a discordant sound, harshness due to unintended vibrations; "a wolf in sheep's cloth-
ing," a person whose evil intentions are masked by friendly
manners; to "cry wolf," to raise false alarms; to eat greedily
and quickly is to "wolf one's food."*

Farley Mowat was, before he wrote his classic *Never Cry
Wolf*, equipped by the Canadian Wildlife Service Department
with what he called one of "the standard works on wolves."
"The wolf," he read, "is a savage, powerful killer. It is one
of the most feared and hated animals known to man, and with
excellent reason." Shortly after reading that, Mr. Mowat had
his first long personal encounter with the "savage," "powerful,"
"feared," "hated" "killers." They were playing tag.

From personal observation, he learned that a female wolf
mates with only a single male, and mates for life. He learned
that when, by the deaths of their parents, wolf pups are left
alone, another pupless pair will take over the job of rearing
them. And he also learned that even on the occasions when he
crawled into a wolf den and surprised the family—and was

totally defenseless in front of them—even then they did not attack him or indeed seem to bear him any malice at all. Finally, he told the story of a wolf "attacking" an airplane:

> Two men in their own light aircraft had flown out from a large city to help rid the world of wolves. During previous hunts they had killed many, and the pilot had become adept at chasing the beasts so closely that his skis would almost strike them. One day he came too close. The harassed wolf turned, leaped high into the air, and snapped at one of the skis. He died in the ensuing crash; but so did the two men. The incident was described in an article in a widely distributed sportsmen's magazine as an example of the cunning and dangerous nature of the wolf, and of the boundless courage of the men who matched themselves against him.

Many years ago a Canadian newspaper offered a reward of $100 to anyone who could prove that a wolf had, unprovoked, attacked him. The reward has never been collected, yet the senseless slaughter of this truly remarkable predator has gone on unabated from the days of John James Audubon to today. The landmark effort to change man's ridiculous vengeance on this animal was an MGM documentary called *The Wolf Men*, which was shown on the NBC network in November, 1969. It included everything from shots of "wolf man" George Wilson entering a wolf den and observing the birth of wolf puppies to a far different type of wolf man engaged in shooting wolves from airplanes and afterward even eating, accompanied by camera smiles, raw wolf meat. The impact of this film was so profound that, when NBC scheduled a rerun of it, the sheepmen pulled out every stop, including demands for an "equaltime" anti-wolf documentary. James L. Powell, president of the National Wool Growers Association, wrote the president of NBC that the man who ate the wolf meat had been, as he put it, "tricked" by a member of the film crew into "putting a piece of raw wolf meat to his mouth." "Any livestock man can tell you," Mr. Powell wrote, "that wolf numbers are increasing in nearly every area of the United States." This, at a time when there were fewer than five hundred wolves running "free" in the entire continental United States, virtually every one of which was either in Minnesota or in a special study sanctuary at Isle Royale in Michigan. And, at a time when the only other wolf left, the red wolf of Texas, was, according to the *Christian Science Monitor*, the rarest mammal in North America.

To its credit, NBC did not agree to an equal-time documentary. To its shame, however, it canceled its scheduled rerun of *The Wolf Men*. Meanwhile, in 1972, Canada's Province of Quebec announced a wolf hunt. In this, it was announced, there would not only be a prize for the most killed, but there would also be, for every hunter who killed a wolf, a trophy consisting of the jaw of the wolf set in an acrylic block, with the hunter's name inscribed on it. The objective was, according to the Montreal *Gazette*, to wipe out two of every five wolf packs in the province. At the last moment, the Quebec hunt was called off, credit for which was primarily due to the television protest of Dick Cavett and a letter-writing campaign initiated by Lewis Regenstein of The Fund for Animals, as well as by Araby Colton, president of the Canadian-American Wolf Defenders.

In the winter of 1973, a new wolf crisis arose when the U.S. Defense Department, through its Defense Supply Agency, incredibly enough issued orders for 368,782 winter parkas trimmed with wolf fur. It was estimated that to fill such an order would have required at least 25,000 dead wolves. Again, public outcry was such that the Defense Department rescinded its order. And here credit went not only to the same figures as above, but also to the remarkable work of Congressman William Whitehurst of Virginia. Indeed, when the Defense Department finally agreed not to use wolf fur but to substitute some other wild fur, it was Congressman Whitehurst who called them to task on this too. Instead he fought for—and won—the use of synthetic fur. The final irony was that not only did synthetic fur prove, by Army tests, as far as warmth went, "an adequate alternative to natural fur," the use of synthetic fur also resulted in the saving, to the taxpayer, of over $1 million.

*

The most remarkable effort to change man's thinking about the wolf was carried out not by a Congressman, by an animal society or indeed by an animal worker—it was, instead, carried out by an animal.

His name was Jethro. A timberwolf, he was born in the Lodi Zoo in California and had no fewer than three owners before he came into the hands of John Harris, a rugged individualist with whom Jethro was destined to spend the remainder of his seven-year life. "Tamed," as Mr. Harris often puts it, but not "trained," Jethro became the world's most famous wolf, traveling hundreds of thousands of miles and personally visiting with and being petted by more than a million people—at schools, in colleges, in shopping centers, theaters, exhibition halls and ecology centers. First by himself, later with his friend and fellow wolf, Clem, Jethro traveled in behalf of the North American Association for the Protection of Predatory Animals, The Fund for Animals, Defenders of Wildlife and many other groups. In Washington, D.C., Jethro and Clem even appeared in the Capitol itself, where, at the behest of a bipartisan committee headed by Congressman

Whitehurst (Republican) and John Dingell (Democrat), they were bipartisanly patted by Senators and Congressmen. At the height of the Minnesota wolf controversy—an effort to make the wolf a "game" animal—Jethro appeared on the steps of the state capitol in St. Paul. On those steps, he was faced with an opposing demonstrator who not only criticized "wolf lovers" but also read from an anti-wolf placard. As if on cue, while photographers took pictures, Jethro moved quickly over and took a large bite out of the opposing sign. In Chicago, at the World Flower Show, Jethro was given the Animal of the Year Award by The Fund for Animals. "Jethro," the plaque read, "Wolf Without Peer and Animal Ambassador Extraordinary. An Ambassador without Portfolio or Collar, who has traveled the country from coast to coast, with patience, understanding and fortitude, to plead the cause of all animals everywhere."

Again, just as I was reading from the plaque and television cameras were recording the event, Jethro found the ceremony a little too long. Gently but firmly he moved forward, grabbed the plaque, put it down between his paws and started chewing. On another occasion, taken through a school library, Jethro ate a book. And on still another occasion, on *The Bob Kennedy Show* in Chicago, when a new guest was introduced, Jethro suddenly leaped across both the new guest and the host and started to eat the sofa. On *The Cromie Circle*, also in Chicago, Jethro apparently decided to close the show shortly before the end. He pulled out of Mr. Harris's restraining hand and, from the end of the set, grabbed a corner of the rug and proceeded to pull Mr. Cromie, Mr. Harris, two other guests and the entire set out of camera range.

Jethro could spot edibles around the corner. At one animal meeting a woman had picked out three tea sandwiches and put them in her pocketbook to take home to dinner. Before leaving, however, she wanted a last pat of Jethro. She came through the line of people waiting to pat him and Jethro was evidently no more aware of her than of anyone else. As she stooped to pat him, however, Jethro made his move. In a flash he had her handbag, first in his mouth, then in his paw, then shaken open. Before the woman knew what was happening, he had eaten all three sandwiches.

On the early morning of July 29, 1973, parked in a locked van on a shady street in Brooklyn, outside the home of Tony Nocera, administrator of the Jethro Lecture Series, Jethro and Clem were fed poison. Jethro was dead by the time Mr. Harris and Mr. Nocera found him the next morning. Clem, in convulsions, died on the way to the animal hospital. A trial of the alleged poisoner proceeded. In the words of John Harris, "Jethro and Clem did not die a natural death. We did not feed them anything that day. They were regularly fed every other day. And we cleaned and watered the van before leaving it. Yet the autopsy clearly showed their stomachs were full of chicken, and there was also chicken inside the van. An eyewitness testified she saw the defendant prying the edge of the van door open. What else do they need?"

However, the judge who tried the case did not admit the autopsy into evidence because it was not brought to court by the veterinarian who performed it. Nor was the fact the wolves had value even discussed—wolves as pelts might be valuable, it was ruled, but not wolves per se. Finally, and incredible as it may see, the judge ruled, "There is no proof here how the wolves died. That would be essential before you could prove anybody guilty of malicious mischief."

It was not enough that Jethro and Clem, who had given so much, who had done so much, had to die such a long and cruel death. It all had to come under the heading of "malicious mischief."

*

Last but not least we come to the very top of our Most-Persecuted List—the coyote. Pronounce him "ki-oat" or "ki-o-tee," either is correct, and he won't care. But mark him well, and do not allow the mystery and marvel of him to be lost in familiarity.

All right, he *is* familiar. He has been located in virtually every state in the Union and he even appears regularly, usually along with the Late Late Show, in Los Angeles' backyard.

He is famous the world over as perhaps the most "American" of all wild animals—indeed, he sometimes seems the very symbol of the American West—but, like so many other animals nowadays, he needs your help and he needs it now.

Highly photogenic, with an eerie, never-to-be-forgotten howl —one with which he sings to the sun, to the moon and in heartbreaking relays to his own kind—he is the little brother of the wolf, yet a close cousin of the dog. If, on the one hand, he is incredibly quick, sharp-witted, cunning and resourceful —no other animal has all *three* senses, sight, smell and hearing, as keen as his—on the other, he is loyal, playful, humorous and even philosophical.

Basically monogamous, coyotes mate, if not for life, for long periods. And, if two unmated males are fighting for the same unmated female, after it is all over she is likely to choose, not the one who won, but the one who lost.

When the pups come, they are taught to hunt, at the age of two months, not by the mother but by the father. And discipline is severe. It is not unusual, for instance, to see a father coyote returning to his den and his pups rushing out to meet him, but, no matter how far away the father is, at a certain invisible line—obviously the greatest distance they are permitted to go from the den—the pups will stop short.

"Next to God," goes the Mexican saying, "the coyote is the smartest person on earth." Even if this is exaggerated—the coyote is, after all, far too smart to be, by human standards, "brave"—the fact remains that he is, if not the most intelligent of all animals, certainly the cleverest.

He would have to be.

Man has made his very name suspect. The second definition for the word "coyote" in the new American Heritage Dictionary is, as we have already noted, "contemptible sneak." For two hundred years, the coyote has faced a steadily increasing campaign to eradicate him from the face of the earth. Many animals have faced such campaigns, but against no other animal save possibly the coyote's big brother, the wolf, has the campaign reached such heights of insane cruelty and brutality.

Some time ago, for example, in Liberty, Kansas, one T. G. Castleberry caught 553 coyotes in 59 days—then draped every carcass on his barn, literally covering its entire front. More recently, Captain Howard Hyde, traveling north of Limon, Colorado, on Highway 71, came upon five strung-up coyotes beside the road, each one with a beer bottle fastened in its mouth. "To be demented," Captain Hyde wrote, "is unfortunate, but to publicly display evidence of one's derangement can lead to no good."

In the old days, the coyote was hunted for his pelt. Then, when pelts dropped in price, he was hunted because he was supposed to be a cattle killer. Then, when it was proven he wasn't a cattle killer—he lives almost exclusively on mice, moles, rabbits, insects and snakes, and even eat fruit for dessert

—we was hunted because he was supposed to be a sheep killer. Finally, when it was proven he wasn't a sheep killer, he was hunted because he was a lamb killer. And when even that was found to be ludicrously exaggerated, he was hunted because he was supposed to kill what man wanted to hunt. Not hunt to eat, of course, but for "sport" hunting. The coyote is classed, simply, as a "varmint."

As such, there is no season on him—for on him it is always open season. Virtually alone among all animals too, for him there are literally no rules of even basic decency, let alone fair play. He is hunted by land, he is hunted by air and, if he ventured on the sea, he would undoubtedly be hunted there. Again, virtually alone among animals, he has learned that the air can be dangerous, and when he even hears a plane, let alone sees one, he takes cover and, like a trained guerrilla fighter, camouflages himself.

The coyote is regularly jack-hunted, by light, by night—— something forbidden by law for most animals. Not, however, in the case of the coyote. "Most hunters," says one hunting magazine about the "sport," "clamp a powerful light directly to their guns and keep it on at all times."

In the winter, snowmobiles hunt the coyote down, with the hunters signaling to each other by walkie-talkies. In the summer trained hunting dogs run him down in relays. Often, indeed, the coyote is chased by dogs riding in automobiles— then, when he begins to tire, the automobiles stop and the dogs are released.

It has been said that the coyote will eat anything that doesn't eat him first. As we have seen, this is not true. But courage he has, and far more than that with which he has been credited. Curiosity is his Achilles heel, wariness his secret weapon. Stories of coyotes outwitting hunters are legion. Coyotes will work in teams, alternately resting and running to escape dogs set upon them. They have even been known to jump on automobiles and flat cars to escape dogs. And they have also successfully resisted bombing. Lewis Nordyke reports that, once when a favorite coyote haunt in Texas became a practice range for bombing, the coyotes left—temporarily. Soon they were back to investigate, and finding that the bombing at least kept people out, decided to stay, meanwhile learning the bombing schedule and avoiding the bombs as well as possible.

Some coyotes have gotten along with their lower jaws shot off. Joe Van Wormer reports that an agent in Idaho captured a coyote whose mouth had been cruelly wired shut. It was able to open it only half an inch, but nonetheless had been able to survive. A coyote in Montana also had her jaw wired shut— she was used by a hunter to "train" his dogs. And a female coyote killed in Tule Lake in northern California was found to have four healthy pups in her den. She had managed to fend for them although she herself had been shot in both eyes with a shotgun and was totally blind.

From some hunts there is, of course, no escape. John Farrar in his *Autobiography of a Hunter* writes of an all-too-typical hunt in the sandhill region of Nebraska. It was, he writes, "a well-planned military maneuver," with a plane overhead to spot the coyotes and, below, hundreds of hunters. "They came in pickups," he says, "armed with short-wave radios, powerful engines, clinging snow tires . . . each nervously fingering a high-powered rifle with telescopic sights."

> At the next section line 12 men awaited his approach. At 100 yards head-on, it began. His faltering speed spared him as bullets churned the snow ahead. As he reached the ditch he sank shoulder deep and floundered desperately. Astonished, ashamed or empty, no one fired.

As he struggled across the road and into the next section he seemed to crawl. As if he were shielded, 30 or more rounds left him untouched. In a weedy draw he could run no further. In cover no more than 12 inches high, he disappeared.

The plane circled and then the men closed in afoot. Talk of letting this one go passed idly. Twenty-five armed men closed in on a terrified, exhausted animal. The enclosed area dwindled to the size of a football field and less. Still no coyote. Some, relieved, hoped he had escaped.

Then he appeared, staggering, worn, mouth agape. He weaved pitifully up the hill among the hunters, as if defying death, or seeking it.

Then man, the rational animal, the pinnacle of evolution, the great humanitarian, gunned him down.

There was little back slapping. Just a sickening, nauseating silence. The day ended. With it ended my coyote hunting.

When the coyote is not hunted, he is trapped. For the coyote there are especially horrible traps—to match his ingenuity. So-called "passion" bait is soaked in a piece of wool and put under a pan. When the coyote investigates, the slightest pressure releases the deadly steel leghold.

Once the coyote is caught, he will often gnaw off his leg rather than remain in the trap. Literally thousands of coyotes have existed for life on three legs. But there are thousands more, too, amazingly, two-legged coyotes. One female coyote in Michigan had only stubs for front legs—she ran like a kangaroo—and yet, when killed, was bearing five unborn pups. A coyote in Colorado existed for more than a year missing two feet—the left front and right hind. In New Mexico a coyote got along, somehow, with both feet missing from his right side, and still managed to raise a family. Trapper Art

Cooper once caught a coyote in two traps at once. One trap caught him by a front foot, one by a hind. The two-trap set was fastened to an iron drag, and when Cooper and a companion came upon the coyote he was trying to cross a plowed field. Seeing the man, the coyote grabbed the drag in his mouth and took off.

Marguerite Smelser tells an even more remarkable coyote trapping story—of two Government trappers who spent weeks tracking down and trying to kill a whole coyote family. First the nursing mother was trapped, then released after the trappers had fastened a collar and tire chain to her. By the trail of the dragging chain, the trappers expected to follow her to her den, where they could then wipe out the pups.

But for two weeks the mother coyote did not betray her family. Her mate brought food to her at night and kept the pups fed. And so, after days of frustration, convinced the mother would never endanger her young, the trappers tracked her down and killed her.

Later, however, they did get a chance at the pups—the trappers came upon them playing at the far side of a dam. At this juncture the father coyote suddenly appeared and, acting as a decoy, managed to divert the trappers' attention until he was shot—and his young had safely disappeared into the brush.

I have on my desk something called a "Humane Coyote-Getter," which is advertised as the "Marvel of the 20th Century." Humane? It is literally a trap gun. A bait is soaked in urine and covered with a jacket, then placed over a bullet cartridge, the whole being set in the ground. When the coyote investigates, the bullet is set off by a spring and shoots the coyote in the mouth with sodium cyanide. This in turn, on contact with the coyote's mouth, or eyes, or wherever it hits him, releases gas, and the coyote gasses himself to death. Or perhaps just blinds himself.

This Coyote-Getter is, by coyote-getting standards, actually humane—at least compared to the more general way of killing coyotes. That is, plainly and simply, by poisoning them. Texas alone, for example, put out in one recent year 300,000 strychnine tablets—tablets which are slipped into an inch square of sheep suet. The death from strychnine is slow and cruel—and the people who put it down admit that at least 70 percent of the baits are picked up by "other animals"—but it goes on.

Even strychnine, horrible as it is, is as nothing compared to the dread Compound 1080, or sodium monofluoroacetate. This is a poison so lethal that there is no known antidote. It is chain reacting—thus, when a meadow mouse eats it and is in turn eaten by a larger animal who is in turn eaten by a coyote who is in turn eaten by a mountain lion—well, 1080 will have poisoned them all.

Perhaps the most horrible thing about Compound 1080 is that it is administered in small doses. Not because it is expensive—unfortunately it is not; it is cheap. But it is administered in small doses so that the coyote will get as far away from the bait as possible before he dies, and thus not be able to warn, by his body lying there, other possible victims. Coyotes have been known to travel as far as twenty miles to die—in incredible agony.

The United States Government has already poisoned more than a million coyotes. The "Poison Map of Northwest Colorado"—one made by a friend of the coyote, Alfred Etter, after his own dog was poisoned—is in itself a study of bureaucracy gone mad. The real irony, though, is not that poisoning is done by your Government, it is that it is done on your land—in other words, public land. It is true that after the scandalous findings of the Leopold Report, the so-called "Predator and Rodent Control Board" had to change its name to "Wildlife Services," but if they thought they were decreasing the irony by changing their name, they were not. The fact remains that the sheepmen graze their sheep on *your* land, public land, which they use for a nominal fee—and then have *your* Government poison *your* coyotes with *your* money, Government money, merely on the suspicion that they kill sheep. And all this despite the Leopold Report's firm warning, "For every person whose sheep may be molested by a coyote, there are perhaps a thousand others who would thrill to hear a coyote chorus in the night."

*

The coyote has had its defenders. Montana State Senator Arnold Rieder early came to the aid of what he called "this gallant little animal." "We wonder," he asked, "if this creature of nature was not meant to have a fairer life. By a twenty-five-to-one ratio, the coyote's deeds have been beneficial to man." So did Oklahoma's Senator Gil Graham, who spent a lifetime among Indians and animals. "I consider the coyote," he said, "the most unjustly accused of all animals." Paul Maxwell, another coyote friend, not only aided orphaned and wounded coyote pups in his own house but also quoted his friend Jimmy Siebert. "I ranched sheep for fifty years," Siebert told him, "and I never had a single sheep killed by a coyote." Then too there was Texas rancher Arthur Lytton, who for forty years ran a twenty-thousand-acre spread. "I would never," he said, "allow a predator to be killed on my land. They are necessary for the balance of nature. Kill them and you're in for nothing but trouble—from rabbits and rodents and everything."

But the vast majority of the sheepmen turned deaf ears to

such voices. Their fury against the coyote knew neither bounds nor even sanity. Frank Dobie told the story of a sheepman who liked to saw the lower jaw off a trapped coyote and then turn him loose for his dogs to tear to pieces. Dobie also wrote of a coyote trapper's way of collecting coyote urine—he would sew up the female's vulva, pour water down her mouth, wait two or three days and then kill her and take the bladder. Stories of skinning coyotes alive are common; coyotes have also been scalped alive. In Washington State not long ago a case was reported to Raymond Davis in the Defenders of Wildlife office of some men who had trapped a coyote and then burned it alive. In the same state, Les Boyd, a Whitman County farmer, finding a dead coyote nailed to a fence post, posted a sign to the same fence. "Attention," he wrote. "This semi-tame coyote, who was eradicating mice from the fields, is the victim of a thoughtless act by man—which is supposedly a reasoning animal."

Farmer Boyd was not joking. Research by wildlife management student Peter Black at the University of Idaho indicated clearly that mice, not sheep, was the coyote's favorite food. Black's coyote autopsies turned up as many as twenty-seven mice in one coyote, and his findings revealed that of the stomach contents of coyotes examined mice constitute 90 percent.

But the revenge—and the poisoning—went on. In 1971, the last year of unrestrained poisoning, the coyote-poisoning program cost the public over $8 million. And of course the program didn't just poison coyotes. In a typical year, the wildlife "body count" was as follows: 89,653 coyotes, 24,273 foxes, 20,780 bobcats, 19,052 skunks, 10,078 raccoons, 7,615 opossums, 6,941 badgers, 6,685 porcupines, 2,771 red wolves, 1,170 beavers and 842 bears.

On December 15, 1971, under the chairmanship of Senator Gale McGee of Wyoming, a hearing was held on the subject of this poisoning. I was merely one of a dozen or more witnesses against it, but, testifying for both The Fund for Animals and the Defenders of Wildlife, as well as for the World Federation for the Protection of Animals, I achieved at least one distinction. "Gentlemen," I began, "on the question before us . . ." Senator McGee stopped me. "I think," he said, "you could be accused of undue influence on the chairman of this committee." At this the sheepmen in the rows behind stirred comfortably. They were certain that I would be brought up short. I did not know what was coming. "Last night," continued Senator McGee, "my daughter attempted to shake me down for fifty cents for a button for your organization. Furthermore, I paid."

At this the sheepmen became very quiet again. I thanked him and continued. "On this question," I proceeded, "there is a man who has, literally, written the book. I would like your permission to place into testimony and put in the record his entire book."

My request was granted. It was a book entitled *Slaughter the Animals, Poison the Earth,* and it was written by a man named Jack Olsen, well-known author and senior editor of *Sports Illustrated.* Mr. Olsen is a rugged six-foot-twoer who at that time lived on a mountain top in Colorado, from whence he could survey vast stretches of land—land on which, as his book described in an utterly unforgettable way, the United States Government was engaged in a poison program of such dimensions that even to read about it and not do anything to help stop it seemed a criminal offense. I finally corralled Mr. Olsen by telephone and asked him to come first to New York and then to Washington. "Listen, bud," he told me, "there's only one way I'll come to New York, and that's handcuffed to a Federal marshal. Since I discovered fresh air, I don't even like talking to New York on the telephone. It's contaminating.

"When you live at nine thousand feet, you don't get many animals," Mr. Olsen told me. "But some nights we get as many as eleven coyotes that come around. I put out Purina dog chow for them, and they really turn out for it. Raccoons come too. They love Purina. People should know that if they live in wild places, even where there aren't many animals, if they'd put out maybe five bucks worth of food a month, they'd get plenty of animals. And, particularly for the coyotes, it would help them in their tough periods—those starving times.

"There's one thing about coyotes, though. They're so smart. If you try to get out to see them, even if you click the front door, they're gone. Once they even went when I clicked my camera from *inside* the house." Mr. Olsen paused. He was obviously thinking about his coyotes. "Yes," he said slowly, "smart. I guess that's why they're surviving."

I asked Mr. Olsen if any of his neighbors—he lived, after all, among people, many of whom were responsible for the poisoning—liked his book. There was a long pause. "Well," he said, "the nearest thing to something like a compliment was said to me by a Colorado game warden quite a ways from here. It was when the eagles started dropping like flies. 'When you came here writin',' the warden said, 'I wasn't sure you knew what you were talkin' about. But you must have known something.' "

Mr. Olsen did indeed know something. His book tells how his work started—for a projected *Sports Illustrated* article about Government trappers:

> . . . for several weeks I roamed the West with crack district field assistants and their supervisors. Gradually it began to dawn on me that even in the presence of an

editor of a prestigious conservation-oriented magazine, these hand-selected government employees were engaged in the wholesale violation of their own rules. I saw them shoot coyotes on private land without authorization, and put out traps that were plainly illegal. I watched them mount murderous campaigns in farm areas where they had been begged to desist. I joined them in long coffee-sessions with rich sheepmen who bragged openly about their violations of state and federal poisoning regulations, while the district field assistants shook their heads and cluck-clucked, apparently for my benefit. I listened as the trappers spoke about their hatred of predators, parroting Mother Goose attitudes and spinning yarns about mountain lions bushwacking fifty sheep at a time and leaving them to die horribly. As they spoke, they seemed neither hypocritical nor insincere, and I came slowly to the conclusion that they were not necessarily villainous or even blameworthy. They were simply poorly directed inheritors of the tradition that had won the West, a tradition that there were God-fearing Americans on the one hand, and every other living thing on the other hand, and the slaughter of anything in this second group—Indians, buffaloes, coyotes—is acceptable. I concluded that there was nothing morally wrong with these men; they were simply trapped in a John Wayne movie; they were locked into another century.

Moving as were those words, Mr. Olsen's conclusion, after 287 pages of detailed documentation of man's insane revenge on nature's greatest and ablest predator, was even more so:

Within a few decades, the last mountain lion will be gone. Bears and bobcats will hold out longer, because there are many more of them, and the wise and canny coyotes will outlast all the other large predators. But unless there are massive changes in the American Way, unless the livestock lobbies and the Federal poisoners release their stranglehold and give up their myths and prejudices, the day will come when the last weak and sickened coyote will drag himself to his feet and lift his voice to the skies there will be no answer. Then the graceful animal that Paul Maxwell called "the smartest and best nature-balancer ever put on the face of this earth" will disappear into the silence of eternity. "When the last individual of a race of living things breathes no more," William Beebe wrote, "another heaven and another earth must pass before such a one can be seen again." We animals of the earth are a single family, and the death of one only hurries the others toward the final patch of darkness.

In February, 1972, President Nixon issued his now historic Executive Order 11643, banning the use of most predator poisons on public land. The Environmental Protection Agency quickly followed suit by canceling the registration of these toxic chemicals, thus banning the interstate shipment of most of them (cyanide, strychnine, thallium and sodium monofluoroacetate, or 1080) for private use. Almost immediately the National Wool Growers Association launched a well-financed pressure campaign to force the White House to reinstate poisoning. Newspaper and wire-service stories began to appear throughout the country as well as advertisements. "EAT MORE LAMB," one said. "20,000 COYOTES CAN'T BE WRONG." The stories told how sheep flocks were being decimated by bloodthirsty coyotes, who didn't even kill the sheep, the stories ran, just drank their blood. Such accounts also complained that since the poison ban the coyotes were proliferating "like rabbits." Lewis Regenstein described the showdown in an article in *Environmental Action* entitled "Gunfight at the D.C. Corral":

> The pressure campaign culminated during the week of January 22, 1973, when the NWGA staged its convention in Washington, D.C. The sheepmen descended on

the nation's capital to have it out once and for all with interior Secretary Morton and these other easterners in government who "just don't understand the problems of the west." Rumors abounded that the ranchers had drawn up a petition signed by several western governors and senators, and planned to present it—amid much publicity —to the White House and the Environmental Protection Agency. The NWGA even managed to corral as their keynote speaker Agriculture Secretary Earl Butz, the President's newly-appointed "super cabinet" member and special advisor for natural resources who theoretically had the power to overrule the Interior, EPA and CEQ and order a massive resumption of poisoning. Conservationists were worried for, in the past, Butz had generally sided with industry in disputes with environmentalists.

But things did not quite turn out as planned. During that same week, the death of Lyndon Johnson and the announcement of the Vietnam peace agreement prevented the NWGA from getting any significant media coverage. Their January 23 press conference was attended mainly by conservationists who had "infiltrated" to find out what the wool growers were up to. The only real notice given to the convention was a front page society piece on their banquet by Washington *Post* reporter Henry Mitchell. He wrote a devastating article reporting that the toastmaster had wound up "linking coyotes, synthetic fibers and other problems with such horrors as polluted rivers, the countryside in shambles, ecologists, editorial writers, homosexuals and the failure of the Ten Commandments in Washington." (With the theme of the evening being a return to old values and patriotism, it was not appropriate to continue discussing why eagles should be shot.) But the final blow to the sheepmen's hopes came when Secretary Butz, in his speech, advised that "the conservation movement is here to stay, and we're going to have to learn to live with it."

Still the sheepmen would not give up. When I wrote an article for *The American Way*, the magazine of American Airlines, entitled "Little Brother of the Wolf," a flood of letters attacked the magazine in general, and the editor, Glenn Walker, in particular. Bill Sims, executive secretary of the Texas Sheep and Goat Raisers' Association, was one of these. He advised that "the man who chaired yesterday's hearing before the Texas House Subcommittee on Wildlife . . . is a close friend of the president of American Airlines," and he also advised that at the same hearing "I heard man after man swear, under oath, that he had lost from five to 300 sheep or goats this past year to coyotes. On many occasions the only thing the coyote did was to slit the throat and suck the blood."

I tried to answer this Dracula charge. I said that any man who would swear under oath that he had lost three hundred sheep or goats to coyotes in one year was a man to whom, at the very least, I'd like to address a few questions. The first of these is how many sets of books he keeps. I presume, like some ranchers, he keeps one for himself and another for the coyotes. I also presume that at night, instead of sheep he counts coyotes. My second question would be concerned with what *he* does to defend his stock. After all, it is hardly the responsibility of his Government both to defend his animals and at the same time give him the opportunity to graze them at practically no cost. At the poison hearings I had defended the rights of the stockmen to defend their animals against predators—with a dog, with a man, even with a gun. But not on public land— your land and my land as well as theirs—with poison. Tom Garrett, Wildlife Director of Friends of the Earth, put it far better than I did. In a letter to the Western Governors, refuting the National Wool Growers Association's claims, Garrett prefaced his remarks by explaining that he was "not an Eastern

academician nor a little old lady in tennis shoes. My grandfather began freighting into the Wyoming territory about 100
years ago. I was born on an isolated ranch in Wyoming . . .
and my views on predator control derive from personal observation spanning almost thirty years." Garrett, who had himself
ranched for twenty of those years, ended his letter strongly.
"The NWGA campaign," he said, "is deepening the public
image of the sheepraiser as a poisoner and misuser of public
land. This hoopla will certainly benefit some well-paid lawyers
and lobbyists, but it cannot have any long-term benefit for
working ranchers and farmers."

Perhaps even more remarkable was the statement presented
to the Subcommittee on Environment of the Senate Commerce
Committee in May, 1973, by a man named Dayton Hyde,
owner and operator of a six-thousand-acre second-generation
cattle ranch in southern Oregon. "In fifty years and two generations," he testified, "we have not lost one single animal to
predators. A small band of stray sheep wintering untended on
my ranch lost not one single animal, although coyotes were
ever-present. . . . Year after year, the same old pairs of coyotes
maintained their same territories and we knew many as individuals. Their pelts were good and knowing where every
mouse run and brown squirrel hollow was in their range, they
made a good living and bothered nothing. Left alone, they did
not increase the food supply. Without my permission, a light
plane flew over my ranch, scattering strychnine and meat.
Within a mile of my house, I found fourteen dead coyotes and
my English setter.

"Poisons do not work," Mr. Hyde concluded. "They kill
many animals but they do not solve the problem. . . . I feel
that the livestock industry has come to believe its own propaganda about predators, and only when it accepts the fact that

poisons are not going to be available and realizes that reduction of predators does not insure an end to losses, will it then look for answers in the areas of research and management. There are things that can be done." Mr. Hyde listed five of these:

> Better fencing of lambing areas.
> Better selection of herders. I have personally found several hundred sheep wandering unattended in forests and the herder drunk in camp.
> Development of repellents or breeds of sheep more able to protect themselves.
> Stricter leash laws to control roaming dogs and to prevent interbreeding of feral dogs with coyotes.
> A better method of determining causes of death among sheep or even a system where livestock owners are reimbursed for losses by predators that can be authenticated.

Unfortunately, to the cry for the coyote which arises not only from humanitarians but also from naturalists, ecologists and biologists, the sheepmen have had, so far, only one answer. This cry is, as one of their publications put it, "the maudlin sentimentalities of the Peewit Twitter Society." Unable to poison on public lands, they have been determined to saturate private lands. In Colorado, for example, in direct violation of the Colorado Division of Wildlife's policy and its own published regulations, the State Department of Agriculture, in 1973, issued 18 permits that list bears among the target species —this for a poison program on 110,000 acres of private land. A pamphlet published by the Cooperative Extension Service of Kansas State University entitled "Controlling Coyote Damage" advised people not only to trap coyotes but also to get their pups. "Plug the hole," it said, "so the pups can't get out." *Defenders of Wildlife News* for April, 1974, told the story of

Bureau of Sport Fisheries and Wildlife employees "denning," as it is called, with gas cartridges:

> Similar to incendiary grenades used on the battlefield, they contain phosphorous and sulphur among other things. Ignited, they burn like a railroad fuse. When the smoke gets heavy in the tunnels and the pups begin to have difficulty breathing, they crawl toward the tunnel entrance. It's not hard to tell when the pups reach the fire of the gas cartridge. You can hear them from quite a distance. The B.S.F.W. personnel who man the Denver, Colorado, research lab should be required to be present when the pups crawl into the fire. With their training, these men should have developed a humane gas for killing coyote pups at least twenty years ago. Perhaps a recording of the sounds of the coyote pups dying might spur their efforts.

Your tax money pays for this, of course. And then, too, there are all kinds of coyote hunting. Two years ago, for example, a coyote hunt took place in Lake Wales, Florida, the coyotes having been introduced into the area from the West by "local fox hunters," as the report stated, "to give their dogs fresh sport." One hunter, Barney Keen, asked why he was hunting coyotes with all kinds of equipment—equipment which ranged from pickup trucks to long wires to fish pups out of dens—was adamant. "Those coyotes," he said, "killed more than 400 lambs, goats and calves on my ranch." In Karval, Colorado, one hunt boasting nine pickup trucks with specially bred "coyote dogs" (mixes of greyhounds with Irish and Russian wolfhounds) penned in quick-release cages in the back billed as "The Biggest Coyote Hunt in Colorado History." Scores of hunters and dozens of dogs hunted all day—their total kill, five coyotes. Rancher Ralph Yoder explained that they didn't like to shoot the coyotes. "That's an insult to these hunters," he said. "They like to let the dogs get them. It's the sport of it."

Such "sporting bloods" notwithstanding, the procedure of the coyote hunt remains essentially the same. The coyote, having been run to exhaustion by trucks and then by teams of fresh dogs and, finally having to fight them, having done his best, at last, when he can fight no more, presents his throat, coyote fashion, in a gesture of submission. The dogs, of course, apparently not understanding the fine sporting sentiments of their coyote-hunting owners, tear him to pieces anyway.

Such hunts—the Karval hunt even included an official "observer" from the Department of the Interior—have outraged coyote friends. The Fund for Animals, for example, has announced an annual award of $500 for prior information leading to the stopping of any such hunt, and also announced that it would back any group engaged in breaking up such hunts by any means short of actual violence. One such Fund-supported group, the Defenders of the Coyote, located in Kansas City, already includes more than a hundred college and high school students as well as businessmen and housewives.

One remarkable defense of the coyote occurred in—of all places—the State of Maine. In 1973, State Representative Roswell Dyar, a hardware and hunting-goods storekeeper, put a bill into the Maine Legislature asking for a $50 bounty on the coyote. It was, seemingly, the right State for it. In Maine, so strong is the "hunting ethic" that even bounties on bears were not challenged until out-of-state hunters began valuing the bears more as trophies than as game. The State has had a bounty on bobcats since 1922; at $15 per cat, it had paid out more than $400,000 for dead bobcats. What chance then for the coyote?

It soon appeared he had much chance. "Dyar and Company," wrote John Cole, editor of *Maine Times*, "had badly underestimated both the number and the variety of the state's coyote defenders. The new voices were coming from quarters that Dyar and his people had never anticipated. The formerly invincible, rural, agricultural, hunting, fishing, farming Maine citizen—the descendant of the settler, the clearer of the forest and the builder of barns and bridges—this patriot was being contested in his own land. Incredibly a varmint was being defended; a four-legged outdoor demon had been recast as a sympathetic hero." Fighting for his bill on the floor of the Maine House, Dyar shouted, "These anti people—and when I say anti, I mean they are anti war, anti motherhood, anti work, and anti you-name-it—they are all against this legislation!"

But, as Cole makes clear, it was not the "anti" voices that proved most effective in killing the bill. Rather it was an elderly, weatherbeaten gentleman named Frank Gramlich, Maine State Supervisor for the Division of Wildlife Services— the very Government agency which had for so long been entrusted with the attempted official extermination of the coyote in the West. Mr. Gramlich's testimony was delivered in quiet, clipped tones:

> For fifty years, my service has shot, poisoned, trapped and clubbed tens of thousands of coyotes. None of it worked. . . .
>
> In Nevada we put out more than one million poisoned baits, which killed other animals too, and we clubbed hundreds of coyote pups. There was no significant reduction.
>
> In California, we spent $8,000 to trap one coyote. And we could spend $15 million in the state of Maine and we still could not exterminate the coyote population.
>
> Our department is against bounties now; all our previ-

ous experience tells us they do not work. It is an archaic
practice. And with the growing forces in this country
against the blood sports, with the eco-awareness of the
'70's, enacting a bounty would only accelerate those
forces and hurt the hunter.

Something that would hurt the hunter! Obviously the bill
would have to be defeated. In the long run, some coyote friends
believe the only answer is to make a pet of him—and there
has been signal success in this regard, the coyote's charm and
loyalty overcoming all difficulties save one. This one, unfortunately, is the law itself. In Kansas City, for example, when
young Greg Rhodus brought home a baby coyote whose
mother had been killed by a plow, the Rhodus family fed it
from a bottle and raised it with, among other things, poodles.
The coyote never acted wild or bit anyone and when partly
crippled by being hit by an automobile, even came through
that. The only thing that finally hurt it was a law the Rhodus
family did not know existed. A conservation officer appeared,
seized the coyote and shot it. The Rhodus family learned, too
late, that wildlife can be kept legally as pets only if purchased
from a licensed wildlife breeder and a "wildlife hobby license"
is purchased from the state. Otherwise anyone who rescues a
wild animal has, at least according to the Missouri Conservation Commission, three alternatives—he can turn it loose, place
it in a zoo or destroy it.

Or, presumably, he can take it out and hunt it and injure
it again. In any case, the Kansas City dog pound refused to
abide such cruelty. When a coyote arrived at the pound and
was slated for extermination, no one in the pound would do
the job. Today the coyote is still the mascot of the pound and
regularly visits schools and colleges for educational purposes.

Still another answer, some believe, is to meet the coyote

literally halfway. Have him, in other words, as he is, half pet and half wild. One who believes this is Los Angeles' Gerald Coward, a man who, on a lonely walk up a canyon a few years ago, managed to make a lasting friend of a coyote. Coward, a photographer and writer, gave up his job and from that day on, for two and a half years, he walked up his canyon. And every day, for two and a half years, his coyote faithfully met him. All day they played, romped and explored together, learning about each other—and then, at the end of each day, they said goodbye. When the coyote mated, he even brought his companion to Coward at the same rendezvous. It was a remarkable idyll that existed until the terrible Los Angeles fire —when Mr. Coward saw his coyote no more. "The coyote," he said, "is the greatest animal there is."

Mr. Coward believes, as Mr. Olsen believes, and this author believes, that when the last coyote howls down the canyon, and there is no answering cry, the handwriting will be on the wall for us too.

A FINAL NOTE:

As this book was going to press, I received the following communication:

Gentlemen:

As a typesetter for [an outdoor magazine name withheld], I came across your statement on and against "sport" hunting among those, pro and con, of other organizations. I had been becoming rather tolerant of hunting in the three months I had been with ———— but still essentially anti-hunting for "sport," if not entirely. (Few conservationist arguments for it are at all convincing; in fact, most are contradictory to my mind.) Anyway, yours was the best argument against hunting

I had heard yet; it didn't pussy-foot around, trying not to alienate our rugged he-men hunters, so big and brave with their guns, as did the Audubon Society "stand." I think it takes a world more guts to love nature and admit it than to kill a helpless animal at a safe distance, hiding in a blind. That's not sport, it's the cruel, cowardly game of power-crazy, trigger-happy children; to them Conservation is only a big word they hide behind.

P.S. Please respect my request for anonymity, if you quote me. (I need my job!)

To me this note says volumes. But to release our wild animals from the bondage of the arms manufacturers and the gun and ammo magazines many things must be done. State laws against cruelty to animals must be applied to wild animals —as they were originally intended to do—and they must be upheld by the courts. Fish and Game departments must be reconstituted, so that the nonhunter may be not only represented, but represented in the proportion that his numbers warrant. State conservation and natural-resources commissions too must be totally reorganized. They have no business in the promotion of this billion-dollar butchery. The animals themselves must be legally realigned. The animals do not "belong" to the individual state any more than you "belong" to your individual state. Then too, the Federal Government's U.S. Fish and Wildlife "Service" must be, in reality, a service. It has taught the whole world "game management"; now it must get out of the "game" and unteach the "management." And, finally, if the National Rifle Association insists to the very end that the slaughter of animals is basic to its cause concerning the right to bear arms, then that cause, or the organization, or both, must go. Somehow, we believe the country will survive the privation.

These things will take time. But, meanwhile, you can play a part. How does the conservation or animal society you support support you? If it does not, either change it or join one which does. Whatever you decide, do it hard. The hour is late and the animals' need is great. It is past high time for all of us to be a voice of the voiceless, to speak for those who can't, to work together for the most oppressed minority of them all.

Index

(For individual animals, See Hunting, Poisoning, Ranching, Trapping, etc.)

Africa, 19–23, 24–26, 30, 33–36, 83, 118, 140, 326
African Game Trails, 26–29
African Safari Club, 92
Aitken, Russell Barnett, 31–32, 133–134, 140
Alaska, 85, 109, 117, 149, 187, 194, 240, 258, 288, 298–305
Alaskan Pipeline, 97
Alaskan Safari, 189
Albrecht, Ernest, 33
Allen, Robert, T., 38–39
Alpert, Herb, 254
Altman, B., 253
American Association of Zoo Keepers, 324
American Bowhunters Society, 176
American Coalition of Patriotic Societies, 10
American Football League, 35
American Forestry Association, 71, 305
American Fur Industry, 277–278
American Fur Merchants' Association, 247
American Game Protection and Propagation Association, 65
American Horse Protection Association, 54
American Humane Association, 17, 76, 238
American Legion, 3, 9, 13, 14
America's Last Wild Horses, 53

American Museum of Natural History, 243–244, 309
American Sportsman, The, 117–122, 171–172, 189
American Sportsman's Club, 11, 151–152
American Way, The, 348
Amos, John B., 160
Anahareo (Mrs. "Grey Owl"), 210–212
Anchorage Daily News, 240
Anderson, Jack, 140
Anderson, Rep. Thomas, 173
Andress, Ursula, 239, 254
"Animals Have Rights, Too," 195
Animal Protection Institute, 241
Animal Welfare Institute, 227, 238, 241, 258
Ann Arbor News, 100, 171
Ann-Margret, 239
Antarctic, 306–307
Anthony, Paul, 110
Aransas National Wildlife Refuge, 177
Architectural Digest, 254
Argentina, 308
Argus Archives, 203, 213
Arizona, 16–17, 110, 111, 138, 148
Arizona Game and Fish Dept., 16, 110
Arizona Republic, The, 16–17
Arizona, University of, 38
Arkansas, 213
Arnett, Ray, 58, 88, 96, 186

Artek Films, 286–289
Asheville Citizen-Times, 274
Asia, 262, 263, 278
ASPCA, 207, 238
Astor, John Jacob I, 197
Atlantic City Press, 273
Atlantic Richfield Oil Co., 96–97
Audubon, John James, 73–76, 329
Audubon Magazine, 73
Australia, 17, 288, 298–304, 312, 315–318
Automobile Association of America, 94
Avery, Ben, 17

Baines, Charles, 317–318
Baird, Reg, 213
Bakal, Carl, 66
Baker, Carol, 239
Bambi, 83, 99, 128, 142
Bank of America, 179
Barnes, Duncan, 157
Barnett, Peter, 32
Bardot, Brigitte, 157
Bartell, Joe, 312
Bartlett, Vernon, 221
Bayh, Birch, 270
Bayh Legislation, 271
Bear, Fred, 132, 171–172
Beauty Without Cruelty, Inc., 261, 298
Beaver Defenders, The, 271
Beckham, Arthur, 10
Beebe, William, 346
Belaney, Archie (see "Grey Owl")
Bell & Stanton, 244
Bell, W.D.M., 19–21, 31
Bender, Marilyn, 225
Bergh, Henry, Mr. and Mrs., 207
Bergstrom, Hilton, 102
Bernhard, Prince, 32, 69
Bernstein, Mrs. Leonard, 229
Bickerton, A. W., 316
Black, Kenneth, 264
Black, Peter, 342
Blair, Frank, 3
Blaisdell, Harold, 42
Blake, Amanda, 231–232
Blass, Bill, 253
Bleakley, Harriet, 169

Bless the Beasts and Children, 16, 88, 189
Bloom, Edith, 225
Blue, Mrs. William L., 54–55
Blue Whale, The, 310
Bolsinger, Joan, 53
Bongartz, Roy, 158–159
Boone & Crockett Club, 64–65, 71, 134–136, 163, 164
Boone, Daniel, 134, 217
Bounties, 128
Bowers, Glenn, 88
Bow-hunting, 106, 161–184
Boy Scouts, 115, 144
Boyce, Martha, 11
Boyd, Les, 342
Brazos River Authority, 177
Breaks, Mrs. John, 293
Breck, Edward, 207, 209
Brezhnev, Leonid, 46
Broadtail, 225
Brookfield Zoo, 322
Brooks Brothers, 225
Brooks, Donald, 224
Brooks, Sid, 120–122
Brown, Mrs. Harold, 227
Brownridge, J.A., 67
Buckley, Mr. and Mrs. William, 229
Bucks, Charles, 158
Buffalo Bill, 17–19
Bundi, Maharajah of, 120–122, 171
Bundy, Dr. Edward S., 142–143
Bunny Bop, 7–14
Bunny, Bugs, 204
Bureau of Land Management, 54, 61
Burrud, Bill, 84
Burton, Richard, 195
Burton, William W., 13
Butz, Earl, 104, 347
Buyukmihci, Hope Sawyer, 271

Caen, Herb, 229
California, 56–59, 94, 101, 103, 149, 151, 152, 205–206, 224, 227, 234, 337, 353
California Fish and Game Department, 58–59, 88, 96, 102, 149, 164–165, 179–180, 182, 186
California Wildlife Advisory Committee, 186

California Wildlife Federation, 57
Calls, 42–45, 113, 164–165
Campfire Club, 65
Canada, 77, 149, 199–201, 205, 207, 209, 234–236, 249, 250, 257, 268, 270
Canadian-American Wolf Defenders, 330
Canadian Association for Humane Trapping, 235, 268–270
Canadian Broadcasting Corporation, 389
Canadian Department of Fisheries, 288
Canadian Federation of Humane Societies, 297
Canadian Wildlife Services Dept., 328
Capote, Truman, 229
Caras, Roger, 15
Cardinale, Claudia, 239
Carlisle, Kitty, 275
Carlsberg, Arthur, 142
Carson, Mrs. Johnny, 229
Carson, Kit, 134
Carson, Rachel, 128
Carpozi, George, 310
Case, Alan, 253
Castet, Frederic, 246–247
Castleberry, T.G., 335
Cavett, Dick, 184, 289
CBS Evening News, 152–155, 235
Central America, 247, 248
Central Park Zoo, 324–325
Cesar, Ed, 235, 237
Chabot Gun Club, 100
Chamberlain, Wilt, 194, 254
Charles I, King, 24
Charles II, King, 197
Charles, Gordon, 100
Chicago Tribune, The, 11, 98, 194, 275
Chincoteague National Wildlife Refuge, 177
Chopin, 256
Christina, 310
Citizens Committee on Natural Resources, 305
Clark, James L., 137
Clede, Bill, 88

Clem, 331–334
Cleopatra, 134
Cody, William ("Buffalo Bill"), 17–19
Cole, John, 353
Colorado, 103–104, 149, 152, 184, 338, 340, 343, 351
Colorado Division of Wildlife, 350
Colorado State Forestry Service, 188
Colton, Araby, 330
Company of Gentlemen and Adventurers Trading into Hudson's Bay, 197
Comstock, Bill, 17–19
Conibear, Frank, 199–201, 209, 234, 282–283
Conibear Trap, 202–203
Conley, Claire, 162–163, 182–184
Connecticut, 104, 173
"Conservation" (word), 46–47
Conservationist, The, 276
Conway, William, 220–224
Cooper, Art, 339
Cooper, James Fenimore, 115
Copper Harbor, Michigan, 112
Corbett, Jim, 31
Cornell University, 104
Corradino, Michael, 327
Cosmopolitan, 144
Council for Livestock Protection, 238
Coward, Gerald, 355
Crockett, Davy, 134, 213
Croft, Dr. P. G., 259
Cromie, Bob, 98, 194
Cronkite, Walter, 231
Crosby, Bing, 117, 119
Crotty, Michael, 324
Cummings, Gordon, 20
Cunningham, Bill, 275
Cusack, Michael, 89

Daktari, 84
Dale, Clell, 44
Daley, E. J., 215
Dallas Morning News, 89
Dalrymple, Byron, 167
Daly, Marcus, 31
Datia, Maharajah of, 21

Datsun, 312–313
Davies, Brian, 291–293
Davis, Jack, 293, 294
Davis, Ossie, 229
Davis, Raymond, 342
Davis, Sammy, Jr., 254
Day, Doris, 231, 234
De Busschere, Dave, 229
Dee, Ruby, 229
Dee, Sandra, 239
Defenders of Animals, 112
Defenders of the Coyote, 352
Defenders of Wildlife, 64, 78, 324, 342, 343
Defenders of Wildlife News, 54, 227, 350–351
Dehaas, Frank, 38
Denney, Richard, 70
Deneuve, Catherine, 239
Des Moines Register, 273–274
Detroit Audubon Society, 314
Detroit Zoo, 325
de Ville, Cruella, 261
Dickinson, Angie, 232
Dickson, Lovat, 210–211
Dior, Christian, 246
Dingell, John, 50, 271, 332
di Sant' Angelo, Giorgia, 222
Disney, Walt, 83, 261
Dixon, Doris, 271
Dobie, Frank, 342
Dolittle, Dr., 86
Donalson, Frank, 240
Donovan, Bill, 44–45
Douglas, Kirk, 34–35
Duchin, Mrs. Peter, 224
Ducks Unlimited, 65
Dudka, Stan, 295–296
Dunaway, Faye, 239
Dyar, Roswell, 352–353

Earth Day, 244
East, Ben, 87–88
Eastman Kodak, 119
Edmiston, Beula, 186
Egan, William, 85
Eisele, Douglas, 10
Endangered Species Act, 15, 221, 240, 311
Endangered Species Productions, 312

Endangered Species List, 316
Eng, Ronald, 150
Ensfield, Mrs. William, 293
Environmental Protection Agency, 346–347
Environmental Quality, 96
Erb, Dick, 273–274
Esquire, 233
Estrada, Julio, 158
Ethiopia, 141, 224
Etter, Alfred, 340
Evarts, Dale, 39
Explorers Club, 139

Facts About Furs, 258, 259–260
Fake (synthetic) fur, 230–233, 237, 278
Fanny Hill, 134
Farkas, Francine, 196
Faunthorpe, John Champion, 22
Faust, Gil, 38
Federation of Sportsmen's Clubs, 266
Fedora, Michael, 173–174
Feezer, Charles, 113
"Fib fur," 225–226
Field & Stream, 46, 73, 82, 94, 99, 123–124, 132, 189, 243
Field & Stream Treasury, 17, 19
Fish and Game Departments (see individual states)
Fisher, Allan C., Jr., 72
Flores, Don L., 42
Florida, 88, 103, 128, 165, 268, 272
Florida Game and Fresh Water Fish Commission, 268, 275
Florida Monkey Sanctuary, 327
Foltz, Donald, 103
Fonda, Jane, 254
Forkan, Patricia, 312
Food and Drug Administration, 175
Forksville Festival, 168
Foss, Joe, 35–36, 118, 122
Fouke Fur Company, 303, 305
Foundation for Environmental Education, The, 243–244
4-H Club, 217–218
4-H Project Book, 217
Fowler, Jim, 260
Frank, Walter, 91

Frankenberg, Regina, 271
Frazier, Joe, 195
Frazier, Walt, 254
Fred, Mr., 225
Friends of Animals, 242, 243, 297
Friends of the Earth, 227–230, 237, 307, 348
Friends of the Earth Wildlife Committee, 270
Friends of the Sea Otter, 56
Friske, Rep. Richard, 173
Frome, Michael, 123
Frye, Fran, 169
Frye, O. E., Jr., 88
Fund for Animals, The, 69, 78, 96, 97, 99, 159, 222, 227, 230, 231, 235, 242, 271, 300, 307, 312, 316, 352
Fun furs, 196, 222–223, 225, 228, 245
Fur Age Weekly, 237, 239–243, 249–257, 261–262
Fur bedspreads, 253, 254
Fur Conservation Institute, 242–245, 272, 275, 281
Fur Conservation Institute Speakers Bureau, 243, 276
Fur farming (*see* Ranching)
Fur Festival Week, 195
Fur-Fish-Game, 90, 215, 272–273, 281
Fur Information and Fashion Council, 193
Fur Pad, The, 253
Fur and Sport, 225
Fur Trade Association, 249
Fur Trade Journal, 249
Fur Workers of America, The, 234
Furs for men, 228, 253

Gable, Clark, 51
Gabor sisters, 239
Galanos, James, 224
"Game Coin," 50, 70, 92, 123
Garbo, Greta, 252
Garrett, Tom, 270, 307–309, 348–349
Gebo, Tom, 276
Gee, Peter, 160
Geier, Harriet, 95

Germany, 202, 255, 288
Georgia, 160, 205, 206
Gibbs Company, 209–210
Gilbert, Bil, 114
Gilbert, John, 252
Gilligan, Edmund, 186
Gimbel's, 226
Ginsberg, Robert, 242
Glassen, Harold, 88
Glenoit Mills, 196
Godfrey, Arthur, 33–34
Goebbels, Josef, 255
Goodman, Mike, 323
Gottschalk, John, 48
Grace, Princess, of Monaco, 195
Graf, Ernest, 272
Gramlich, Frank, 353
Grancel, Fitz, 137
Grauman's Chinese, 179
Gray, Prentiss, 136
Great Britain, 19–23, 31, 32, 37, 69, 202, 229–230, 249, 258, 261, 288, 298, 307–308, 311
Great Game Animals, 133
Greenberg, Henry, 216
Greenwood, Michael, 314
"Grey Owl," Mr. & Mrs., 210–211
Grey, Zane, 132
Grosscup, Bill, 128–133
Grundlach, Jan B., 59
Guajolote Ranch, 156–157
Guelph University, 269
Gurahian, Judge Vincent, 162
Gutermuth, C. R., 69
Great Swamp, 92
Grzimek, Bernard, 288
Gun Week, 98

Hamilton, W. J., 213
Hamm, Mrs. William, 227
Hammond, Celia, 298
Handley, Virginia, 195, 271
Harbour, Dave, 174
Harriman hunting party, 78
Harris, Helen, 275
Harris, John, 331–334
Harrowe, Bob, 239, 240, 241, 251
Hart, Philip, 271
Harvard, 194

Harvard Club of New York, 139
Hawaii, 33, 109, 149
Hecht, Irvin, 248
Hediger, Heini, 321
Hefner, Hugh, 195
Hemingway, Ernest, 25, 26, 114, 132
Hemingway, Mary, 25, 26
Henry VIII, 251
Herberg, Marilyn, 88
Herrington, Alice, 242
Herrington, Dr. R. P., 174–175
Hide and Fur, 278
High, Harold, 238
Highway Action Coalition, 96
Hill, Dave, 311
Hodge, Guy, 271
Hoghunters Annual, 22
Hood, Samuel Stevens, 30
Hopi Indians, 13
Howard, Dr. T. R. N., 144
Howe Massacre, 54
Hubbard, Wynant P., 24
Hudson, Rock, 254
Hughes, Robert, 265
Hughes, Tom, 296
Humane Coyote Getter, 339
Humane Information Services, 238
Humane Slaughter Act, 258
Humane Society of the U.S., 227, 238, 302
Humane Trap Development Committee, 269–270
Hunt, Mr. and Mrs. Harry, 112
Hunter, Francis, T., 139
Hunter, J. A., 20–21, 31
Huntress, Frank, 156
Hunt-the-Hunters Hunt Club, 3–6
Hunting, 1–179
  Antelope, 10, 115, 141, 152
  Aoudad, 155
  Armadillo, 159
  Badger, 108, 173
  Bear, 39, 64, 75, 76, 106, 111–112, 115, 123, 132, 136, 145, 147, 152, 156, 171–172
  Beaver, 64, 108, 109, 139
  Bighorn sheep, 135–139, 146–149, 156, 186
  Birds, 33, 39–40, 48, 69, 75–76, 82, 115, 130, 152, 173

Blackbuck, 156
Bobcat, 108, 109, 111, 173, 352
Boars, 160, 168, 169–170
Buffalo, 16–21, 27, 115, 139, 144, 145, 156
  Cape buffalo, 24, 33–34, 144
Caribou, 136
Cheetah, 27
Chipmunk, 108, 168
Coyote, 108–11, 132, 152, 173, 335–355
Crows, 39, 64
Curlew, 115
Deer, 40, 45, 52, 64, 113, 123, 130, 131, 136, 137, 140, 152, 157, 159, 162, 165–166, 172, 174, 176, 178–179, 182–184
Dolphins, 313–314
Doves, 48, 113, 152
Eagles, 73, 110, 115, 184, 238
Elephants, 19–21, 27, 35, 119, 143, 171
Elk, 40, 44, 110, 152, 186
Fisher, 108
Giraffes, 28, 321–322
Geese, 15, 41, 48, 125–127
Gophers, 39
Groundhogs, 108
Great Auk, 16
Hawks, 64, 110
Heath hen, 115
Hippopotamus, 27, 139
Ibex, 156
Jaguar, 23, 44
Javelina, 110–111
Kudu, 34, 38
Kangaroos, 245, 315–318
Leopard, 23, 26, 27, 34–35, 144
Lion, 21, 27, 139, 144
Lynx, 109
Mink, 173
Muskrat, 109
Moose, 40, 136, 149
Mountain lion (cougar puma) 52, 57, 58–59, 108, 115, 184
Mustang, 51–53
Opposum, 108–109, 173
Ostrich, 29
Owl, 64
Passenger pigeon, 115

Hunting (*cont'd*)
Penguin, 307
Pig, 22–23, 33, 152
Prairie dog, 39, 42, 75
Porcupine, 108, 173
Quail, 48, 128, 173
Rabbits, 7–14, 39, 41, 48, 64, 108–109, 162, 173
Ringtail cat, 109–110
Raccoon, 52, 64, 75, 108, 110, 112–113, 152, 168
Sea lion, 109
Skunks, 52, 64, 108, 110, 173, 321–322
Sloth bear, 122
Snakes, 39, 168, 173, 321–322
Springhaas, 27–28
Squirrels, 64, 108, 173
Tigers, 22, 39, 120–122, 145, 171
Turkey, 41, 101
Walrus, 109
Weasel, 108, 173
Whales, 311–313
Woodchuck, 39, 108, 173
Wolf, 52, 74–75, 109, 115, 132
Wild Ass, 140
Wild Goat, 109, 145, 160, 169–170
Wild Horse, 51–53
Wild Sheep, 109
Wapiti, 138
Whooping Crane, 177
Hyde, Dayton, 349–350
Hyde, Captain Howard, 335

Ice, Cecil, 246
Idaho, 54–55, 108, 149, 337
Illinois, 177
India, 21–22, 47, 120–122, 171, 255, 288
Indiana Department of Conservation, 103–104
Interior, U.S. Department of, 50, 54, 89, 90, 127, 205, 217, 221–222, 245, 248, 273
International Association of Game, Fish and Conservation Commissioners, 305
International Fur Corporation, 248
International Professional Hunters Association, 92

International Society for the Protection of Animals, 296
International Union for the Conservation of Nature, 124, 140
International Whaling Commission, 311–313
Iowa, 104, 274
Ishi, 163
Italy, 69, 83, 197
Ivy League, 252
Izaak Walton League, 65, 71

Jacopetti, Gualtiero, 326
Japan, 288, 300, 308, 310, 311–313
Javits, Mrs. Jacob, 229
Jefferson, Thomas, 251
Jethro, 331–334
Jiminez, Manny, 96
Johnson, Jennifer, 271
Johnson, Lyndon, 47, 227
Johnson, Rev. Roy, 219
Johnston, Velma, 51–52
Jones, LeRoi, x
Jones, Robert, 161–164
Jones, Vernon, 159, 160
Jotham, Neal, 269

Kahn, Ben, 223, 272
Kansas, 108, 205
Kansas City Dog Pound, 354
Kansas State University, 350
Kaplan, Georges, 224
Kaplan, Jacques, 221, 223
Karakul, 262
Karpel, Craig, 159, 178–179
Kaye, Danny, 229
Keith, Ronald, 297
Keen, Barney, 351
Keever, Homer, 7
Kellogg, Francis L., 70
Kennedy, John F., 66
Kentucky, 108, 176, 209
Kimball, Thomas L., 66, 186
Kipling, Rudyard, 285
Kline, Dede, 277
Kolisch, Dr. J. M., 164
Kosten, Charles, 273
Kourtides, Ellen, 223
Koury, Carol, 271

Kramer, 16, 88
Kroehler Manufacturing Company, 194
Kulik, A., 186

Lacey Act, 148, 248
Landon, Mrs. Walter, 227
Lawford, Mrs. Pat, 224
Lee, Dale, 44
Lee, Helen, 225
Leghold trap, 198–283
    banned in Florida, 268
    Massachusetts, 226
    South Carolina, 226
Lehrer, Tom, 126
Leopold, A. Starker, 123, 188
Leopold Report, 341
Le Resche, Robert, 186–187
Lewis, George, 323
Lexington Bluegrass Army Depot, 176
Liberace, 253, 254
Liebling, A. J., 233
Lillie, Dr. Harry, 235, 286
Lindsay, John, 229
Lindsey, Gilbert, 181–182
Lindsey, Robert, 246
Line, Les, 148–149
Linzmeier, Florence, ix
Lion Country Safari, 325
Littman, Art, 237
Logan, Mrs. Joshua
Lollobrigida, Gina, 194
London Times, 69
Look, 233
Los Angeles Times, 142–144, 148, 274, 323
Los Angeles Zoo, 323–324
Louis' Big Game Preserve, 156
Louis, Jean, 224
Louisiana, 104, 200, 204, 205, 213
Lovell, Capt. James, 156
Lucas, Tom, 278
Lucey, Gov. Patrick, 112
Lust, Peter, 286–288, 290
Lytton, Arthur, 341

MacFarlane, John, 238
MacGraw, Ali, 229
Magdalen Islands, 287–291

Magnuson, Warren, 271
Maine, 352
Maine Division of Wildlife Services, 353
Maine Times, 353
Manning, Mrs. Allen, 272
Margetts, Josephine, 264
Marine Mammals Act, 87, 109, 305–307, 314
Mark Twain National Wildlife Refuge, 177
Marnich, J. R., 166
Marty, Carl, 165–166
Mason, Bill, 68, 222
Massachusetts, 108, 194, 209
Massachusetts SPCA, 238
Matagorda Island, 177
Maxwell, Paul, 184, 341
Maxwell, Tom, 263
Maxwell, Valerie, 263–264, 266–267
McCall's, 233
McElroy, J. C., 142, 143
McGee, Gale, 343
McIntyre, Joan, 227
McMahon, Frank, 302
McMaster University, 269
McMillan and Wife, 278
McNellis, Maggi, 278
McQueen, Steve, 254
McRunnels, Clyde, 154–155
Meadows, Jayne, 232
Meadowview Wild Life Preserve, 153–155
Messel, Professor Harry, 316
Mexico, 23, 44, 113, 219, 247
Michigan, 50–51, 59–60, 82–84, 88, 103–104, 111, 131, 156, 171–172, 213, 281, 338
Michigan Bow Hunters Association, 173
Michigan Fish and Game Protection Fund, 281
Michigan Out-of-Doors, 278
Miller Family, 104
Minnesota, 93–94, 205, 213, 330, 332
Misfits, The, 51
Misizka, Joe, 214
Mississippi, 108, 174–176

Mississippi Game and Fish
Department, 175
Missouri, 140, 281
Missouri Conservation Commission,
354
Missouri Trappers' Association, 281
Mitchell, Henry, 347
Mitchell, Hugh G., 10
Mitchell, Patt, 271
Mongolia, 146, 225
Monroe, Marilyn, 51
Montana, 109, 146, 337, 340
Montreal Gazette, 330
Moore, Mary Tyler, 231–232, 233,
239
Moore, Thomas, 117
Morford, Gordon, 233
Mowat, Farley, 309, 328, 329
Mueller, Gene, 94–95
Muir, John, 77–78
Mundis, Jerrold, 105
Murphy, Hon. Lionel, 316
Museum of the City of New York,
277

Namath, Joe, 195, 253
National Anti-Steel Trap League,
207–209, 226, 235
National Association to Keep and
Bear Arms, 50
National Audubon Society, 71–72,
76, 125, 148–149, 305, 312,
314, 356
National Beagle Club of America,
184
National Catholic Society for
Animal Welfare, 227
National Council of Women of
South Africa, 262
National Field Archery Association,
183
National Geographic Society, 71–72
National Guard, x
National Hunting and Fishing Day,
62, 251
National Muzzle-Loading Rifle
Association, 62
National Park System, 116
National Reloading Manufacturers
Association, 62

National Rifle Association, 50–51,
62, 79–82, 88, 98, 102, 115, 127,
128, 281, 305, 356
National Safety Council, 102
National Shooting Sports
Foundation, 38, 50, 63, 81–84,
86–87
National Society for the
Conservation of Bighorn
Sheep, 149
National Sporting Goods
Association, 62
National Trappers Association,
235
National Wildlife Federation,
57–58, 66–69, 71, 115, 182,
186, 305, 312
National Wildlife Magazine, 71–72,
91
National Wildlife Refuges, 127–128,
130, 177–179
National Wool Growers
Association, 329, 346–349
Nebraska, 55, 337–338
Nelson, Garry, 16
Nevada, 51–52, 148, 152, 353
Newhouse, Mr. and Mrs. Samuel,
195, 200
New Mexico, 92, 93, 111, 148,
338
New Jersey, 92, 155, 216, 263–268,
271, 273
New Jersey Fish and Game
Council, 216, 266
New Jersey Trapping Hearings,
263–268
Newman, Marian, 316
Newsweek, 233
New York Cooperative Wildlife
Research Unit, 104
New York Daily News, 206
New York Post, 223
New York, 55, 111, 113, 149, 151,
160, 203, 205, 207, 213, 216–
218, 219, 221, 227, 242, 243,
250, 276–278
New York State Conservation
Department, 276–277
New York Times, 53, 69, 158, 220,
223, 232

New York Zoological Society,
71–72, 133, 221
New Yorker, The, 233
Niarchos, Stavros, 32
Nichols, Margaret, 243
Nissan Motor Corporation, 312–313
Nixon, Richard, 47, 304, 346
Nocera, Tony, 333
Noerenberg, Wallace, 85
Nordyke, Lewis, 336
North American Association for
the Protection of Predatory
Animals, 331
North American School of
Conservation, 60
North American Shooting Preserve
Directory, 151
North American Wildlife and
Natural Resources
Conference, 38, 90
North American Wildlife
Foundation, 305
North Carolina, 7–14, 274
North Dakota, 104, 213
Northeast Ohio Fur Takers, 273
Northernair, 165
North-South Skirmish
Association, 50
Norway, 202, 205, 285, 288, 291,
296, 298, 306, 308, 310
Norwood, Peter, 295
Nowak, Johanna, 272

Oakley, William, 225
O'Connor, Jack, 36–38, 101–102,
147
O'Hara, Maureen, 239
Ohio, 108, 176, 273
Ohio State University, 217
Ohrbach's, 226
Oklahoma, 104, 149, 213, 340
Old Farmers' Almanac, 186
Olin, John, 151
Olney, Warren, 153–155
Olsen, Julius, 246
Olsen, Jack, 343
Onassis, Aristotle, 309–310
One Hundred and One Dalmations,
261

Ontario Fashion Institute, 249
Ontario Humane Society, 296
Orchard, Harry, 30–31
Oregon, 53, 104, 149
O'Rourke, Bill, 45
Outdoor Life, 36, 58, 87, 132, 189
Outdoor Recreation Resource
Review Commission, 56
Outdoor Writers of America, 88,
96, 128
Owings, Margaret, 56–58
Owings, Nathaniel, 227

Page, Warren, 82–84
Pahlavi, Prince Abdorreza, 158
Papert, Reuben, 237
Pappas, Ike, 235, 236
Parent-Teachers Association, 193
Parent, Tom, 239, 240, 251–252,
261
Pasqual, José Maria, 222
Patterson, Stanley, 281
Paul, King, 32–33
Peace Corps, 115
Peacock, O. L., Jr., 268
Peck, Major Paul, 214
Pennsylvania, 88, 104, 149, 167,
171, 209, 274, 281
Pennsylvania Game Commission,
167, 169, 170
Pennsylvania Game News, 167–169
Peru, 310
Petrie, Gordon, 292
Phelps, Chester, 88
Philip, Prince, 32, 69
Phipps, Herb, 185
"Pied Pipers of Coro," 260
Pieffer, Caine, 273
Pinchot, Gifford, 47
Pines to Palms Wildlife Committee,
164–165
Pittman-Robertson Act, 58
Pittsburgh Press, The, 274
Playboy, 195
Plimpton, Mrs. George, 224, 229
Poaching, 220
Poisoning, 210, 340, 342, 345, 355
Body Count, 342
Poland, 205
Polo, Marco, 100

Poole, Daniel A., 89–90
Pope and Young Club, 163–164
Pope, Dr. Saxton, 163
Popowski, Bert, 44–45
Porte, Violet, 196
Portnoy, Irene, 171
Poser, Joseph, 247
Possum Kingdom Lake, 177
Powell, James L., 329
Preston, Ruth, 223
Pribilof Islands, 299–305
Price, Overton, 47
Probst, Marian, 272
Project Jonah, 311
Project Monitor, 311
Pugh, Michele, 324

Queen Christina, 252
Queen Elizabeth Park, 326
Quig, James, 291–292
Quinn, Governor, 33

Racine Zoo, 324
Ragsdale, Ed, 177
Ranching
  Beaver, 204
  Broadtail, 262–263, 278
  Chinchilla, 204, 238, 254, 259
  Fox, 204, 260
  Karakul, 262
  Mink, 204, 257–258
  Nutria (Coypu), 204
  Persian Lamb, 262
Ranching, methods of killing,
  258–260, 262–263
Ranger Rick, 67–68
Ravenna Arsenal, 176
Rawlins, George, 11
Reader's Digest, The, 186, 233
Red Data Book, 15
Reed, Nathaniel, 50, 90, 248
Reed, Rex, 254
Regenstein, Lewis, 69–70, 243–245,
  330, 346–347
Reid, Edwin, 273–274
Remington Arms Company, 136
Reuters, 246
Rhodus, Greg, 354
Rieder, Arnold, 341
Rikoff, James, 92

Right to Bear Arms, The, 66
Ripley, Malcolm, 238, 277
Ritter, Benjamin, 223, 244, 247
Robertson, Assemblyman, 266
Robertson, Cliff, 119
Robichaud, R. J., 289, 293
Rockefeller, John W., 41
Rockefeller, Laurance, 56
Rogers, Roy, 34
Roosevelt, Jonathan, 29, 30
Roosevelt, Kermit, 27
Roosevelt, Kermit, Jr., 29, 30
Roosevelt, Theodore, 25–31, 64, 65
Ross, Diana, 239
Roswell, Dr. Harry, 306
Roth, Mrs. William Matson, 227
Rowland, Sandy, 271
Royal Hunting Preserve, 160
Royal SPCA, 258
Rupert, Prince, 197
Russell, Buck, 94
Russia, 146, 200, 205, 207, 223,
  249, 300, 308, 311–313
Ryan, Ruth, 172
Ryden, Hope, 53

Safari Club International, 141
Sagendorf, Robb, 186
Saint James, Susan, 278
Saks Fifth Avenue, 222, 261
Saldana, Lupi, 43, 140, 148
Salvation Army, 97–98
Sanderson, Derek, 254
San Diego Zoo, 306
Sand Lake National Wildlife
  Refuge, 125–127
San Francisco Zoo, 324
Sargent, Gladys, 271
Satran, Dan, 105
Saturday Evening Post, The, 114,
  186
Saturday Night Special, The, 66
Save a Kangaroo Committee, 317
Say Goodbye, 84–87
Schaefer, Marion, 277
Scheffer, Victor B., 302–303
Schipper, Sidney, 249
Schirra, Wally, 156
Schnapp, Max, 261
Science World, 89

Sealing, 225, 228, 244, 254,
　　283–309
Seater, Steve, 271
Seaver, Tom, 195
Sedlak, Pat, 214–215, 218
Seeger, Pete, 229
Segal, George, 229
Seton, Ernest Thompson, 210
Seventh Avenue, 245, 250
Shaw, Dale L., 188–189
Sherrill, Robert, 66
Sherwood, Glen, 125
Shields, Patrick, 17
Shikar Safari International, 140
Sheppard, Eugenia, 274
Shooting Preserves, 150–160
Show-Me-Big-Buck Club, 140
Siebert, Jimmy, 341
Sierra Club, The, 76–78, 265, 312
Simon, Mr. and Mrs. Weil, 229
Simpson, Colin, 317
Simpson, Dr. Elizabeth, 290
Singer's Midget Circus, 322
Small, Dr. George, 310–311
Smelser, Marguerite, 339
Smith, Dodie, 261
Smit, Van de Sandt de Villiers, 261
Snares, 74, 214, 220–221, 269
Snead, Sam, 35
Snow, Robert, Jr., 160
Society for Humane Legislation, 112
South Africa, 20, 70, 140–141, 144,
　　248, 261, 262, 306, 311
South America, 23, 44, 260–261,
　　301, 306, 308, 310
South Carolina, 104, 209
South Dakota, 35, 125, 245, 246
Southern California Archery
　　Association, 181
Southwick, Hiram, 93
Space, Fred, 267
Spencer, William I., 144
Sport Fishing Institute, 305
Sports Afield, 11, 174, 189
Sports Illustrated, 157, 161–162,
　　343
Sportsman's Alliance of Michigan,
　　50–51, 98
Sportsman's Club of Texas, 98
Spring Maid, 254

Stack, Robert, 91, 118
Stadt, Henri, 292–293
Stans Foundation, 141
Stans, Maurice, 140–141
Starnes, Richard, 94
Stevens, Connie, 239
Stevenson, Robert, 180
Stewart, James, 141
Stevens, Craig, 120–122
Stevenson, Mrs. John Fell, 227–228
Stockton, Marjorie, 303–304
Stofsky, George, 248–249
Stone, Dr. Ward B., 243, 276–277
Stoughton, Col. William, 176–177
Stowers, Henry, 89, 98–99
Stringer Family, 104
Sturm, Jerome, 246
Sullivan, Leonor, 271
Sunday Mirror, The, 69
"Swakara," 262, 272
Swanson, Gary, 148
Swarthout, Glendon, 16
Sweden, 93, 111
Sweeney, Richard, 324

Taiwan, 143
Talbert, "Cap," 109
Tanzania, 143
"Tap's Tips," 46
Taylor, Angela, 223, 224
Taylor, Elizabeth, 195, 239
Taxidermy, 136–137, 145–147
Tell, William, 180
Tennessee, 206
Tennison, Harry, 50
Ternes, Allen, 243
Texas, 109, 130, 149, 152, 158–160,
　　177, 260, 278, 337
Texas Committee for Wildlife
　　Protection, 178
Texas House Subcommittee on
　　Wildlife, 348
Texas Parks and Wildlife
　　Department, 109, 156, 177
Texas Sheep and Goat Raisers
　　Association, 348
They Take So Long to Die, 235
Thomas, Robert L., 16
Timme, E. F. & Co., 230–231
Tioga Boar Hunting Preserve, 160

Today Show, The, 3
Together Magazine, 185
Toker, Cyril, 77
Tors, Ivan, 84
Town & Country, 275
Track, 92
Traplines, 235
Trappers, 212–219
Trapping (and killing for fur),
  193–282
  Alpaca, 254
  Badger, 205
  Baranduk, 223
  Bear, 207, 279
  Beaver, 199, 205, 210, 211–212,
    218, 276, 278–279
  Bobcat, 205, 278
  Cats, house, 225, 260–261
  Cheetah, 247
  Chipmunk, 223
  Civet Cat, 254
  Coyote, 205, 236, 261
  Coypu (Nutria), 204
  Dogs, 261–262
  Ermine, 223, 236, 278
  Fisher, 205, 228, 279
  Fox, 204, 215, 222, 225,
    245–246, 254, 272, 278–279
  Jaguar, 247
  Leopard, 220, 230, 247
  Lynx, 196, 200, 205, 210, 213,
    223, 228, 244, 272, 279
  Lynx cats, 279
  Margay, 247
  Marten, 205
  Mink, 195, 197, 205, 213, 222,
    225, 257, 279
  Mongolian cat, 225
  Monkey, 223, 245
  Mountain lion (cougar, puma),
    195, 247
  Muskrat, 199, 205, 216, 217, 274,
    279
  Nutria (coypu), 204, 205
  Ocelot, 228
  Oppossum, 195, 205, 228
  Otter, 199, 205, 210, 213, 244,
    247, 279
  Persian lamb, 262
  Pony, 225

  Porcupine, 235
  Rabbits, 216, 225, 254
  Raccoon, 205, 215, 225, 228,
    244, 278, 279
  Ring-tailed cat, 205
  Sable, 278, 279
  Skunk, 205, 213, 245
  Snow leopard, 220
  Squirrel, 216
  Tiger, 117–122, 194, 229, 230,
    255
  Vicuna, 230
  Whiskeyjays, 235
  Wolf, 194, 219, 222, 228, 240,
    244, 253, 254, 279
  Zebra, 245
Trapping Tips for Young Trappers,
  217
Traps
  Conibear, 202–203, 269
  Diamond Walloper, 201
  Gin, 198
  Humane, 201, 209, 269–270
  Jump, 198–199
  Spring pole, 199
  Stop-Loss, 198
  Stop Thief, 201
  Triple Clutch, 201
  Two Trigger, 207
  Victor Stop-Loss, 202
Trefethen, James, 135–138, 164
Trophy Hunting, 140–149
Trout Unlimited, 305
Trudeau, Pierre, 294
True Magazine, 32, 139, 162, 182
Tule Elk Committee, 186
TV Guide, 99, 117
Twain, Mark, 30–31

Uncle Wiggily, 99
Unexpected Wildlife Refuge,
  271
United Nations, 10
United Nations Conference on the
  Human Environment, 312
U.S. Air Force, 258
U.S. Fish and Wildlife Service, 15,
  48, 49, 90, 125, 177, 351, 356
Utah, 108, 152, 204
Uzielli, Mrs. Gianni, 229

Van de Water, F. F., 208
Vanderbilt, Amy, 196
Van Gelder, Richard, 244
Van Hoy, Pierce, 9, 10, 13, 14
Van Wormer, Joe
"Varmints," 112–113, 132, 336
Vermont, 111, 149, 273
Vermont Times, 273
Vesely-Forte, 247
Vietnam, 314
Virginia, 156, 177
Virginia Mason Institute, 300
Vilas-Oneida Wilderness Society, 166
Vogue, 196, 200, 233
Voigt, Les, 88
Voltaire, 251
Volk, Mrs. John, 272
Von Furstenberg, Betsy, 229

Walker, Glenn, 348
Walkup, Gerald, 236
Wall Street Journal, The, 70, 80, 100, 274–275
Washington, 149, 213, 215, 260, 275, 342
Washington Department of Game, 275
Washington Post, The, 347
Washington Star-News, 94–95
Watson, Wade, 260
Weather Winky, 225
Webb, Samuel B., 138
Weber, Dr. Henry, 114
West, Mae, 195
Westra, Jim, 64
Whale for the Killing, A, 309
Whales, 309–313
Whitaker, Elmer, 278
White, Robert, 311
Whitehurst, William, 331
Whitlam, Gough, 316
Wild and Free-Roaming Horses and Burros Act, 54
Wilderness Society, The, 65, 71
Wild Horse Annie, 51–52

Wild Kingdom, 260
Wildlife Management Institute, 66, 89, 90, 305
Wildlife Preserve Society, 265
Wildlife Society, The, 71, 305
William II, King, 100
Williams, Stuart, 124
Wilson, George, 54, 329
Wing, Morgan, 174
Wisconsin, 88, 112, 151, 166, 237
Wolf Men, The, 329
Wolper, David, 84–87
Wolper Productions, 85
Women's Lib, 251
Women's Wear Daily, 229, 277, 279–280
Woodcock, Joseph, 264
Woodstream Corp., 287
Woodward and Lothrop, 226
Woody's Fur Storage, 226
World Convention on Endangered Species, 248
World Federation for the Protection of Animals, 343
World Safari Taxidermy, 148
World War II, 255
World Wildlife Fund, 32, 69–70, 117, 230, 305
Wray, Phoebe, 312
Wring-off, 198
Wyler, Gretchen, 271
Wyoming, 162–163, 184, 205, 343

Yandell, James, 11, 12
Yarbrough, Mrs. J. C., 160
Yoder, Ralph, 351–352
Y. O. Ranch, 157–160
Young, Art, 163
Young, Loretta, 224
YWCA, 98–99

Zachary, Frank, 275
Zambia Safaris, Ltd., 143
Ziggy, 322–323
Zern, Ed, 73
Zistel Era, 63–64, 206
Zurich Zoo, 321

74 75 10 9 8 7 6 5 4 3 2 1